289.3
WHY   Why I believe

D0960873

presented in
memory of

Liz Paulson

by

Buddy King Family

Valley of the Tetons Library

WHY I
BELIEVE

WHY I
BELIEVE

BOOKCRAFT

SALT LAKE CITY, UTAH

© 2002 Intellectual Reserve, Inc.

All rights reserved. No part of this book may be reproduced in any form or by any means without permission in writing from the publisher, Deseret Book Company, P. O. Box 30178, Salt Lake City, Utah 84130. This work is not an official publication of The Church of Jesus Christ of Latter-day Saints. The views expressed herein are the responsibility of the authors and do not necessarily represent the position of the Church or of Deseret Book Company.

Bookcraft is a registered trademark of Deseret Book Company.

Visit us at www.deseretbook.com

Library of Congress Cataloging-in-Publication Data
    Why I believe.
    Includes bibliographical references.
    ISBN 1-57008-723-7
    1. Church of Jesus Christ of Latter-day Saints—Apologetic works.   2. Mormon
Church—Apologetic works.
    BX8635.5   .W48   2001
    289.3'32—dc21
                                                                          2001004532

Printed in the United States of America   72082-6830
Publishers Press

10   9   8   7   6   5   4   3   2

Contents

INTRODUCTION

Readers will have a treat in the pages to follow as they learn of the deep, religious convictions—the testimonies—of over half-a-hundred individuals who have written briefly about "Why I believe." Even though the "I" represents individuals of widely divergent backgrounds, their "Whys" will be strikingly similar, since the inclusive gospel net gathers "of every kind." (Matthew 13:47.)

In an age of reticence about religion in which many communicate through bumper stickers and stereotypes, the openness of these writers, who are not merely "passive believers," shows they are "not ashamed of the gospel of Christ." (Romans 1:16.) Yet, though high achievers, the writers do not seek to draw attention to themselves but rather to the "whys" of their testimonies.

Some, in order to write about "why," also write about "what." Others write about defining moments, including difficulties and doubts in the development of their faith. Still others focus on gospel doctrines particularly powerful for them or on the rewards of gospel living. As impressive as each individual's expertise is in various fields, each would be quick to acknowledge that he or she is still learning and developing, growing and progressing.

The Church of Jesus Christ of Latter-day Saints has over 11 million members located in 162 countries. Its growth constitutes what one non-Mormon scholar says is "the birth of a new world religion." (See Rodney Stark, *Review of Religious Research*, September 1984, v. 26, no. 1, page 7.) In the testimonies of these accomplished individuals one can sense "what makes the Church tick," concerning which the conscientious reader will come away with a much better understanding.

To individuals who would like to know more, but not everything, this reader-friendly volume is dedicated.

—Elder Neal A. Maxwell
Quorum of the Twelve Apostles

The glossary will be helpful in defining terms unfamiliar to many readers. Likewise, there are significant foundational documents appearing at the end of this volume concerning the Articles of Faith, The Living Christ, and The Proclamation on the Family which speak for themselves.

Scripture citations other than those from the Bible are from the Book of Mormon, the Doctrine and Covenants, and the Pearl of Great Price, which Latter-day Saints accept as scripture along with the Bible.

DANNY AINGE

It was the summer of 1962, and I was three years old. My family and I went on a long vacation to Salt Lake City, a bus ride that, from Eugene, Oregon, took fifteen hours. The purpose of our trip was to be sealed, or united, as a family for eternity. My parents, Don and Kay Ainge, had been baptized as members of The Church of Jesus Christ of Latter-day Saints just a year and a half earlier.

I will never forget that day in the temple. To this day, I have a vivid picture in my mind of our family in the temple together.

Most of my growing-up experiences were not that serene, however. I went through my school years full of energy, taking chances, running through glass doors, and somehow always avoiding danger. Even now I wonder how I have made it this far without injury. I played 18 years of professional sports without a fracture or surgery.

When I was eighteen years old, the top universities in the country recruited me heavily. I was most sought after as a receiver in football. But I was 6'4" tall and weighed only 165 pounds, so I knew football was out.

I weighed my options for college basketball and baseball and knew I wanted to play in the Pacific 10 Conference. It had the greatest exposure and would give me the greatest opportunity to achieve my childhood dream of playing in the pros. I had often imagined myself being Lew Alcindor or Lucius Allen, the UCLA greats, or Freddy Boyd, Paul Westphal, or Ronnie Lee, all PAC-10 heroes of mine.

I went to various universities on recruiting trips. Each school showed me the best their school had to offer. I saw the basketball facilities, met with professors, and was introduced to a few members of the basketball team. At night I was escorted around town by a couple of selected players.

At each university, the "visit" turned into a typical college party. I had been to parties in high school, so I was not naive about what would happen at these campus stays, but I was still sickened by the environments. The players thought they were impressing me, but I didn't want my life to be anything like theirs.

One university even informed me that a tutor would be provided to complete all my course work and take all my tests. I'm embarrassed to say that I was seriously tempted.

On another visit I was offered cocaine. I was not tempted.

Then an unusual set of circumstances developed that gave me an opportunity to visit Brigham Young University. I was a little apprehensive about going to BYU because four years earlier my older brother, Doug, had accepted a basketball scholarship to BYU. He had left after just one year. Plus, it was the Western Athletic Conference, not the PAC-10. I didn't even know any players from the WAC. Nevertheless, I eventually accepted an invitation to visit BYU.

When I arrived at the BYU campus, I went through the same routine as at the other schools. I met the coaches, toured the campus, and visited with professors in communications, which was my choice of a major. I don't know if it was coincidence that Marie Osmond was eating in the same cafeteria I was taken to, but I thought it was pretty cool.

Later that night I was turned over to my escorts. We played some basketball, went to dinner, and got into a snowball fight with a couple of little cowboys trying to impress their girlfriends. They actually tried to fight 6'11" Mark Handy, a center on the basketball team. The fight didn't last long. The evening ended at a party. But this party was amazingly different than any other party I had been to. There was dancing, cake and ice cream, and only juice and root beer to drink. I had a great time.

After the party, I stayed up late talking to Scott Runia, an all-state player from Utah, who had started as a freshman. I asked him if they ever did any crazy stuff at BYU. He told me that during a recent snow-storm, he and a friend had called the police on themselves while driving snowmobiles all around campus. The officers had no chance of catching them.

I laughed and laughed. I could relate to that type of prank. He told me of the trouble their starting center was in. He was on probation for throwing a freshman out the window of his dorm room on the second floor. When I asked why he'd done that, he said, "Because the kid got his homework wet with a water balloon." That was my type of center.

One of the things I did while in Provo was attend the baptism of a teammate, Mike May. I felt something at that baptism I had never felt before in my life. As I watched these big athletes stand with humility and testify of their knowledge of their Savior, Jesus Christ, their love for one another, and their testimony that the Book of Mormon was truly an ancient scriptural record that testifies of Christ, my eyes started to water, and my body started to tremble. I wasn't sure if what they were saying was true, but I was sure I wanted to feel that way again. I was sure I wanted to be around these people. I was sure I was going to BYU.

I called my brother Doug when I got home from my visit. I asked him if he thought I would like BYU. He responded, simply, "If you want to follow the rules, it's a great school, and you will like it." That's why I wanted to go there. I wanted to be around people that lived the rules and liked it.

The task of calling the other coaches who had recruited me was not an easy one. I thanked them for their consideration but announced that I had chosen to play for BYU.

The local newspapers were not kind to me, calling me a traitor for leaving the state of Oregon. It was not easy to tell people why I was leaving. I've always felt it was a private experience, only to be shared by those who could understand my feelings. I knew it was the right choice and feel even stronger about it today.

I planned on playing both baseball and basketball at BYU, so I kept playing baseball with my American Legion team at home in Eugene. My plans began to change when, a couple of weeks before the major-league amateur draft, a scout from the San Diego Padres arrived at school and got me out of class. He took me out to the baseball field, timed my sprints, and watched me throw. After a few days, the Padres approached my father and invited me to be the number-one pick in the baseball draft in 1977. It only took a few discussions with the Padres for my father to realize how determined I was to go to BYU to play basketball, and we graciously declined the offer, even though the money was very tempting.

When the baseball draft came, I was drafted by the Toronto Blue Jays in the fifteenth round. They sent me letters to report to their farm clubs for assignment and sent me contracts in the mail. I trashed them all, sent no response all summer, and just continued with my summer American Legion program. The Blue Jays sent their general manager, Pat Gillick, and hitting coach, Bobby Doerr, the ex–Red Sox great, to watch me in person. One day after a double header, my father suggested the idea of playing college basketball at BYU and playing for the Blue Jays in the summer. The Blue Jays promised not to interfere with my college, so I agreed to do it. How could I go wrong? It would give me a chance to live two dreams at once and even get paid.

Choosing BYU over the rest of my options is one of the best decisions I have ever made. All the great things that have happened in my life have come as a direct result of the Holy Spirit guiding me in the right direction at a crucial time in my life.

It guided me to my wife, Michelle, who has been the single greatest blessing in my life. I think about how close I came to making a decision that would have changed my course so dramatically, and I am thankful that the Lord was leading me in the direction He knew I needed to go.

I felt like Amulek, in the Book of Mormon, when he said, "I never have known much of the ways of the Lord, and his mysteries and marvelous power. I said I never had known much of these things; but behold, I mistake, for I have seen much of his mysteries and his marvelous power. . . . Nevertheless, I did harden my heart, for I was called many times and I would not hear; therefore I knew concerning these things, yet I would not know; therefore I went on rebelling against God, in the wickedness of my heart." (Alma 10:5–6.)

I was raised in The Church of Jesus Christ of Latter-day Saints, and yet I couldn't see its beauty or feel its truth until some of those defining moments at BYU.

The baptism I attended on that recruiting visit changed my life forever. That day I decided to obey God. I won't say that I haven't had many struggles with day-to-day life; I just decided never to quit. At that critical time in my life, my Savior was there for me. I am often tempted and weak, but I can never deny the Spirit that first manifested itself to me that glorious day and has confirmed my feelings many days since.

After my first year of school, I headed to Syracuse, New York, to start my first season of professional baseball. Although I couldn't make it to spring training, I did have a couple of days with the BYU baseball team to prepare. I found out quickly that AAA baseball is a big jump from American Legion. For the first time in my athletic life, I was struggling.

To make things worse, my teammates hated me. A team favorite, Hector Torres, was waived to create my spot. He was a good man, had five children, was in his thirties, and had high hopes of getting back to the majors. I felt bad for him, and my teammates blamed me for his misfortune. My teammates, the media, my manager, and the fans all made the transition difficult. I could handle all of it except being hated by my team.

I would go to get a meal in the hotel restaurant after a game, only to find my drunken teammates, who threatened my health if I came near them. Sometimes there were no other places to eat that late at night, so I would be forced to skip dinner. On the field each day we played a game called flip during warm-up. In the game, you can't catch the ball with your glove; you just bounce it off your glove around and across the circle of players like a hot potato. If someone bounces it off a player and it hits the ground, that player is eliminated. I knew that the players didn't want me in their game, but I played out of boredom and loneliness. They flipped the ball at me as hard as they could to eliminate me first every game. I knew they wanted me to quit.

That kind of treatment went on for a couple of weeks. One day a major-league player, Garth Iorg, was sent down to our minor-league team. It didn't take Garth long to see what was going on. During the warm-up flip game, Garth saw the attack on me. He immediately started flipping the ball back as hard as he could at the ringleader teammate. A fight broke out, and Garth, not a big man, embarrassed the pest easily. No one messed with me, or with Garth, again.

Garth and I became good friends. The next year I was called up to the big leagues at Garth's position. I knew it wasn't fair; he was better than I was, and he should have been the one called up. But Garth, never bitter, wished me good luck and gave me some pointers on what to expect in the show.

Garth was a member of The Church of Jesus Christ of Latter-day Saints. He was proud to be a member, and he was a feisty one, like me. I think that's why we hit it off so well. He was also older than I was, had started his family, and had a lot more answers about life than I did. He encouraged me to study the Book of Mormon.

Because of Garth's urgings and his example, I read the Book of Mormon for the first time, cover to cover. I prayed with a sincere heart and real intent, having faith in Christ, to know of its truth. I never felt something to be truer. Since then, I have read the Book of Mormon many times. I love how it complements the teachings of the Bible. I know if I apply its teachings to my life, I can never be led away from God. The more I read, the happier and more certain I am of my intended path.

I learned a lot that summer. The trials I faced helped me prepare for my life ahead. I learned not to quit. I learned compassion for others, especially those who might be struggling. But most important, I learned to rely on the Lord.

In addition, I've been surrounded by good people. When I played for the Toronto Blue Jays, there were four other players on the team who were members of the Church: Jerry Garvin, Barry Bonnell, Luis Gomez, and Garth, who eventually came back to the majors and had a long career. Then, when I played for the Celtics, there were two other Latter-day Saints on the team, Greg Kite and Fred Roberts. When I started coaching in Phoenix, another Church member, Danny White, the former Cowboys quarterback, was already coaching the arena football team owned by the Sun's owners. Their presence alone made it easier for me to be a member of the Church.

How lucky I've been to be surrounded by good people. Although they are not really angels, they are men of God. Through their examples I have seen that families, faith, service, and humility bring more happiness than worldly success ever could.

Truly an angel from heaven, my wife, Michelle, has been my greatest motivator. She is such a model of consistency and obedience. Her toughness, her unwavering faith, and her ability to endure me and my career, with our six children, have been remarkable. She knows everything about me and still loves me. That's not easy. If my actions are ever not in line with our family rules, which we established together, she reminds me of what I need to do. And I need that.

I always thought I could juggle all the facets of my life until I became addicted to the intensity and competitiveness of coaching the Phoenix Suns. One day I was reading in Matthew 6:24: "No man can serve two masters: for either he will hate the one, and love the other; or else he will hold to the one, and despise the other. Ye cannot serve God and mammon."

And again in Matthew 6:20–21, I read, "Lay up for yourselves treasures in heaven, where neither moth nor rust doth corrupt, and where thieves do not break through nor steal: for where your treasure is, there will your heart be also."

My treasures were at home, yet my thoughts were constantly on the court. I would read good books and listen to inspired words and then apply them, not to my personal life but to coaching and my team. My true treasures, my beautiful wife and children, were often neglected. I could have continued in this way, as I did for four years, but I was robbing both my family and my team. Both deserve a full-time leader. I finally decided to resign as head coach of the Suns, and it was one of the best decisions I've made in my life.

My testimony of the gospel has come in two ways. The first way was at the shining moment of realization, when the Holy Ghost testified to me that the gospel was true. The second way is more of an evolution, a gradual realization that my early testimony was deficient, as I continue to recognize and more deeply appreciate more truth in the gospel.

This has been a long explanation of why I believe, but my life experiences have helped me to see truth, to find my path, and to lighten my load. I am indebted to countless people in my life, including my parents, my siblings, Michelle's family, my children, and my friends. But the person I am most grateful to, and to whom I owe the most, is my Savior, Jesus Christ. I am thankful for His life, thankful that even as a mortal, He lived perfectly. His unwavering love inspires me daily. His atonement is the source of hope in my life. Without it, I would be lost. The knowledge of His life puts my life in perspective. I can link the past, present, and future together, knowing that I, with my family, can be reconciled with God forever.

Danny Ainge grew up in Eugene, Oregon, where he shined as a young athlete in both baseball and basketball. His two-sport dominance extended into his collegiate days as he played professional baseball for the Toronto Blue Jays during the summers while attending BYU. During the winters, Danny led the Cougar basketball team, scoring in double figures in all 118 games and averaging 20.9 points. In 1981 he won the John Wooden and Eastman Awards and was an All-American selection as well.

After the Celtics selected Danny in the second round of the 1981 NBA draft, he gave up baseball to concentrate on basketball. His contributions to the great Celtics teams of the '80s were invaluable, and he was an All-Star selection in 1988.

Danny spent the early '90s with Sacramento, Portland, and Phoenix, helping the Blazers and Suns to the finals. He recently stepped down as the coach of the NBA Phoenix Suns to spend more time with his wife, Michelle, and their six children. Currently living in Gilbert, Arizona, Danny is an NBA color analyst for TNT.

NOLAN D. ARCHIBALD AND
MICHAEL K. YOUNG

As a young man, I was attending Weber State University in Ogden, Utah, where I played varsity basketball for Dick Motta (who eventually became the third-winningest coach in NBA history). Basketball routinely required a daily three- to four-hour time commitment, as well as extensive travel to away games. I was also a serious student who hoped someday to attend the Harvard Business School. In the midst of these demands on my schedule, my bishop asked me to accept an assignment in our church that would require a substantial commitment of time. I struggled with this decision for several days, but, after prayerful consideration, I informed the bishop that I would accept. It required a great deal of organization in my life, but things did work out.

I felt equally challenged when my wife and I moved to Boston to attend the Harvard Business School. I was again asked to accept another time-consuming assignment in the Church. I was newly married, becoming accustomed to a new city, and, coming from Weber State University, intimidated by the need to compete against classmates who had graduated from Ivy League and other well-known colleges. But I again determined to do what was asked.

A few years ago, life repeated itself yet again. I was CEO of a multi-billion-dollar corporation, father of eight active children, serving on the boards of several major corporations, and active in community service. Yet none of this deterred my stake president from calling me to serve as bishop (the presiding authority) of my local congregation. I knew this assignment could easily take upwards of thirty hours a week. Nevertheless, without hesitation, I accepted the call.

I feel now, as I did so many years ago at Weber State and again at

Harvard, that I have been abundantly blessed by the Lord—blessed with a wonderful family, professional success, and countless opportunities to serve. But I also firmly believe that many of those blessings have come to me precisely because of the service I have been privileged to render in the Church.

Nolan D. Archibald

I too recall times when I was so overwhelmed by secular concerns that it did not occur to me that I could easily accommodate additional responsibility. The Lord was not to be deterred, however.

Some years ago, I had just completed my first year at Harvard Law School and had been invited to become a member of the Harvard Law Review. I knew that this position could easily require seventy to eighty hours of work each week, in addition to all my classroom work and my normal family responsibilities. I also knew I was competing with classmates who had far more writing and editing experience than I did. Just as I thought absolutely nothing else could be added into an impossibly busy schedule, my bishop asked me to accept a calling that would require not only a significant time commitment on Sunday but also a substantial expenditure of time at least one or two evenings a week. I accepted, knowing that somehow the Lord would provide and that this opportunity would, in the end, provide more blessings and benefits than any of the secular activities in which I was engaged. I was not wrong.

A few years later, we had moved our young family to Manhattan to accept a teaching position at Columbia Law School. I not only had significant teaching and administrative responsibilities, but I also had to publish, and publish well, to secure tenure. To make matters even more complicated, I had chosen to specialize in Japanese law, a decision that required me to conduct virtually all of my research in Japanese-language research materials, thus requiring substantial additional time for research than might be necessary for colleagues similarly situated.

In the midst of trying to raise a young family in Manhattan and publish *enough articles and books of sufficient quality to earn a permanent position on an Ivy League university law faculty, I was called to serve as president of our local stake, a position that I knew would require many hours a week. Again, after consultation with my wife, I knew there was no other course for me but to accept this position and fulfill these responsibilities to the best of my ability. While it was seldom easy, that call began six of the most wonderful years of our family's life. And the blessings and opportunities of that wonderful assignment still redound to our family's benefit.*

Michael K. Young

What is perhaps most unusual about both our stories of accepting time-consuming assignments to serve in our Church without remuneration and in the face of significant family, work, and community responsibilities is that there is nothing unusual at all about them—and that is one of the reasons we believe. Two thousand years ago, Christ organized His church, serving as its head and calling others to various positions for the feeding of "his lambs" (John 21:15) and "the perfecting of [his] Saints" (Ephesians 4:12). They were fishermen, carpenters, tax collectors, lawyers, merchants, and laborers; but, despite the personal sacrifice, they all responded to the call.

Two thousand years later, The Church of Jesus Christ of Latter-day Saints is organized in the same manner as Christ's church in the meridian of time. We believe that our current prophet and President, Gordon B. Hinckley, was called by Jesus Christ, as was Peter of old. Like Peter, who served in a presidency with James and John, President Hinckley presides over the Church with two counselors, forming the First Presidency of the Church. Twelve modern-day apostles are also called and function as the apostles of old, administering the spiritual and temporal affairs of the Church. They, in turn, are assisted by five Quorums of Seventy, many of whom live all over the world, wherever members of the Church are found, and who carry out assignments from the First Presidency and the Twelve.

Countless other members of the Church also serve in a variety of leadership and pastoral positions in the Church, but only the members of the First Presidency and the Quorum of the Twelve are called to serve for the entire remainder of their lives. Members of the First Quorum of the Seventy, comprising only about fifty men in all, serve until age seventy. And only they, their counterparts in the Second Quorum of the Seventy, the three-man Presiding Bishopric, and the members of the First Presidency and the Quorum of the Twelve Apostles serve in full-time, ecclesiastical positions.[1] In other words, with the exception of the small number of men described above, numbering just over 100, all other members are called to serve temporarily, sometimes for a period of years, sometimes only for months. These presiding authorities who have responsibility for the entirety of the Church are called General Authorities. All other members serve in part-time or more limited capacities.

But serve they do! Members of our Church are organized into local congregations, usually geographically based, called wards (or branches, in the case of smaller congregations). These wards, which at the end of 2000 numbered nearly 26,000, generally comprise between 400 and 600 people and are under the direction of presiding authorities called bishops (or branch presidents, in smaller congregations), who are

---

1. There are two other full-time ecclesiastical callings: (1) mission presidents and their wives, who are called for a period of three years to preside over one of the Church's 300-plus missions around the world; and (2) temple presidents and their wives, who are called to preside over the Church's larger temples. These people are asked to leave their homes and full-time occupations and devote full-time work to the supervision of the mission or the temple for which they are responsible. The service of these individuals is slightly different from that of the other authorities described above, not only because it is limited in geographic and substantive scope, but also because upon completion of three years of service, these individuals return to their previous lives. There are approximately 340 mission presidents and about 60 temple presidents of larger temples serving in this manner at any given time.

called from among the members of the congregation to serve in this part-time capacity. They may be teachers, plumbers, doctors, lawyers, CEOs, farmers, carpenters, or salesmen. But whatever their background and their other responsibilities, they are expected to—and invariably do—minister to the affairs of the ward and attend to the needs of their ward members, all entirely unpaid. They and the two men called to assist them as counselors and advisors seek guidance and heavenly inspiration in order to call others in the ward to serve in other essential Church positions. They teach, counsel, perform ordinances, minister, and preside over all ward functions and activities.

The bishop also calls a woman from among the congregation to preside over the ward's Relief Society, comprised of the women eighteen and over in the ward. This organization is one of the oldest and largest women's service organizations in the world. The president of the Relief Society and her two counselors are also called to look after the temporal and spiritual needs of the women and their families in the ward. The men of the congregation are divided into Melchizedek Priesthood quorums through which they receive instruction and further opportunities to serve. These quorums and all the teachers and officers within them are also called from among the male members of the congregation. The youth and adults are usually divided into age groups and meet in weekly Sunday School classes, where they receive instruction from a teacher also called by the bishopric.

The young men of the ward (ages twelve to eighteen) are, if worthy, ordained under the supervision of the bishop to positions in the Aaronic Priesthood. (See glossary.) The Aaronic Priesthood is divided into quorums, and the young men are instructed and serve under leaders called by the bishop. Most young men are also active in the Scouting program, participating in ward-based Boy Scout troops, which are also an integral part of the training and service opportunities the Church provides for young men. The young women of equivalent age belong to the Young Women organization and receive lessons in the gospel and service from teachers and leaders, also prayerfully and carefully selected by the bishop. The younger members of the congregation (ages five to eleven) attend Sunday classes in the children's organization called Primary.

All told, a fully staffed ward may have more than 250 people serving in different assignments, all without compensation and all for limited periods of time.

In addition to these specific calls to serve in some leadership or instructional capacity, virtually all adult men and women in the Church are also assigned a certain number of families or individuals to visit on a frequent basis, usually monthly, to assist the families or individuals with any needs, either spiritual or temporal, they might have. The men are designated as home teachers, and the women as visiting teachers. The men report back regularly to their quorum leaders and their bishops, while the women report to their Relief Society presidents.

Wards are, in turn, grouped together into geographically defined areas called stakes. The word *stake* comes from the Old Testament. (See Isaiah 54:2.) Stakes were used to keep the tent or tabernacle secure from the influences of the weather outside. Today's stakes help keep members of the Church safe and secure both temporally and spiritually.

A stake president presides over the stake. A typical stake is comprised of six to ten wards. Worldwide, there are more than 2,500 stakes in the Church, with new ones being created almost weekly. The president of a stake is assisted by two counselors, twelve high councilors, stake clerks, and a stake executive secretary, as well as other members who serve in various advisory capacities. These various stake officers help train and instruct the various ward officers who hold corresponding positions at the ward level. A fully staffed stake may engage as many as fifty to seventy-five members in various callings. These positions are filled by members from the various wards within the stake boundaries.

But perhaps the singular manifestation of service most identified with the Church today is the young man or woman serving a full-time mission in countries throughout the world. Today some 60,000 young men and women have put their schooling, careers, personal and family lives, and everything else on hold to accept an assignment from the president of the Church. Young men serve for two years, while young women serve for eighteen months. They receive no monetary compensation; indeed, they either pay their own way or are assisted by their families or other Church members. The work is extraordinarily demanding; missionaries are expected to work twelve to fourteen hours a day, six and a half days a week, with no vacation or holidays. The separation from family and friends is likewise never easy.

Both the authors have more than a little experience in this regard. One of us spent two and a half years in Japan as a missionary many years ago. That author's son also served in Japan, under a mission president to whom, as it turns out, the author had taught the gospel twenty-five years earlier in Japan. And that same author's daughter just recently resigned her coveted position as a cadet at the U.S. Air Force Academy and is serving a nineteen-month mission in Kobe, Japan.

The other author served a mission in the southern part of the United States a number of years ago. He now has seven sons and one daughter. His six oldest children have covered the globe in missionary service, including Switzerland/France, Finland, England, and Australia. Two are currently serving missions in Canada and Taiwan.

Since the restoration of the Church, more than 750,000 individuals have served as full-time missionaries. By one estimate, these young missionaries provide annually almost 7 million hours of unremunerated Christian service.

Though brief, this overview captures a number of important and distinctive features of leadership and service in The Church of Jesus Christ of Latter-day Saints. First, and most important, as articulated in our fifth Article of Faith: "We believe that a man must be called of God, by prophecy, and by the laying on of hands by those who are in authority, to preach the Gospel and administer in the ordinances thereof." Our members are taught neither to seek nor decline Church callings. Appointments to service are made by the presiding authority after much thought, prayer and, on occasion, fasting.

Both authors affirm from firsthand experience the receipt of such inspiration in extending these callings—another reason we believe in the divinity of the Church. While neither of us claim revelations or manifestations like the one Joseph Smith received when the Father and Son appeared to him in a grove of trees in upstate New York, both of us have felt spiritual promptings and divine guidance when extending calls to ward and stake members. Both of us can testify from experience to the truth of our Article of Faith: men and women are *called of God, by prophecy*.

Second, members serve without any form of remuneration or even compensation for living expenses.[1] Rather, members perform their assigned tasks, even the most demanding ones, while holding down full- or part-time jobs, raising families, and otherwise living their normal, everyday lives.

Third, our members are not taught or trained in special seminaries or colleges for the ministry. Nor are wealth, education, or social position factors relevant to the position to which a person is called to serve. A bishop with little formal college education may well preside over a ward full of highly educated doctors and lawyers. A stake president with few financial resources may supervise and direct a bishop

---

1. Mission presidents may also receive modest living stipends, if necessary, during the term of their service.

who is CEO of a major corporation. The Lord looks not to the bank statement or the educational pedigree but to the heart and the soul.

Fourth, with the exception of the president of the Church, the counselors in the First Presidency, and the members of the Quorum of the Twelve Apostles, our members serve for limited periods of time in their callings. A Relief Society president, upon her release after an appropriate period of service, may next be called to lead the Primary children in song every Sunday. A bishop or stake president, upon his release, may be asked to teach a youth Sunday School or priesthood class, as were both the authors when released from those positions.

This continual rotation of callings and positions has a tendency both to ensure that members remain enthusiastically engaged during their entire term of service within their callings and to increase members' understanding of all aspects of the gospel and Church service. Since members do not choose their own callings, moreover, there is no necessary correlation between what people perceive to be their own strengths and weaknesses and the requirements of the position to which they are called. Accordingly, members are continually encouraged to study and learn about their callings. A lifetime of learning ensues.

A small manifestation of this is found in the way in which we conduct our main Sunday worship services, which are called sacrament meetings. Though the bishop presides over the ward, he does not do the bulk of the "preaching" on Sunday. Rather, the members of the ward are assigned to speak on various Sundays throughout the year. Significant personal gospel insight and greatly strengthened personal testimonies inevitably flow from this process. Even young people from ages twelve and up are given the opportunity to speak to the entire congregation. At least one youth speaker is featured on almost every sacrament meeting program.

Among the most remarkable features of this organizational system, moreover, is the simple fact that it works. Service is provided to members and nonmembers alike on a broad scale. Worship services occur on a regular basis and tend to be well ordered and well organized. Instruction and counsel are given. Social, cultural, and athletic events are held. Simply put, this massive organization, with only the most limited full-time clergy, runs regularly and with appropriate efficiency.

It is also our experience that a term in a position of leadership is perhaps the best way to learn to be a good follower, a true disciple of Christ. Broad-gauged leadership experience teaches a member not only to rely more devoutly on the Lord but also to follow more humbly the person that now occupies the position the member once held. We also tend to be more forgiving of the mistakes and weaknesses of our leaders, having served in similar positions and having ourselves made mistakes and exhibited weaknesses and foibles for all to see. We do not expect our leaders to be perfect. They are men and women like us, and, try as they might, they, like us, sometimes fall short of the mark. Our faith is in the only perfect man, our Savior, Jesus Christ, and we all understand that these leadership experiences and service opportunities are designed to help us strive to be like Him, to more closely approach perfection, though perhaps not in this life and certainly not in any assignment that either of the two authors has attempted to carry out.

We also learn from firsthand experience that we are all one with Christ. In a Church in which today's Sunday School teacher may be, literally, tomorrow's bishop or stake president, hierarchy, preference, and status from one's title or position of leadership have little if any meaning. The eye cannot say it has no need of the hand, nor the head that it is superior to the feet. (See 1 Corinthians 12:21.)

Finally, virtually all of the active members of our Church, even members as young as twelve and thirteen, serve in some sort of calling. This has a number of important consequences for us as members.

First, this constant service tends to engender a high degree of engagement and activity on the part of most active Church members. Second, and more important, this organizational structure puts the concept of service to others squarely at the center of all our worship and devotional activities. Indeed, in the most real and important way imaginable, service to others defines membership in The Church of Jesus Christ of Latter-day Saints, as well as our commitment to our fellowman and to our Father in Heaven and His Son, Jesus Christ.

Third, and perhaps most important, constant attention to service inevitably generates a tremendous degree of personal growth, drawing us closer to our Savior and making us better able to obey His commandments and follow His lead. From an early age, our members learn, through their service, to forget self and focus on the needs of those around them.

The organizational structure of our Church profoundly affects our growth and spiritual development as members. Through this divinely inspired and directed service, we draw closer to the Lord, we better understand the true nature of our responsibilities to our fellowman, and we more clearly comprehend the divine purposes of our Savior and His glorious mission. We and our families have been both firsthand observers and blessed beneficiaries of this inspired plan. It is yet one more reason why we believe and testify that this is indeed Jesus Christ's Church, restored through His prophet, Joseph Smith, in these latter days, and guided by His hand even today through His living prophet, Gordon B. Hinckley.

Nolan D. Archibald is chairman of the board, president, and chief executive officer of The Black & Decker corporation, a $5 billion company with products sold in more than 100 countries. *Fortune* magazine named Nolan one of the "10 Most Wanted Managers" in the U.S., and *Business Week* named him one of the best managers of 1987.

Nolan was an All-American basketball player at Dixie College and an Academic All-American at Weber State University and was invited to try out with the Chicago Bulls. In 1993, the National Association of Basketball Coaches named Nolan, along with four other former All-American basketball players, as their "Silver Anniversary" NCAA All-American basketball team. He earned an MBA from the Harvard Graduate School of Business.

Nolan serves on the board of directors of the Brunswick Corporation; the National Advisory Council, the Marriott School of Management, Brigham Young University; and the International and Government Affairs Committee for The Church of Jesus Christ of Latter-day Saints.

He is married to the former Margaret Hafen, and they are the parents of seven sons and one daughter. He is currently president of the Washington, D.C., Stake.

Michael K. Young is currently dean and professor of law at the George Washington University Law School. He is also a member of the U.S. Commission on International Religious Freedom, the Committee on International Judicial Relations of the U.S. Judicial Conference, and the Board of Visitors of the U.S. Air Force Academy; and a Fellow of the American Bar Foundation.

Prior to his present position, Dean Young was the Fuyo Professor of Japanese Law and Legal Institutions at the School of Law of Columbia University, where he also served as director of the Center for Japanese Legal Studies, the Center for Korean Legal Studies, and the Project on Religion, Rights and Religious Freedom.

During the administration of President George Bush, Dean Young served as ambassador for trade and environmental affairs, deputy undersecretary for economic and agricultural affairs, and deputy legal advisor to the U.S. Department of State.

He is a 1973 graduate of Brigham Young University (B.A., summa cum laude) and Harvard Law School (J.D., magna cum laude, 1976), where he served as note editor of the *Harvard Law Review*. Before beginning his teaching career, Dean Young served as law clerk to Supreme Court Justice William H. Rehnquist.

Dean Young served a mission to Japan and as president of the New York New York Stake for The Church of Jesus Christ of Latter-day Saints. He is married to the former Suzan Stewart, and they have three children.

MARILYN ARNOLD

How is it that I, trained in the academic profession at one of the finest graduate schools in the country, turned out to be a believer rather than a nonbeliever? Among some academicians there is the notion that scholars are supposed to be religious skeptics, even cynics. But there is an odd phenomenon in The Church of Jesus Christ of Latter-day Saints. The more educated a Latter-day Saint is, the more likely he or she is to be active and committed in the faith. [1]

Recently I participated in an international literature seminar, and the subject of religion came up in a late-night conversation with several colleagues. We sat out on the deck of a large conference lodge, gabbing, gazing at the sky, listening to the crickets, and enjoying each other's company. One of the women in the group turned to me and said, "You're a Mormon, aren't you?" And I answered, "Yep, I'm a believer." She seemed surprised that I would say openly, without qualification, "I'm a believer," and she confessed that she was deeply touched by my statement. "Most people don't say that and mean it in quite the way I sense that you do," she said. "Especially not scholars."

Then I pointed out that in the Church, I was the norm. I'm educated; I believe.

Then another person asked why the Church kept growing and thriving when it had so many "rules." I laughed and replied that maybe it thrived *because* it had a lot of rules, because it wasn't especially easy to be an active Latter-day Saint. Don't most of us grow to love the thing for which we sacrifice? I asked. Don't we value the thing that

---

1. See Stan L. Albrecht and Tim B. Heaton, "Secularization, Higher Education, and Religiosity," *Review of Religious Research* 26 (September 1984):43-58.

requires something more of us than a warm body in a pew once a week, or once in a while? And the more we give, the more we devote our energies and resources, the more that cause or person becomes part of us and precious to us. Anyone who has had children, or who has chosen to care for an aging parent, knows that.

Then I said that when this seminar was finished, I would be putting my younger brother and his wife on the plane for Russia where they would serve in one of the missions—he as president of the mission, she as companion, adviser, and missionary. Since their call, they have been learning the Russian language through a tutor and their own study, they have attended a month of intensive language training, and they have sold their beautiful home along with many of their belongings. They are leaving four sons and three adorable grandchildren, with two more on the way whom they will not see until the little ones are nearly three years old.

"This is why the Church is strong and growing," I said, "because people like my brother and his wife know it is truly the Church of Jesus Christ, and there is nothing they would not do for it and for Him." I also mentioned that all four of their sons, as nineteen-year-olds, served two-year missions at their own expense—one to England, one to Germany, one to Taiwan, and one to France. And these are bright, able, funny, wonderful young men. Two are currently doing medical residencies, one is in a school of orthodontics, and the youngest will enter law school in another year. Every one of them is any mother's dream for a son-in-law. And do you know what? I have never heard one of them utter so much as a cussword or tell an off-color story. And I have played with these kids all their lives—on hikes, camping trips, tennis and basketball courts, and picnics. And, I have worshiped with them. Could anyone possibly think that they are less free than their unbelieving counterparts because they observe the Sabbath, pay a full one-tenth of their earnings as tithing to the Church, prefer wholesome music to unholy noise, and don't use foul language, drink alcohol, smoke, use drugs, or have extramarital sex? One need only look in their faces to see how free they are.

The day after that conversation on the deck, the woman who had seemed touched by my comment approached me again. "I still can't get over it," she said, "that you would say you were a believer right out loud—at an academic conference, no less." She paused, then added, "I'm glad you did. It's given me a lot to think about." What I didn't explain, but what she probably understood, was what I meant by describing myself as "a believer."

Perhaps I should have said that I believe in a Godhead composed of three distinct personages—the Father, His divine Son, and the Holy Ghost. I also believe that only through Jesus Christ can we mortals be redeemed from temporal death and from spiritual death. Temporal death results from the fact that we have mortal bodies, spiritual death from that fact that we commit sin. We need redemption from both temporal and spiritual death. I believe, too, that Christ restored His full gospel of salvation, and the attendant holy priesthood and ordinances, in modern times, through a devout young prophet named Joseph Smith. And I believe that He still reveals His will through living prophets. I further believe that the Bible is not the only recorded word of God. The Book of Mormon, paramount among latter-day scripture, is the most powerful testament of Jesus Christ ever published, a worthy companion to the Bible.

This woman's kindly curiosity set me to thinking. Why, indeed, am I a believer? And, perhaps more to the point, why am I a Latter-day Saint? That's an easy question on the surface of it. I was born into the Church, and our family was always actively engaged. My parents arranged for me to pay tithing when I was just a tot so that I would develop the habit, and now it is as natural to me as rain. So, too, are the other countless offerings of money, time, and service that are part of everyday life in the Church. Outside observers tend to focus more attention on what Church members are instructed *not* to do rather than on what they are. I would be naive if I pretended that all believers toe the line in all departments all of the time. But what I can say is that most of us try. And most of us thank the Lord every day for the principle of repentance.

What is it that drives such a flurry of sacrifice and good works? Is it this thing called "belief"—faith? Where does it come from? How is it born? How do I know I have it? Even as I contemplate the subject of belief, I realize that I have been speaking mainly about what believers do rather than what they are. That's a tougher one. Now that I am home and back in the customary routine of my life, my thoughts keep returning to that late-night conversation under a humid night sky, far from the crisp, dry air of my desert landscape. I said I was a believer, but do I really know what that means? It is easy to toss off a statement like that without giving it much thought at all. It *is* true; I'm a believer in the sense that I have described here. But am I a believer in the sense that Paul takes up the subject in connection with the unfailing practice of charity, or what the abridger of the Book of Mormon calls "pure love," the "pure love of Christ"? (Moroni 7:47.) No. I fail in charity every day.

Of course, what we do is often a measure of what we are, as in the case of my younger brother and his family. It is also true of my older brother and his family, who would not describe themselves as active believers, but who operate out of a deep, unpublic, undefined belief, serving their fellow beings whenever and wherever there is a need, better and more generously than I do. A case in point: In the last years of my parents' lives, my older brother took care of our parents' needs in exceptional ways, very nearly devoting his life to them. I helped as best I could, but without him, the floundering ship would have sunk long before it did.

I truly have been awakened spiritually; I cannot deny that for an instant. I know that Christ lives, and yet perhaps like most people I fall short when it comes to translating belief into practice. And yet, I often remember Peter's faltering steps as he sought the Lord across the water, and his failure of courage as he faced his accusers before the crucifixion. I remember these moments and take comfort. I remember, too, the words of Jesus and the words of the man who asked Jesus that his son be healed of a vexatious spirit:

> Jesus said unto him, If thou canst believe, all things are possible to him that believeth. And straightway the father of the child cried out, and said with tears, Lord, I believe; help thou mine unbelief. (Mark 9:23–24.)

"I believe; help thou mine unbelief." I take comfort in those words because what the man said was apparently enough. Jesus cast the spirit out of his son. Perhaps few mortals are perfect in their belief. What is required is the desire to believe, and a conscious effort to live as a believer would live. "If thou canst believe . . . ," Jesus said. But I must never forget, either, that after Peter had seen the resurrected Christ, he never faltered again, even to the point of martyrdom.

Marilyn Arnold is an emeritus professor of English at Brigham Young University, where she also served as dean of Graduate Studies, as assistant to former university president Dallin H. Oaks, and as director of the Center for the Study of Christian Values in Literature. She was awarded a Ph.D. in American literature from the University of Wisconsin—Madison and went on to receive various research awards, teaching awards, and lectureships. An internationally recognized scholar on the writings of Willa Cather, and a widely published writer and speaker in academic circles, she has also authored several nonacademic books, including three novels that grow out of her spiritual roots and her deep attachment to the desert country of southern Utah. An avid hiker, skier, and tennis player, Professor Arnold continues her long association with BYU through the Women's Research Institute.

ALAN C. ASHTON

With all my heart and soul I believe that the gospel of Jesus Christ as taught by The Church of Jesus Christ of Latter-day Saints is true. My assurance is certain and unwavering; it goes beyond mere hopeful belief. It is rooted in confidence, trust, faith, feeling, and experience. I have complete confidence that Jesus Christ can and will save those who come to Him with a broken heart and a contrite spirit. I have implicit trust that God the Father will keep His promises made in the holy scriptures. I have faith that the word of God contains power unto salvation. I have felt manifestations and promptings of the Holy Spirit, and I have experienced the sweet joy and peace that come from the tender mercies of the Savior and from following His commandments.

These are bold statements, but I don't mean to be proud in making these assertions. On the contrary, I regard my faith as a gift from God, and I am deeply grateful for the knowledge that has been granted to me concerning the truth of these things. I recognize that without the Savior and His loving atonement, I could not have this assurance. (See John 15:5.)

My purpose in writing this essay is to explain, as well as I can, the reasons for my strong convictions, and to elaborate why I believe so assuredly. My testimony is a personal assurance based on feelings I have felt and experiences I have had. It may be difficult for a reader who has not had such experiences and feelings to understand what I am trying to communicate.

For example, it is difficult to explain to someone how a particular food tastes. If a person has tasted the food before, he or she would understand much more completely the adjectives used to describe its taste. However, if the person has not tasted the food before, no matter how the taste is explained, it cannot be fully understood. So it is with feelings that are of the Holy Ghost. I have received and felt the warmth and reality of spiritual promptings, and those feelings form a solid base for my faith and trust in the truth of my convictions. I have felt the presence and influence of the Holy Spirit as I have read and studied the scriptures, as I have pondered their meanings, as I have prayed about their truth, as I have taught their principles, and as I have heard others teach and bear testimony of their truth.

A major pillar upon which my testimony securely rests is the knowledge I obtained concerning the truth of the Book of Mormon. As I graduated from East High School in Salt Lake City, Utah, I was accepted into the 23rd National Guard Army Band, where I played the trumpet. That summer I spent six months at Fort Ord, California, for my army basic training. During this training I carried a pocket-sized Book of Mormon with me, and each hour at our ten-minute breaks I read it. After a few weeks I finished reading the Book of Mormon, and I determined to put the prophet Moroni's exhortation (see Moroni 10:3–5) to the test. He promised that to those who receive the writings of the Book of Mormon, who ponder them and think of the dealings of God with men throughout the ages, and who ask God in the name of Christ if the book is true, asking with a sincere heart, with real intent, and having faith in Christ, He will manifest the truth of those things through the power of the Holy Ghost. I desired to have such a personal witness, so one night I climbed down from my top bunk and went alone into an adjoining classroom in our barracks. It was a large, empty room with folding chairs stacked away neatly against one wall. I walked barefoot across the cold linoleum floor to a far corner of the room, where I knelt in prayer. I asked God directly if the Book of Mormon was true. I had felt good about the teachings and precepts contained therein as I read it, but I desired a greater witness. As I asked, a feeling of warmth and certitude came over me that I could not deny. Just as it is difficult to say where the wind comes from and where it goes, so is it with this experience. I felt a definite peace, warmth, a prickling sensation, and the assurance of the Spirit confirming the truth of the Book of Mormon.

When I got off my knees upon experiencing that wonderful encounter with the Holy Spirit, I knew that the writings of the prophets contained in the Book of Mormon were true and from God. I also knew how the promptings of the Holy Ghost felt. My knowing that the Book of Mormon was true meant that surely Joseph Smith was a prophet of God and that the gospel of Jesus Christ was the way to eternal salvation and happiness. I knew that Jesus Christ was the literal son of God, that He lived and died to bring eternal salvation to those who come unto Him, and that He restored His true and living church upon the earth in these latter days through Joseph Smith.

Since that time, I have read and listened (on tape) to the Book of Mormon scores of times. In addition to the Book of Mormon, I have also read and studied the Bible, the Doctrine and Covenants, and the Pearl of Great Price regularly. I have seen the same gospel in them all and have felt the sweet, spiritual assurance of the truth of God's word as contained in each of these holy books. That constant nourishing by the Holy Spirit has kept my belief strong and active.

I have felt the same warm, confirming spirit many times in my life. I felt it as I knelt in prayer with people investigating the truth of the gospel as I served as a missionary of the Church. Not only did I feel the witness of the Holy Ghost, but I also saw that others experienced it as well. I understood what they felt as they described their feelings because I had felt it too.

I have felt the warm love of the Savior and a spiritual assurance as I have taught the scriptures, as I have counseled with each of my eleven children, as I have had important business decisions to make, and as I have taught and administered in priesthood callings in the Church.

I have sought spiritual guidance throughout my life, especially at critical times. Definite answers to prayer came and were sacred. Inspiration came from on high as I found my wife, Karen; it came as I sought for help regarding my dissertation topic; and it came concerning the starting of a word-processing business, which became WordPerfect Corporation. I humbly acknowledge the hand of the Lord in all successes that have blessed my life.

When Bruce Bastian and I first attempted to start our word-processing business, unexpected setbacks caused us to abandon our initial plans. That caused me to wonder somewhat about the strong and definite spiritual prompting I had received concerning our starting such a business. However, relying upon that feeling, I had faith that we would indeed be successful, and I mentioned to Bruce that we should stay in touch and that in the future we might be able to get together again to do our computer word processing. Bruce took a full-time job elsewhere, and soon an opportunity presented itself to us that allowed us to work together on our word-processing program. That effort blossomed into the successful WordPerfect word-processing company.

Besides the deep spiritual roots I have talked about, there are many practical experiences that add to my faith and knowledge of the truth of the gospel of Jesus Christ. I have seen its consistency as it is contained in all of the standard works. I have seen that this same gospel is taught and preached by modern prophets and apostles of the Lord Jesus Christ. I have seen the happiness and stability the gospel has brought to others, especially to those in my family. I have observed the peace and well-being that righteous principles have brought about. I have been the recipient of the concern and love of others, primarily of my wife, parents, and children. I have seen the healing power of the Lord's atonement in people's lives.

A number of years ago, my daughter and her husband lost their four-year-old son in a tragic bicycle accident. As his casket was closed, his younger brother cried, "Don't shut it. Bryan is in there." His seven-year-old sister immediately replied, "It's okay. Bryan is not in there now; he is with Heavenly Father." She expressed confidence that we would see Bryan in the future as a resurrected person.

I have seen that living the gospel of Jesus Christ brings love, peace, and contentment into family life. I have experienced and enjoyed this love in the families of my seven married children. I have witnessed the fruits of joy and happiness as my children and their children are striving to live the commandments of God.

When my wife and I had many small children, we were concerned about the amount of contention and bickering that was going on in our home. We decided to follow the admonition of latter-day prophets and began reading the Book of Mormon with our children every morning. It wasn't easy to start this new program with them. At first they didn't want to rise earlier in the morning to do the reading, but they did it. At times, as they were stretched out with their blankets on the floor and sofas, we wondered if our children were getting anything out of the reading, but we soon saw definite results in our home. The children were less quarrelsome, they were more considerate of each other, and there was an increase of love and harmony in our family.

I know that the gospel of Jesus Christ is God's power unto salvation, and that it brings happiness, trust, faith, and love to all who obediently follow its covenants and who come unto Jesus Christ.

Alan Ashton and his wife, Karen, have eleven children and seventeen grandchildren. He is the co-founder of WordPerfect corporation and past president and CEO. He is a director of Deseret Book Company, Whizbang Labs Inc., Candesa, and eRooms Systems Inc. and has served on other boards. He was a co-chairman of the BYU Lighting the Way capital fund campaign and was the chairman of the Board of Trustees of Utah Valley State College. He serves on the Utah State Department of Business and Economic Development Board. He and Karen are the founders and owners of Thanksgiving Point in Lehi, Utah.

THURL BAILEY

My parents weren't "every Sunday" churchgoers. We kids went to Sunday School at the Baptist church, and all the while I was growing up I felt like I always believed in God and in His Son, Jesus Christ. But there were a few elements that weren't clear to me, things that I was always searching for, even subconsciously. I had succeeded in pretty much everything I'd attempted in life, but sometimes I would think there was just something more.

When I first stepped off the plane in Salt Lake City to play NBA basketball for the Utah Jazz, I felt immediately acclimated to the beautiful surroundings as well as to the people themselves, who I thought were very, very cordial. I always got a gift when I met someone, and it was always a Book of Mormon—so I have a stack of about thirty of those in my library.

It didn't mean anything to me at first, but after a while I got curious, and anyway I was interested in knowing a little something about the people I would be spending a lot of time around. So I would pick the book up and take it with me on travels and read it. I'd done some research when I was in college and had to write a paper on the LDS people, but I really didn't have much knowledge of their religion. I'd heard some things, of course, especially about how blacks at that time were not eligible to be ordained to the priesthood, but until you meet people and understand how they live, you don't see it clearly. I decided to study and search for myself, because I've had judgment passed on me before, and I hate to do that to anyone, any group of people.

Then I met and married Sindi Southwick. Some individuals close to her were concerned that I was not a member of the Church. We had to be patient. We were ostracized for a while. Sindi was just fantastic, though—she didn't seem to care what anyone said. And she never pressured me about religion. She told me, "I'd like my kids to be raised in the Church," and I didn't have a problem with that. She never abandoned any of her beliefs; she just lived what she knew and led by example.

It wasn't until my NBA life slowed down that I had an opportunity to really delve into and learn in-depth what the Church was all about. The offer came up for me to go to Italy to play ball. I gave up my NBA career to go to a basically last-place team, with the money less than half of what I was used to making. But for some reason, I felt like I was prompted to do that.

So, I went to Italy by myself—my wife wasn't due to join me for several weeks—and I started to assess my life. I had that nagging, empty feeling inside like there was something else beyond the success I had achieved by worldly standards. I was definitely searching.

I called the missionaries of The Church of Jesus Christ of Latter-day Saints, thinking maybe they could answer some of my questions. When they introduced me to their mission president, Halvor Clegg, I knew right away that he was going to answer all the questions I had. It was kind of funny, really. I mean, here's this man who is maybe 5'8" or 5'9", and *he* intimidated *me*. It wasn't his look; it was the feeling I had when I shook his hand. There was a strong, strong spirit in that room. That night, although I didn't tell anyone, I knew the direction I was going. I knew that I would be a member of the Church.

When I called Sindi, I didn't say anything for a long time. I just cried. Finally I said, "I'm going to be baptized." And then *she* started to cry. There was really no talking going on—there was a bunch of crying on both ends of the phone.

So, here I am. It hasn't been an easy process, but I've learned a lot about patience and forgiveness. A lot of people I've encountered insist on telling me this is a racist church, but I say, "Hey, there's racism everywhere in the world. You can't spend your time blaming imperfect people." I searched for my answers with an open heart, without blame, and I got them. Anyone can do the same.

This I can say: My life just keeps getting better and better—receiving the priesthood and attending the temple. There's nothing to compare with gifts like those. It's the truth, plain and simple. I'm grateful every day that I believe.

 Thurl "Big T" Bailey was born April 7, 1961, in Washington D.C., but grew up in Cedar Heights, Maryland. His parents, Retha and Carl Bailey, also raised four other children: Sharon, Carl Jr., Inga, and Saul.

While Thurl's love of basketball didn't come until he was fourteen years old, few know that Thurl had spent most of his time in music interests, academics, and other school activities. Now, after twelve years in the NBA (nine with the Utah Jazz and three with the Minnesota Timberwolves), one year in Greece, and three years in Italy, including playing on the Italian league championship team, Thurl has undertaken other pursuits and is a TV color analyst for the Utah Jazz and KJZZ television.

Thurl, who has recorded two professional music CDs, lives in Salt Lake City with his wife, Sindi, and their two children, BreElle and Brendan (ages four and two).

Michael Ballam

Who has not stood in astonished awe at the ceiling of the Sistine Chapel and Michelangelo's depiction of the creation of man? Who has not felt a quickening of the pulse as Beethoven proposes in his Ninth Symphony that "all mankind can be brothers?" Who has not wept and committed to greater service when reading about the Bishop of Digne's forgiveness of Jean Valjean in Hugo's *Les Misérables?* Music and art have tremendous power to transcend politics, language, or social and economic status. They have the remarkable ability to communicate where words alone fail, and they bring joy and hope when other means falter. They are one important reason why I believe.

At an early moment in my life, seated next to my parents at a concert of Handel's *Messiah,* I felt the sweet calm that can only come from the presence of the Spirit. It has been my lifelong quest and passion to regain that moment of connection with His Spirit and share it with others. Having gained that first spiritual experience, I am not surprised that Handel credited divine inspiration as the source of the majesty of his immortal oratorio: "I did think I saw all heaven before me, and the great God himself!"[1]

J. S. Bach, probably the most spiritually devout of all composers, related in 1708 that his life purpose was "to create well-regulated church music to the Glory of God," noting that "music's only purpose should be for the Glory of God and the recreation of the human spirit."[2]

---

1. Patrick Kavanaugh, *Spiritual Lives of the Great Composers* (Grand Rapids, Mich.: Zondervan, 1996), p. 3.
2. Robert W.S. Mendl, *The Divine Quest in Music* (New York: Philosophical Library, 1957), p. 59.

Similarly Joseph Haydn, speaking of his oratorio *The Creation*, said: "Not from me—it came from above. . . . I would quietly and confidently pray to God to grant me the talent that was needed to praise him worthily."[3] Mozart, in a letter to his father Leopold, confided: "God is ever before my eyes" and "I prayed to God for His mercy that all might go well, to His greater glory, and the symphony began."[4]

Johannes Brahms, in Arthur M. Abell's *Talks with Great Composers*, describes the source of his inspiration: "I immediately feel vibrations that thrill my whole being. These are the spirit illuminating the soul power within, and in this exalted state, I see clearly what is obscure in my ordinary moods. Then I feel capable of drawing inspiration from above, as Beethoven did. . . . Straightway the ideas flow in upon me, directly from God, and not only do I see distinct themes in my mind's eye but they are clothed in the right forms, harmonies and orchestration. Measure by measure, the finished product is revealed to me when I am in those rare, inspired moods. The power from which all truly great composers like Mozart, Schubert, Bach and Beethoven drew their inspiration is the same power that enabled Jesus to work His miracles. It is the power that created our earth and the whole universe."[5]

It is no wonder that Latter-day Saints have been great supporters of symphony orchestras, oratorio societies, great choruses, and opera companies. Music and art help us understand beyond our normal capacity. The Apostle Paul commented on this phenomenon when he explained the teaching of the Spirit: "And the peace of God, which passeth all understanding, shall keep your hearts and minds through Christ Jesus." (Philippians 4:7.)

---

3. Herbert F. Peyser, *Joseph Haydn, Servant and Master* (New York: Philharmonic Symphony Society of New York, 1950), p. 50.
4. Alfred Einstein, *Mozart, the Man and the Artist Revealed in His Own Words* (New York: Dover Publications, 1965), p. 95.
5. Arthur M. Abell, *Talks with Great Composers* (New York: Philosophical Library, 1955), p. 5.

An example of that took place on Christmas Eve, 1944, on an island in the South Pacific. Every night for a week, the Japanese forces had climbed under the cloak of darkness to a position of advantage at the top of the island, whereupon they opened fire at midnight. On this particular night, the Allied soldiers heard the stealthy approach of the enemy forces taking their posts as usual. Then, just before the stroke of midnight, a courageous soldier in his foxhole began to sing "It Came Upon a Midnight Clear." It started out as a solo but soon became a duet, a trio, and a quartet, and ultimately the entire hillside was filled with the strains of that carol. Then the soldiers sang "O Little Town of Bethlehem" and finally "Silent Night," which aptly describes the evening—silent. No shots were fired. The enemy retreated in relative peace. What had happened? Is it possible that the Japanese were moved by the text or the familiarity of the tunes. No! It is highly unlikely that they had any recognition of text or tune. What was it, then, that caused their change of heart? It is the essence that can be found in all inspired works of music and art. It is found in the sweetness of a Brahms lullaby and the stirring crash of a Beethoven symphony. It hovers on ethereal wings in Michelangelo's depiction of the creation of man on the ceiling of the Sistine Chapel and in the immortal words of a Wordsworth or a Shakespeare. It is the light of Christ, the divine essence that is recognizable regardless of religion, race, or creed. It is that link between God and man which keeps communications open. God speaks through the words of holy scripture, the crash of thunder, the glory of a sunset, and the inspired moments of music and art. There is seldom an autograph, except in those moments when the Creator ascribes divine intervention, but it is audible and visual to all those who, as Moses said, have "eyes to see, and ears to hear." (Deuteronomy 29:4.)

In these difficult times, a closeness of the Spirit and full recognition of God's unconditional love for His children is crucial for me. It is becoming increasingly more important to rely on personal inspiration. I have sought the constant companionship of His spirit through reading His holy scriptures and surrounding myself with divinely inspired art and music. I have a firm, unshakable, solid knowledge that He lives and loves us. I have heard His voice in the crash of thunder and the crescendo of Beethoven's Ninth Symphony. I have felt His love in the writings of King David and Victor Hugo. I am a witness to His unconditional love and His desire to communicate with us in a myriad of inspired ways. Though this knowledge has come through the assistance of masterful teachers, composers, authors, and artists, it stands independent and personal. It is my anchor in the continual challenges of life.

Michael Ballam has received critical acclaim with the major opera companies of the USA and a recital career in distinguished concert halls on four continents. His operatic repertoire includes more than 600 performances of over 70 major roles. At the age of twenty-four, Mr. Ballam became the youngest recipient of the degree of Doctor of Music with Distinction in the history of Indiana University. An accomplished pianist and oboist, he is the founder and general director of the Utah Festival Opera, which is fast becoming one of the nation's major opera festivals. He is the author of more than thirty publications and recordings in international distribution and serves on the board of directors of four professional arts organizations.

MERRILL J. BATEMAN

My belief in The Church of Jesus Christ of Latter-day Saints began early as I listened to the convictions of my parents and grandparents and was taught to pray and discover the truths for myself. The belief was strengthened as a sixteen-year-old teenager when I was assigned to teach a class of eight-year-olds in Sunday School. For the first time in my life, I became a student of the scriptures. I read the Bible and the Book of Mormon daily in connection with a study of the lesson materials for the Sunday class. I developed warm feelings for the truths found in both books. I marveled at the consistency of the scriptural principles as a foundation for a happy life, and at the ease with which the principles could be explained to young children even though their complexities stimulated adults. The teenage calling began a lifelong odyssey with the Holy Word that continues to fascinate and warm me fifty years later.

But the story I wish to tell is not my own but that of a group of remarkable young people with whom I have been acquainted for the past few years while serving as president of Brigham Young University. In most respects they are typical of the young people of The Church of Jesus Christ. BYU students number approximately 30,000 and come from all fifty states and more than 110 countries. They speak sixty languages, with more than 50 percent having lived in a foreign country for eighteen months or more. Two-thirds speak a second language. The common element among them is an abiding faith in our Heavenly Father and in His Son, Jesus Christ; faith in the gospel and the Lord's divine Church as restored by the Prophet Joseph Smith; and obedience to gospel principles as taught by Church leaders.

Most of the students come to the university with a firm conviction of these principles even though they are only eighteen years of age. Their spiritual beliefs are personal and stem from study, prayer, and experience. Most have had a spiritual witness that has confirmed their beliefs. And the evidence of their faith is illustrated by their behavior. Jesus Christ told His listeners on one occasion, "A good tree cannot bring forth evil fruit, neither can a corrupt tree bring forth good fruit. . . . Wherefore by their fruits ye shall know them." (Matthew 7:18, 20.)

These young people are by and large honest, clean, and well-groomed, and they show respect for others. In a recent survey of students at twenty-two academic institutions, 92 percent of BYU students reported that they had never seen someone cheat at the university, compared to 55 percent for the norm group of students.[1] BYU students perennially rank number one as the most "stone-cold sober" in the nation.[2] In contrast, many university officials at other institutions are worried about alcohol-related problems among students, including absence from class and deaths associated with binge drinking. Another national student survey determined that BYU students study significantly more hours per week than other students even though they work more hours to earn funds for their schooling. They also pay a greater share of their expenses compared with students at other institutions.[3]

All students attending Brigham Young University agree to live by the BYU Honor Code, which is modeled after the Church's thirteenth Article of Faith. The article reads as follows: "We believe in being honest, true, chaste, benevolent, virtuous, and in doing good to all men. . . . If there is anything virtuous, lovely, or of good report or praiseworthy, we seek after these things."

---

1. "Academic Integrity Study," Center for Academic Integrity, Duke University, fall 1999.
2. "The Best 331 Colleges," *Princeton Review*, 2000 edition, p. 43.
3. "College Student Experiences Questionnaire (CSEQ)," Winter 1997; "National Survey of Student Engagement (NSSE)," The Carnegie Foundation for the Advancement of Teaching and The Pew Forum on Undergraduate Learning, Winter 2000.

The code was not developed by the administration or trustees but by a group of students many years ago. As outlined in the code, students are expected to demonstrate in their daily living on and off campus the moral virtues encompassed in the gospel of Jesus Christ. These include honesty in dealing with other people as well as honesty in the classroom. Cheating on a test or plagiarizing a paper is a rarity at BYU. Also, students are expected to live a chaste and virtuous life. This means that students are not to engage in sexual activity except within the bonds of marriage. Further, students are to use clean language, respect others, and abstain from alcoholic beverages, tobacco, tea, coffee, and substance abuse. Finally, students are to dress modestly and be clean and neat in appearance.

In 1996 an ambassador to the United States from a major foreign country visited Brigham Young University. During the course of his visit, he gave a lecture at the Kennedy Center to a large group of students. Afterward, a question-and-answer session ensued. Suddenly, the visitor realized that almost everyone in the hall spoke Spanish—his native language. Moreover, it became apparent that many of the students had lived in his country. Following the lecture and a tour of the campus, he came to my office for us to become acquainted. During the course of the conversation, he asked two questions that I will always remember. The first was "Are all the buildings new?" The answer: "No! Some are almost one hundred years old." His response: "But they are so clean!" The second question then followed: "Why are the students so happy? Everyone seems to be smiling." He and I discussed the selection process for admitting students, including their willingness to live the BYU Honor Code. I told him of their background in the Church, the strength of their families, the feelings they have about Christ's teachings, and their understanding of life's purposes. It was a marvelous exchange as he gained a deeper appreciation for the remarkable young people on the BYU campus.

Two years later, another government official from a different foreign country visited the campus. His routine followed much the same pattern as the ambassador's. At noon he joined me for lunch. He, too, was impressed with the students, whose questions illustrated an awareness of the issues confronting his nation. The exchange with the students demonstrated their appreciation for his country, his people, and his culture. During the meal he leaned over and said, "Last week I was on another campus in another state. The students on that campus are different from yours. If I were to bring those students to this campus, would they soon act like your students?" My answer was, "No! We would have to start with their parents first." In most instances, the appearance and behavior found among BYU students is the result of many years of training in the home by parents who believe in the same principles exemplified in the Honor Code.

The two experiences are related not to suggest that BYU students are better than students on other campuses. But they are different in appearance and behavior because of their beliefs. In point of fact, they are not different from other Latter-day Saints students or young adults who adhere to the principles taught by the Church.

Recently, I learned of a student initiative that has blessed the lives of children in a foreign land. Two women students, Chelsea Jensen and Annette Orlando, learned of an overcrowded and understaffed orphanage in Romania. They decided to visit the orphanage as a service project for a sociology class. After their classmates helped them raise money for travel and the orphanage, the two young women made their way to Europe in April 1998. The intrepid duo did not speak Romanian, had no accommodations, and knew little of the culture, but their sense of charity carried them forward.

They found infants and toddlers confined to cribs, their little minds and bodies underdeveloped because of the dearth of human contact. The six regular staffers were overwhelmed by the eighty children in their care. After assisting in various ways for six weeks, the pair returned to BYU and reported to their classmates. Others immediately volunteered to continue the tradition of service and learning, and the example set by Chelsea and Annette has now blossomed into a regular work-study program administered by the David M. Kennedy Center for International Studies at Brigham Young University. Every semester, between five and ten carefully screened students arrive in Romania to teach and love the children at the orphanage.

Students spend a minimum of six hours a day with the children applying a clinically-proven child-development program that uses a series of teaching steps that help improve a child's physical and emotional development. The babies learn to grasp and pass small objects between their hands; how to sit, crawl, and walk; and how to speak short Romanian phrases. Our students, mostly pursuing various social science and family life degrees, carefully chart the children's progress as they build from one class to another.

Chelsea and Annette are typical of thousands of BYU students who combine service and learning at the university. Domestic and international projects are carefully defined to integrate student service with academic learning. Faculty members work closely with students in project design, monitoring activities, and evaluating outcomes. The campus motto of "Enter to learn, go forth to serve" is a reality. Recently the *Chronicle of Higher Education* reported that the number of BYU students engaged in foreign internships and study-abroad programs was the largest of any campus in the United States.[4] In addition, thousands of BYU students are engaged in service-learning activities domestically.

My time at the university will soon total fourteen years—four as a

4. "More Students Study Abroad, but Their Stays are Shorter," *Chronicle of Higher Education*, November 17, 2000, p. A74.

professor, four as a dean, and six as the president. In the past six years approximately 60,000 students have been on campus, and over the fourteen years the number must approach 140,000. The quality of these young people is extraordinary. They are bright and quick-witted, but more important, they are good. Their belief in the principles associated with the gospel of Jesus Christ and the manner in which their behavior has exemplified them has strengthened my conviction of the Church and its teachings. I know why they are happy: they are true to their convictions and live accordingly.

 Elder Merrill J. Bateman is the president of Brigham Young University, having served in that capacity since January 1996. At the time of his appointment he was serving as the presiding bishop of The Church of Jesus Christ of Latter-day Saints. He has been a Church General Authority since June 1992. Prior to his Church callings, Elder Bateman served as dean of Brigham Young University's business school, as an economic consultant to governments and multinational businesses, and as a professor of economics. He received his Ph.D. in economics from the Massachusetts Institute of Technology. He is married to Marilyn Scholes Bateman, and they are the parents of seven children.

JOYCE M. BENNETT

I have the opportunity of meeting a lot of outstanding women in my role as the wife of a United States senator. I have traveled extensively with my husband and have met and talked with the wives of many world leaders and ambassadors, as well as other Senate wives. These are caring, religious women; we pray together and share problems and successes. When we get into religious discussions, we find that we have much in common, and I'm always asked about my own religious background.

The first reason I am a member of The Church of Jesus Christ of Latter-day Saints is because my parents and grandparents were. I grew up in Salt Lake City learning about the principles of the gospel. I was taken to church every Sunday and went to Primary (the children's organization) every Tuesday after school. During my teenage years I attended the Young Women's organization every Wednesday night.

My home was stable. My parents loved each other, and I had three older sisters but no brothers. I was taught by example how to live up to the teachings of Jesus Christ and to create a Christ-centered home.

I was different in one respect: My grandfather, David O. McKay, was president of The Church of Jesus Christ of Latter-day Saints. To me, he was two people—the loving grandfather who never forgot my birthday and was always punctual to Sunday dinner, and the striking, white-haired prophet who spoke in the Salt Lake Tabernacle at the Church's worldwide general conference twice a year and guided the membership of the Church. My parents traveled with him on occasion, and I heard stories of remarkable happenings on these trips abroad (a hurricane that veered off its course, barely missing their airplane; children in Germany who came from behind the Iron Curtain to shake hands with the prophet and then took his handkerchief back to their ill mother, who was healed; and many other similar accounts).

More routinely, I watched my own mother and father fast and pray for friends who were ill and then take a ham or a casserole to the family. I watched them spend many hours in church service of various kinds. I participated when our family prayed together not only in special times, as when my father had a small stroke, but every morning, when we would say family prayers. I would hear my parents pray for every child by name. (This continued into their old age, when they had a little trouble remembering all of the grandchildren. I remember hearing my mother interrupt Daddy by saying, "Don't forget the Parmley family!")

The second reason I believe in the gospel of Jesus Christ is because, as an adult, I have seen what it does in the lives of others. Latter-day Saints are happy people. When my daughter was taking Suzuki violin lessons in California, her teacher commented that she always liked to teach in Utah because the people there are so happy and friendly. She wondered what made them that way, and could she become like that? I told her that the first thing she would have to do was believe in Jesus Christ. She said that might be difficult as she was Jewish. However, she had recognized that the Latter-day Saints have a sense of contentment, a faith in where they came from, and an understanding of why they are here in this life and where they are going after it is over. They have a strong foundation on which to build their lives.

I realize that the Church doesn't take away problems and difficulties, but it does help people to deal with them. I have a Latter-day Saint friend who went through a difficult divorce, leaving her to cope with five children by herself. When I asked her how the Church responded to her needs, she said that the leadership in her congregation had been extremely supportive and helpful. They had especially been sensitive to the needs of her growing children, who now had no father. For example, one of her teenage sons suddenly felt "different" because his father had walked out on the family. She did her best to reassure him, but it was the concerted, Church-encouraged actions of his Latter-day Saint friends, rallying around, that helped her son understand that his personal worth was not dependent on his father's presence. The Church was her rock of support in difficult times.

The final reason I believe is because the Church has done a great deal for me. It has been the center point of my husband's and my life together. We have always been unified in our beliefs, giving our home a solid foundation. We believe that because we were married in the temple, our marriage is eternal, which further strengthens it.

I have felt the influence of the Lord in small ways in dealing with my family. One day I was driving to our home and felt that I should drive by the high school. I didn't usually take that route, although it wasn't far out of the way. When I did, I found out that my daughter had been in a minor car accident. While it wasn't a serious accident, she was upset and needed her mom there to help with police details such as car registration and insurance. I've always sought the Lord's help in dealing with any issues with our children and have felt Him near me.

The Church has also given me an incredible opportunity for growth as an individual and as a woman. Some of the skills I have developed as a result of my activity in the Church include public speaking; the capacity to organize and serve a dinner to three hundred people; the ability to direct a choir; the ability to teach classes to adults, youth and children; the opportunity to direct an orchestra and create a musical production; the experience of organizing women's conferences; and going on backpacking trips and learning outdoor survival skills. It has given me a lifelong opportunity to serve and nurture others.

One insight into how much I have gained from the Church came from a friend outside of it. When I was the choir director, I leaned heavily on a neighbor who was a professional musician and had been a choir director in other churches. She taught me a lot about choral conducting, even coming as a guest conductor once or twice. After I had served in this calling for about two years, I was called to serve in a leadership position elsewhere and had to give up the choir post. My friend couldn't understand why I was asked to change positions when I had just been trained in the choir job and was doing well there. She felt that the Church promoted mediocrity by switching people around so much. What she didn't understand was that one of the purposes of the Church is to help us grow and progress. The new assignment taught me a great deal.

I have had many opportunities to direct choirs since then, so my training has been put to good use. Incidentally, this particular friend investigated the Church further, joined it herself, and now understands.

I am grateful to be a member of The Church of Jesus Christ of Latter-day Saints. My faith in Jesus Christ is the backbone of everything I think and do. I can't imagine how I would exist without it.

Joyce M. Bennett has reared six children while maintaining her professional skills as a flute performer and teacher. She holds a degree in flute performance from American University, has played with the Utah Symphony and the Pacific Palisades Symphony, and was president of the Utah Flute Association. Married to Senator Robert F. Bennett, she currently teaches Suzuki Method flute on the faculty of the Levine School of Music in Washington, D.C., where she has served as first vice president of the U.S. Senate Spouses as well as a member of the boards of Meridian International Center and Washington Performing Arts Society.

ROBERT F. BENNETT

A cynic would say, "Of course Senator Bennett says he believes in The Church of Latter-day Saints. He runs in a state where 70 percent of his constituents are members of it. If he doesn't say he believes, he doesn't get reelected."

Will you stick with me long enough for me to explain why there is more to it than that? Let me start by telling you my history (briefly).

I have had what some people charitably call "a checkered career," which means that I have had a lot of different jobs, in a lot of different cities, in a lot of different fields. I have worked for a paint company in Salt Lake City, run a PR firm in New York and another one in Washington, managed a marketing operation in Japan while doing consulting for another one in France, been president of a NASDAQ-listed firm in California, and done marketing for the Howard Hughes hotels in Las Vegas. I have been part owner of a group of radio stations in Nevada and Hawaii.

I have served as a staffer in Washington, D.C., first with a congressman and then with a senator. After that I was a corporate lobbyist. Then I served in the Executive Branch, at the Department of Transportation, during the Nixon administration. I have been vice president of an airline and was the CEO of a company that started with four full-time employees and is now listed on the New York Stock Exchange. I have worked as a political consultant to a variety of campaigns, including some presidential ones, and, as a result of one of those campaigns, am now a U.S. senator.

Why is any of that relevant? Only because it means that I have met a lot of people in my life.

I believe in the teachings of The Church of Jesus Christ of

Latter-day Saints because I have watched those teachings affect the lives of people.

I have seen the Church make things better for people wherever it has gone. I have watched people have better marriages, become better parents and better neighbors, gain confidence in themselves and achieve success, and find comfort in adversity and faith in their questioning, all as a result of their affiliation with and service in the Church.

The reason I have been able to watch all this happen is because the Church has no professional clergy. We have to do everything ourselves. Wherever we have lived, my family and I have been involved in Church activity, and we have seen, firsthand, what it does to people, regardless of the culture from which they may have come.

The experience that gave me the most insight into the Church's impact on people's lives was when I was asked to serve as a bishop. I had a congregation of more than three hundred people to deal with. Since I still had to earn a living outside of the Church, my time was volunteered, as was theirs. I had two men, or counselors, who helped me, directly, and the three of us asked nearly a hundred others to take some role in keeping our congregation going. We organized the meetings, preached the sermons, shoveled the snow, visited the sick, conducted the funerals, taught the classes, and went hiking with the Boy Scouts, among lots of other things. When you go through something like that, you get to know people, and God, very well. I mention God because I spent a lot of time on my knees, asking for His help in all of this, as did the other teachers and workers in our group.

His help was taken as a given. It was written into the instruction manuals. Those manuals would tell you what to do up to a certain point, and then they would say, "Pray about it and follow the promptings of the Spirit."

That can be a very scary thing. I have been in some tight circumstances in some of my Church assignments, where people were looking to me either for advice or for the performance of some spiritual ordinance in some truly difficult situations, and I knew that I wasn't up to it. But He—God—was. He always came through.

He is throughout the Church, running it, and not just at the top. I have felt His hand in tiny little gatherings, in far-off places, as people of faith have turned to Him and asked for help that was beyond human capacity to give. I have seen that help come, and lives change, always for the better. That's one of the reasons why I believe.

Most of the people I have met have not been members of The Church of Jesus Christ of Latter-day Saints. Let me talk about a few of them for a minute.

I was in a city in Europe with a colleague, sitting in a hotel lobby waiting to go to dinner, when an attractive woman walked by. My associate surprised me by asking if I thought she was a prostitute. I said I hadn't really thought about it—I was not in the market for one—and that triggered a conversation. He was amazed, he said, that I wasn't even curious about what it would be like to have a sexual partner other than my wife. He had had plenty, and he told me that I should at least try it. "You can always go back to being faithful if you don't like it," he said.

While he said he was very happy with his current wife, he had had several before her, as well as a large number of girlfriends in between. He insisted that there was very little downside to that kind of life.

But I have seen too many examples of what that sort of behavior leads to. I have no desire to live as my friend lives. As one of my friends who did try it told me, "When you become an adulterer, you learn to be a really good liar." Why is that a good idea?

When I look at what would happen to my life if I adopted the lifestyles I see followed by some of my friends, I know I don't want to go there. That's another reason why I believe.

I have met many important people in my life. I have been close to power—real power—in terms that the world understands, and I have seen what it can do to people who do not have a mooring in something greater than themselves. The Bible says that the love of money is the root of all evil, but I believe that power is the ultimate temptation. When Satan had his dialogue with Jesus, he tempted Him first with appetite and then with fame. When neither one of those did the trick, Satan's final offer was power.

Lord Acton said, "Power tends to corrupt—and absolute power corrupts absolutely."[1] Look to history for examples. Hitler killed up to ten million, convinced that he alone was right in his theories. Lenin and Stalin killed many times that number, filled with the same conceit.

We don't have to go back that far. I lived through the Watergate era. I knew many of the people who went to jail during that time—some of them had been my friends and co-workers in the first Nixon administration. Most of them were decent people who had been seduced by the power that came with the positions they held. As their careers crumbled, I saw how transitory their power really had been, power that they had worked so hard to acquire.

I don't agree that power automatically corrupts, because I have met many important men and women who use their power to serve others, who genuinely seek to do something positive with the positions they hold. These people all have one thing in common—humility, usually rooted in a deep religious belief.

So, what about power in the Church? Not long ago a major newspaper decided to write an "exposé" about the Church. Following the time-honored maxim to "follow the money," they did a complete financial profile of the Church. The reporters chased down every lead, probed every file, interviewed every source they could to find out how

---

1. John Emerich Edward Dalberg Acton, *Essays on Freedom and Power*, selected by Gertrude Himmelfarb (Boston: Beacon Press, 1949), p. 364.

much the Church was worth and how its leaders used that financial power. When they were done, the paper reported that there were no instances of corruption—not one. No one in the Church had used his position to enrich himself.

That didn't surprise me. Throughout my life I have watched the people who hold power in the Church (and not from too far a distance, because I have been related to some of them). I know they make mistakes, because they are human, and human beings make mistakes all the time. However, the leaders in our Church are, as a group, unusually humble and anxious to use their power to serve others.

I think there is a reason for that. I think they spend more time in prayer than I did as a bishop; I believe they are truly concerned that they do what God wants them to do, and they try every day to find out what that is. God has answered their prayers and touched their lives in a way that blesses the Church and its members continuously. I've seen that, close up, and that's another reason why I believe.

Have I always believed? Well, I never *disbelieved*—never latched onto something else and said, "This proves that the Church is false." But there was a time when I entertained the notion that it might be, when I was far more concerned with other things. There was a time when "belief" was not something to which I paid much attention.

It was in my late teens that I decided I had better start paying attention. I had said prayers, perfunctorily, all of my life, but I seldom *prayed*—really prayed. One of my friends challenged me to do that. I did.

I didn't hear a voice. I didn't see a light. I didn't have any sort of manifestation. But I did get an answer, an answer that told me nothing more specific than the fact that God was there and had heard me. There were more prayers, sometimes with specific problems in mind, and more answers, and, bit by bit, my conviction grew. And then I started noticing people, in all the ways I have described here and many more, and I knew that God was in their lives too, in the Church. I knew that I was not the only one who knew that it was the truth.

I started studying. I wanted to be comfortable, intellectually, with the doctrine and the history of the Church. Faith transcends intellect, but it was important to me to find out if the concepts of the Church "hang together," if they make sense. I read commentaries written by both friends and foes, and I discovered that the Church offers what one of its leaders calls "a rational theology."[2] I found that everything fits together magnificently.

Since that beginning, I have lived almost half a century. As I've said, I have gone a lot of places, seen a lot of things, met a lot of people, read a lot of books, and said a lot of prayers. The totality of my experience teaches me that I still believe.

Sometimes I don't act as I should, as a believer. There are times when I have let the pressures of life move me away from where I should be. But I know, as I found out as a teenager, that if I pray— really *pray*—God will be there, listening. He'll help me. He'll help anyone. I know that.

And that's why I believe.

 Robert F. Bennett is a U.S. senator from Utah. His primary focus in the Congress has been on economic and high-tech issues. He was chairman of the Senate's Y2K Committee and the Republican High Tech Task Force, and in the 107th Congress he is vice chairman of the Joint Economic Committee. His other committee assignments include Appropriations, Banking, and Governmental Affairs. His previous career was as a businessman; *Inc.* magazine named him Entrepreneur of the Year in the Rocky Mountain region in 1989. He is the author of *Gaining Control*.

2. John A. Widtsoe, *A Rational Theology* (Salt Lake City: Deseret Book Co., 1937).

SUSAN EASTON BLACK

"I extend a call to you and your wife to serve a brief mission on Easter Island," said Elder Dale Miller, a General Authority of The Church of Jesus Christ of Latter-day Saints serving in Santiago, Chile. To my dismay, my husband accepted the assignment despite my discreet nudges to the contrary. Realizing that I couldn't count on him for an acceptable excuse, I blurted out, "It took all the courage I had to spend this summer in Santiago. Easter Island is out of the question. Perhaps you have forgotten that I am a professor on leave from Brigham Young University and haven't made plans for giving real Church service—just a few lectures in designated metropolitan chapels will be fine for me."

Elder Miller must not have heard my comments, for he spoke of faithful members on the island needing my help. "How can that be?" I asked. "What could I possibly offer a people that live 2,300 miles west of Chile on the farthest eastern outpost of the Polynesian world? Surely the native population would be better served by anyone else. What I know about the mysterious Moai statues can't sustain a conversation, and I have no illusions of returning to the university with tales of being an adventurous Thor Heyerdahl. Just give me a room full of books in a quiet library in Santiago, and I will be entertained for weeks."

Elder Miller's enthusiasm for the balmy temperature and clear water at the island did nothing to sway my opinion. Instead of focusing on his discourse on tuna fishing, primitive boats, and sandy beaches, I was remembering my readings of slavery raids, smallpox epidemics, and a leper colony associated with the island's history. Nothing that the Church leader said piqued my interest about the island or its people, but his anticipation of my affirmative answer to serve a brief mission in the island posed a huge dilemma for me.

I had always taken my religion seriously and had never thought of not accepting a Church assignment before. A hand-embroidered statement from the prophet Joshua, "Choose you this day whom ye will serve; . . . as for me and my house, we will serve the Lord" had been our family motto for years. (Joshua 24:15.) Since childhood I had been taught that the Lord speaks to His prophets and other Church leaders. This knowledge had been confirmed through research and study and in prayer in the quiet of my home.

For nearly twenty-five years in academia, I had focused my library efforts on the founder of the Church of Jesus Christ, Joseph Smith. I had read and memorized his words and knew that he was a prophet of God. The Book of Mormon: Another Testament of Jesus Christ had been my favorite reading for decades. As I read its contents, the Spirit of the Lord testified to me that it was the word of God. I had studied the mortal life of Jesus Christ and resonated to the words of Isaiah: "His name shall be called Wonderful, Counsellor, The mighty God, The everlasting Father, The Prince of Peace." (Isaiah 9:6.) I knew by careful study that The Church of Jesus Christ of Latter-day Saints was the Lord's Church upon the earth.

But more important than my academic efforts was the knowledge I had gained through life's experiences. Through fasting and prayer, I knew that what I had studied of Jesus Christ and Joseph Smith was true. I knew that the power of the priesthood, the authority to act in the name of God, was restored to the earth, for I had seen loved ones healed of afflictions by those holding the holy priesthood. My desire was to share my thoughts and testimony with those residing in Santiago, not with those living on Easter Island. Frustrated by my dilemma, I excused myself from Elder Miller.

Needless to say, my husband was deflated by my expressed

thoughts. "I can't go," I told him, and, "I won't go." Returning to our apartment, I opened the scriptures, seeking a defense for my adamant stance. Perhaps it wasn't a coincidence that I read of those who hearkened to the words of ancient prophets and those who did not. The blessings that followed faithful service and the trials that came to those who disobeyed prophetic counsel seemed clearly applicable to my circumstance. Certainly my choice wasn't of the magnitude of Cain or Jonah, yet I did have a choice to make.

Even as my confidence waned, my spirit soared as I knelt in prayer. I recognized the familiar voice whispering peace to my soul and felt a renewed sense of courage assuring me that I could serve on the island. Before I lost that choice feeling, I telephoned Elder Miller and told him that I would accompany my husband to the remote island. He was pleased. It seemed like the right choice at the time, but days later as I stepped onto the airplane questions arose again.

As the plane arrived at the island, natives carrying leis and selling souvenirs greeted passengers in the terminal. The greeting and profiteering was reminiscent of Hawaii, and my thoughts turned to crowded shopping centers and white beaches. "Easter Island may not be so bad," I said to my husband. But a taxi ride on dirt roads quickly eroded my newfound hope. The driver's boast, "I own one of the few cars on the island. Most natives travel by horseback," did nothing to calm my nerves. And then, as if to distress me further, he bragged, "We have a hospital on the island. There are two doctors that work at the hospital. One is a 'people's doctor' and the other is a veterinarian."

At length the driver stopped his monologue and taxi in front of our destination—a clapboard dwelling that served as a chapel and now our home. The building was a far cry from home, but it would do. It wasn't until I washed windows, waxed the floors, and polished the furniture that my sense of well-being returned. I had a purpose, a moment in time, and I must not fail to find out why I was needed at the island.

That purpose did not unfold until the first Sunday. As I watched the island families enter the chapel, I noticed that some were carrying scriptures, others babies, and one man a piano keyboard. After I greeted the man with the keyboard, he asked in a unique blend of Spanish and the native language, Rapanui, "Can you play this?" I nodded, "Yes."

In my opinion the favorite and classic Latter-day Saint hymn "Come, Come, Ye Saints" was never sung better than that day at the island. There, in the humble circumstance of a small chapel, the Saints of God sang with gusto the hymn of thanksgiving. The singing brought tears to my eyes, and the tears increased as one after another of the islanders shared their testimony of the gospel of Jesus Christ. I didn't understand all of their words, but I felt them—especially the testimony of an eleven-year-old boy named Marcos.

When the Sunday meetings ended, Marcos asked me if I would teach him to play the piano. I assured him that I would try. Every day Marcos came to the chapel to practice on the keyboard, and every day he brought me avocados. Although I wondered how I could eat so many avocados or how it was possible to have such severe acne from eating the avocados, I looked forward to his visits. His keyboard expertise was questionable, but he was determined. I was surprised at his consistent ability to hit the wrong notes but even more surprised at my patience and the love I felt for his goodness. He sincerely wanted to learn the hymns of the Church, and by the end of our stay on the island, he was becoming pretty good. In fact, together we carried the keyboard to the hospital so that he could play for the patients. His smile and musical talent, or lack thereof, cheered up the patients and presented opportunities for my husband and me to teach the gospel of Jesus Christ.

I hadn't anticipated how difficult it would be to say good-bye to Marcos, but I had books to read, and my summer leave from the university was over. Wanting to savor the memories of my favorite musician on Easter Island, I determined to send Marcos a keyboard from the States. It wasn't a rational decision, for the island lacked a postal delivery service. Packages picked up on the day they arrived at the post office could be claimed. If the packages were not claimed the first day, their contents became the possession of postal workers.

What were the odds that Marcos would go to the post office to retrieve his package the day it arrived? Calculating that the odds were against his receiving the keyboard, I didn't write him about the forthcoming gift. I made my purchase and mailed it with a prayer in my heart that somehow the gift would reach him.

Months passed, and as university assignments crowded my life, Easter Island became a distant memory—until a day in February 2001 when a long-distance telephone operator asked, "Will you accept a collect call from Easter Island?" As I stammered, I heard the voice of Marcos saying, "It's me." After I accepted the call, he exclaimed, "I prayed to God for a piano. Today I went to the post office and God sent me a piano. I can still play 'Come, Come, Ye Saints,' 'I Know That My Redeemer Lives,' and 'We Thank Thee, O God, for a Prophet' [other Latter-day Saint hymns]."

Scoffers may reject the miraculous nature of this story and claim that it was a coincidence that Marcos was praying for a piano or that he went to the post office the day the package arrived at the island. But Marcos and I know better. God hears and answers prayers. He answered the prayer of a bespectacled professor and the prayer of an eleven-year-old boy. I would never have known the joy of having a young Rapanui friend if I hadn't accepted the mission assignment to serve on Easter Island.

The truth has been restored. God hears and answers prayers. Because of prayer, I have a friend on Easter Island who knows, as I do, that The Church of Jesus Christ of Latter-day Saints is God's church on the earth.

 Susan Easton Black is a professor of church history and doctrine and a past associate dean of general education and honors at Brigham Young University. Dr. Black has received many university awards and fellowships for her research and writing over the past twenty-five years, including the Karl G. Maeser Distinguished Faculty Lecturer Award in 2000, the highest award given a professor at Brigham Young University. She has authored, edited, and compiled more than ninety books and as many articles. She is married to Harvey Black, and they are the parents of eight children.

HAROLD C. BROWN

My great-great-grandfather, Anson Call, joined The Church of Jesus Christ of Latter-day Saints in 1835, following the example of his father. The decision was difficult for him. He tells of Brigham Young, John P. Greene, and Almon Babbitt's coming to his home and teaching him from the Bible and the Book of Mormon. These visits were not always pleasant. The missionaries knew the scriptures well, and Anson was unable to answer their questions or present his point of view.

To prepare for one visit, he determined that he would study the Bible and Book of Mormon from cover to cover. His diligent study brought a witness of the truth in both of these books. He now faced the decision of whether or not to join this newly formed, little-understood, and unpopular religion.

After struggling with the decision for some time, Anson finally approached the Lord in serious prayer, asking for "the courage to face the world in 'Mormonism.'" He said that after his prayer, he never again feared what men could do. His determination carried him faithfully through many trials and tribulations, including the long trek to the Salt Lake Valley, where his life was one of service, unselfishness, and sacrifice.

Just as many of my ancestors came to believe through their own study, prayer, and sacrifice, so have I. I have learned that one of the important ways we come to believe in God is by unselfishly serving others.

We hear much of those who are selfish and unkind, who harm others, or who are involved in other shameful acts. On September 11, 2001, we saw an unbelievable display of terror, cruelty, and inhumanity to man in the eastern United States. However, the majority of mankind cares about other people and does much to relieve their suffering. Many would do more if they had the means to do so.

My belief in God and His goodness is strengthened as I see man's humanity to man. We learn about God as we see His character and qualities manifested in those who spend time in the service of others. Those who serve others more often sense the power of God within themselves. Those who receive assistance feel God's love and concern for them. Both givers and receivers are blessed. Both gain more understanding of God's goodness and His love for His children.

My own parents set an example for me. My mother was a wonderful cook. Our home was filled with the aroma of bread, pies, cookies, cakes, and casseroles. However, we learned to ask before we assumed that this food was for us. Often it was prepared with loving hands for a mother with a new baby, a neighbor, a friend, or someone else in need.

The fact that our family had little of this world's goods was not a deterrent to helping others. Our home was modest and a little older, and while we enjoyed the necessities of life, there wasn't much left over beyond immediate needs.

I remember a single woman who lived in our community. She was alone, trying to raise a son. She had little education and produced only a small income by cleaning homes and offices. She was a friend of my parents; they often visited together. She did not have a license to drive a car, and my parents helped her with transportation.

On occasion she would work in our home, washing and ironing, cleaning, and papering walls. I wondered why my parents paid someone to work for us when we had such meager circumstances ourselves. My mother was ambitious and able, and my three sisters knew how to work. It was only later that I came to understand their desire to help this woman. My mother and father could have managed without her service, but they seemed unable to manage very well without serving other people. My father firmly believed that if he would help the poor and needy, he would always have enough for himself and some to spare.

For many years I have been employed in the work of caring for the poor and needy throughout the world. The rewards and satisfaction I have felt are immeasurable, and my faith in a loving God increases as I witness the generosity and kindness of others.

Recently, a request went out to the Relief Society women of the Church. They were asked to provide quilts for refugees who had fled from Kosovo. Winter was coming soon, and there were hopes that 30,000 quilts could be provided.

The women of the Church went to work. Others soon joined in. Some were members of the LDS Church—others were not.

The response was heartwarming, and the feelings were tender. Quilts came in one at a time, by the armload and by the truckload. Families gathered together and made quilts. Mothers, grandmothers, and daughters together made quilts. Children made quilts. Even young men made quilts. Notes were frequently attached to the quilts, many of them unsigned. One note simply said:

> Dear Children of Kosovo:
> We love you!
> We pray for you!
> We have faith in you!
> From children of The Church of Jesus Christ of Latter-day Saints.

Another note came from six young men in Southern Utah. It said:

> Hi, We live in Ivins, Utah. Our town is about the size of your family pet. . . . We worked long and hard on this quilt and hope it helps. Six people made this quilt, and we got poked by needles and cut by scissors. Tyler was the main

man, the sewer. Kayde was another sewer. Kayson, me, was the cutter. Brandon was in charge of first-aid procedures. Jason was the relief cutter, and Dallen, um . . . brought personality to the group. We are members of the LDS Church. We did this service project to aid in the world effort to help people in need. We hope this warms your heart.

Women in a nearby prison made 500 quilts, and groups in Denver and Kentucky made quilts. When the quilts were counted, more than 140,000 had been contributed to the Church's Humanitarian Center in Salt Lake City. Soon they were on their way to Eastern Europe and other parts of the world.

Even the poorest of the poor have room in their hearts to give what they have to others. A young missionary living among the people of Oaxaca, Mexico, tells the story of being invited to eat dinner with what he describes as "possibly the poorest woman" in the area where he labored.

She gave us beans and two little tough, tough pieces of meat along with a few tortillas. After we ate them, she asked if I would like some more beans. I said, yes please. Later she asked if we would like a little egg. It was a very small egg from her chickens, and we accepted the offer. After the meal we were sharing a scripture with her to thank her for the meal. Afterward she said that when we wanted more beans, her heart filled with joy, and she was so happy—so happy for what she had to share. She thought we did not like eating with her, but that when we did, her soul just filled with joy and happiness.

I believe in God when I read of Him in Holy Writ. I feel His presence when I pray. I sense His majesty through the wonder of His creations. But I know Him best as He manifests Himself through the kind acts and loving care of His children, one toward another. I felt His arms around me when my mother held me as a child. I sensed His kindness as I worked in my neighbor's field by my father's side, and I saw His loving hands as a young woman in Africa reached out to an orphaned child.

I am thankful for a great-great-grandfather who followed the convictions of his heart. I have tried to follow his example and the example of others who generously give of their time and means in the service of their God. I know that God lives and that He loves us. For this and other reasons, I too believe.

Harold C. Brown is the managing director of Welfare Services and chairman of the Board of Trustees of LDS Family Services. Before this, he served nine years as commissioner of LDS Family Services. In his present assignment, he provides overall direction for Welfare Services activities worldwide, including employment, Deseret Industries, food production and distribution to the needy, LDS Family Services, and humanitarian relief services. He serves also as an area authority seventy in the Fifth Quorum of the Seventy. Elder Brown received his bachelor's degree from Brigham Young University and a master's degree in social work from the University of Utah. He and his wife, Penny, have ten children and fifteen grandchildren.

F. ENZIO BUSCHE

I grew up in Hitler's Germany without any religious background, turning fifteen when the Second World War came finally to an end. At the age of fourteen I had been drafted into the German army. Since the beginning of the war, when I was nine years old, I had not been able to attend any regular, serious schooling. During these chaotic, distressing years of insecurity and panic, I witnessed how the vast majority of the cities of my homeland became almost completely destroyed, including the destruction of my hometown with all of its suburbs and the burning down of my family's house.

For three years of my life I had no roof over my head. My mother, my four sisters, and I slept in the ruins of our house, not knowing whether our father was still alive or not. For the better part of three years after the war, physical survival was the only thing on our daily agenda. As you can imagine, I was in deep emotional pain and definitely unfit for any halfway challenging academic training, even if it had been available. Everything looked empty and vain to me; and in the feelings of melancholy and destructive self-pity, I turned my attention to Oriental philosophy, inspired by reading works from the poet Herman Hesse.

My father, who was exactly forty years older than I, finally came home more dead than alive, after having spent two years in a British prisoner-of-war camp. Soon he became very alarmed about my absentminded, self-centered, and destructive behavior borne out of my misguided thinking. I owe it to my father's loving, caring patience and wisdom that I gradually could let go of my dangerous way of thinking and get back to the pragmatic task of survival.

About two and a half years after the war, I became seriously ill with spinal meningitis. I survived this disease, which had killed many teenagers in my neighborhood, including a brother of my later-to-be spouse.

In 1956, when finally the missionaries of The Church of Jesus Christ of Latter-day Saints knocked on my door, I was twenty-six years old, had been married a little bit longer than a year, and had just survived another deadly disease. This time it was Hepatitis B, which brought me, shortly after my wedding, for five months into a hospital. The things I learned at this time became the background for my conversion to Jesus Christ as a living reality. As much as I had liked these young elders from the United States, the message they wanted to bring to us seemed at first so unusual that it took some direct intervention from the Lord and the total commitment of some particular missionaries to finally bring us to our baptism on the 19th of January 1958.

About twenty years later, in October 1977, I was called by Church president Spencer W. Kimball to serve as a General Authority of the Church. I had previously gained all my understanding of the gospel from service in leadership positions among the most humble people in the most humble places in the heavy industrial Rhine Ruhr area in western Germany.

Most of the instructions that we received regularly from Salt Lake City did not fit our local situations, so I was encouraged to look for the principles in the instructions and then to decide as guided by the Spirit.

This time of my early membership in the Church became the most important period for my own learning. Not only did I have to learn how to adapt into my life the sacred covenant of baptism, but I had also to learn how to have my own successful family and how to build up the family business. Doing the latter soon became imminent because of the early death of my father. In this crucial time I had no other choice than to surrender my life totally into the arms of the loving Christ, as I had learned it through the Spirit as taught by the missionaries, and by my own serious study of the scriptures and my own fervent prayers. At this time I learned to trust unshakably in the Lord Jesus Christ: "Draw near unto me and I will draw near unto you; seek me diligently and ye shall find me; ask, and ye shall receive; knock, and it shall be opened unto you. Whatsoever ye ask the Father in my name it shall be given unto you, that is expedient for you." (D&C 88:63–64.)

I can honestly say that in this time I received a strong and unshakable conviction that the Lord is the only lasting reality in our lives, that He knows us by name, and that He never leaves His servants without guidance when we are totally focused on Him, having a most humble heart and a contrite spirit.

When I look back today at the early years of my membership, I am overwhelmed with feelings of astonishment and gratitude. I readily acknowledge that I did not take a single step in the business world without first speaking earnestly with the Lord about the various possible options. How often was I confronted with the threatening powers of adversity from all corners of life, finding myself totally helpless, sobbing on my knees. Never, ever has the Lord forsaken me. He was always ahead of me, preparing people to give much-needed help, opening doors that I could not have opened myself, and inspiring me as to what was the next thing to do and how to do it most effectively.

In the same way, I am astonished at how He has helped my wife and me in our personal family life. With our baptism, my wife almost totally lost contact with her family, and in the beginning my own mother and several of my sisters turned against me. These circumstances of isolation made it possible for my wife and me to become very close to one another, uniting us in our need to plead always with the Lord. There was hardly a day when He did not inspire us to come together in some kind of emergency family council. Learning is never easy, and my wife and I went through a large variety of personal learning crises, but our family became finally, as it is only possible under the influence of the Spirit of the Lord, a strong, proven unit, with a oneness that we both have in all humility accepted as the greatest gift and blessing from the Lord.

I believe that it was not an accident that in the very first weeks of my service as a mission president, I was blessed with another devastating illness. I had phlebitis with several serious blood clots. I feel it was the learning I acquired during this illness that made me finally capable of handling my sacred calling of being a mission president; it also gave me the very important preparation for my soon-to-happen move to the United States.

When Jutta and I and some of our children finally arrived in Utah, faith in Jesus Christ was the only element that mattered to us, because it became the key for our spiritual survival and the only source of joy in life. Faith in Jesus Christ was for us a gift that needed to be industriously developed on an ongoing basis and always be kept strong in focus. Faith in Jesus Christ was something that could never be taken for granted; it would be there only when we focused on it in an ever-controlled sharpness. Only then, when our faith was strong, were we living under the vibrant influence of the Spirit. Then we felt an abundance of joy, and we felt sheltered and guided by the hand of the Lord, who comforted us in all our learnings.

Under the influence of the Spirit, everything becomes easy, our fear is gone, and our testimony becomes so powerful that we will be amazed to see even the most challenging circumstances changing, as miracles will happen to bring us relief, and everything inside of us will be like the brightness of the perfect day.

Born April 5, 1930, in Dortmund, Germany, F. Enzio Busche lived in one of the heavily-bombed parts of Germany during World War II. In the last year of the war, at the age of fourteen, he was drafted into the German Army. When the war ended, he was in an American prison camp.

Elder Busche finished his schooling by pursuing studies in economics and management at Bonn and Freiburg universities and taking graduate study in technical printing. After his education, he began his work in the printing industry, and for twenty-two years he served as chief executive officer and co-owner of a large publishing and printing company.

In 1955 he married his lifelong childhood sweetheart, the former Jutta Baum. The gospel was brought to them by missionaries in 1956, and after two years of investigation, they were baptized in 1958. In 1977 Elder Busche was sustained as a member of the Church's First Quorum of the Seventy. He has also served as president of the Frankfurt Germany Temple. He and his wife have four children and fifteen grandchildren.

RICHARD LYMAN BUSHMAN

I have lived an academic life ever since I graduated from Harvard College in 1955 and then later received a Ph.D. in the history of American civilization from that same institution. Since then I have taught at Brigham Young University, Boston University, and the university of Delaware, been visiting professor at Brown and Harvard universities, and now am Gouverneur Morris Professor of History at Columbia University. In these many years as an academic, I have never been belittled for my religious beliefs or felt excluded. I have published books, contributed to conferences, entered into scholarly controversies, and had my share of honors without once feeling that my well-known faith raised a barrier.

Only now and then have I caught a glimpse of the wonder my colleagues must feel that a rational, modern man believes the stories and doctrines of the Latter-day Saints. Soon after I was hired as professor of history and chair of the department at the University of Delaware, a member of the search committee invited me to lunch. While we were driving along, I mentioned my work on a biography of Joseph Smith, the founder of the Latter-day Saint Church. My colleague, doubtless to reassure me, turned quickly and said, "Dick, we took all that into account and decided it didn't matter." Apparently he was thinking of the peculiar tic in my intellectual makeup that allowed me to hold these strange beliefs. A similar reaction greeted me on coming to Columbia in 1989. Introduced to a member of the faculty, he said jovially, "Oh, you're the Mormon," an entirely amiable remark meant to make me feel at home. But one can imagine the repercussions if a new faculty member at Brigham Young University was greeted with "Oh, you're the Jew," or "Oh, you're the Catholic."

The extravagant nature of the Latter-day Saint religion probably accounts for the perplexity of my colleagues. Christian and Jewish doctrines, weathered by time, no longer strike people as bizarre or unusual. One can hold to one of the moderate versions of these ancient religions without startling one's friends. But Joseph Smith saw the angel Moroni less than two hundred years ago and then brought home gold plates and translated the Book of Mormon. These miraculous events, happening so close to home, strain one's credulity. How can anyone in this day of science and skepticism believe that God sends angels to speak to humans and requires such unlikely acts as the translation of an ancient history with the aid of a Urim and Thummim? My sophomore tutor, the distinguished historian of science, I. B. Cohen, once coyly mentioned to me that many people thought LDS beliefs were pure garbage. He doubtless was trying gently to bring me to my senses after my sheltered upbringing as a member of the Church.

For reasons I cannot completely explain to those who have not embraced LDS doctrine, I have not abandoned my beliefs after forty years of scholarship. I believe in the gold plates, the translation, and the angels, just as I did when I sat in I. B. Cohen's office in Widener Library as a sophomore. I did go through a period of doubt that year in college, beset by questions on every side, from philosophical logical positivists (who did not accept anything not learned through the senses) to the deep skepticism of Nietzsche. When I left for a two-year mission in New England at the end of my sophomore year, I frankly was not sure what I believed. When the mission president asked if I had a testimony, I said no. He made no objections but simply handed me a Book of Mormon and asked that I try to find an explanation for it. After three months of poring over the book and pounding my brain, I admitted to him that I believed the book was right—it was an ancient history as Joseph Smith said it was. I haven't wavered from that conviction since.

A lot has been written in opposition to the Book of Mormon and even more in its support. I have tried to keep up with this vast literature without claiming to command it all. Apart from all of the technical arguments, I am impressed with the fact that Joseph Smith published this immensely complex book when he was just twenty-four. He had little education, had not attended church as a boy, could scarcely write a letter according to his wife, and yet produced 588 pages of sermons, prophecies, and history that most experienced authors would be hard-pressed to match.

I had this extraordinary fact in mind while visiting the country house of my daughter-in-law Harriet Bushman's parents in Cornwall, England. Christopher Petherick, her father, casually mentioned the remarkable feat of Charlotte Brontë in writing *Jane Eyre* at age twenty-eight, causing a sensation in London literary circles. Her work seemed to come out of nowhere. Wondering if Brontë's life paralleled Joseph Smith's, I asked if the house library contained a biography of Charlotte Brontë, which it did. She grew up, I learned, in a provincial parsonage, somewhat like the isolation of Joseph Smith in upstate New York. But I also found that the parsonage was loaded with newspapers and books, and that from childhood Brontë wrote plays and stories with her sisters, all building up to her first novel. No build-up of any kind can be found to the Book of Mormon—no preliminary drafts, no attempts at other kinds of literature, no wide reading that we know of. Joseph Smith dictated the entire work in less than ninety days, going on page after page without interruption or review of what was written. His wife, who watched him while he dictated (and took down some of it herself), said no manuscript was in sight. It all came from the mouth of this plain, visionary farmer.

While I consider the very existence of the Book of Mormon an intellectual puzzle that scholars have yet to explain, in the final analysis the marvels of the book are not the reason I believe. I don't think you can build a life on a few intellectual reasons. My real reasons for believing all these years are more abstract and more powerful. The fact is that I find goodness in my Latter-day Saint life that I find nowhere else. When my mind is filled with scripture, when I speak to the Lord in prayer, when I comport myself in the way of Jesus, I am the man I want to be. I feel wisdom, concentration, compassion, and comprehension to a degree beyond anything I have known as a scholar or a teacher. I do everything better under the influences that radiate from the Latter-day Saint religion. I am a better father and husband, I give more to my children, I connect with the poor and needy, I counsel my students more truly, I am more unselfish. Moreover, I like what the religion does for my fellow Saints, both longtime members and new converts. It welds us together into a community of mutual trust and aid. Latter-day Saints, in my experience, are people of goodwill. They give to each other and to worthy works of every kind. We care for each other the way Jesus said we should. These experiences in my own congregation have persuaded me that nothing is more likely to improve the world than conversion to the beliefs I have treasured all my life.

As a scholar, I know full well the doubts of agnostics. I know that the scientific worldview, now dominant among intellectuals, appears to exclude traditional belief. I have dealt with the arguments against belief all my life. But over against these, I place my own intimate experience of goodness among the Latter-day Saints. I do not see how, as a rational man, I can give up what I have known directly and powerfully for the messages of doubt coming from distant authorities in the realms of science and philosophy. I feel like the disciples who were asked by Jesus in a crucial moment, "Will ye also go away?" and they replied, "To whom shall we go? thou hast the words of eternal life." (John 6:67–68.)

Richard Bushman, Gouverneur Morris Professor of History Emeritus at Columbia University, was born in Salt Lake City but grew up in Portland, Oregon. He received his Ph.D. degree in the history of American civilization from Harvard University in 1961 and taught at Brigham Young University, Boston University, and the University of Delaware before joining the Columbia faculty in 1989. He and his wife, Claudia, are the parents of six children. He is the author of *Joseph Smith and the Beginnings of Mormonism* and other books on American history. His latest is *The Refinement of America: Persons, Houses and Cities*.

ARIEL BYBEE

"Five minutes, Miss Bybee!" calls the stage manager through the door of my dressing room deep in the bowels of the Metropolitan Opera. After one final check of that vexed passage in scene I of Strauss's *Elektra*, I kneel and ask Heavenly Father to help me use my talents to the best of my ability. I believe that Leonie Rysanek is doing the same in her dressing room next to mine. As I hurry down the hall to the stage, I wave to my dresser friend Arlene, stopping for an instant to watch her teach my seven-year-old daughter to crochet. Another night the opera is *The Tales of Hoffmann*, and Alfredo Kraus is ahead of me as I reach the stage. Just before we are to step onto that wonderful, terrifying platform, he crosses himself and bows his head for a moment. We enter, singing.

This may not be everyone's stereotype of the behind-the-scenes goings-on at a major opera house, but during thirty-five years as an opera singer, including eighteen seasons at the Met, it *was* what I experienced. I had numerous acquaintances of all sorts, but every single one of my many close friends in the world of opera was religious. Sometimes I may not have known that a singer I was drawn to was a person of faith until after we had begun to form a friendship. What was always clear from the beginning, however, was that, more than our art, our common approach to life brought us together. There was always a sense of mutual respect and less of the narcissism common to all sorts of performers. These like-minded singers of all faiths tended to be family-oriented people who knew that, in a crunch, their children were more important than their careers. I remember with great fondness the times such great divas as Leona Mitchell and Frederica von Stade shared occasions of family togetherness with my family. I think of my dear friend Batyah Godfrey, who became Batyah ben David when her husband, whom she helped convert to Judaism, launched his own successful singing career—as a cantor.

I am aware of members of my own church who share the common misconception that it is impossible to enjoy a successful career in the performing arts as a committed Christian. Of course, it may have been the case that elsewhere backstage at the Met a married tenor pursued a chorus girl and an enraged diva shouted obscenities at her clumsy dresser. Those were realities at the opera, too, as they are in many places of work. People everywhere tend to find whatever it is they are looking for. My friends and I agreed, in general, on what we were looking for. Though I am painfully aware that there have been times when I have been spiritually distracted, whenever I have allowed the gospel of Jesus Christ to direct my attention—to guide my efforts to find fulfillment inside as well as outside the theatre—the fruits of these efforts have brought unmistakable affirmation of the rightness of gospel principles held in common by all people of faith. They have also affirmed my belief in those principles peculiar to The Church of Jesus Christ of Latter-day Saints.

Early in my career, I learned that life, as Oscar Wilde so cleverly tells us, can indeed imitate art. Singing the title role in *Carmen* at the San Francisco Opera, I began to notice the temptation to carry the character out of the theatre, to feel that I didn't have to follow the rules any more than the fiery gypsy girl did. Soon after, when the part of wild Jenny in *The Rise and Fall of the City of Mahagonny* brought me the beginnings of renown, I found that I didn't want the show to end with the curtain. It was my LDS perspective telling me such feelings were stupidly immature that helped me grow up into my true identity—that of an LDS woman. What was interesting to me was how this realization brought with it a mutually reinforcing seriousness toward both my art and my religion.

At a very young age, I learned that when my actions were in harmony with the teachings of the Church, I felt calmly happy; when they were not, I felt miserable. It was pretty black and white. For instance, the Church teaches the literal law of the tithe: we should return one tenth of our increase to the Lord to be used for His work, not just make a "goodwill offering" of any amount we happen to come up with on our own. As a very little girl, when I first began to give the specified, "Lord's tenth," I felt the Spirit's confirmation that that was the specific, right thing to do. Through the years since then, repeated acts of obedience to the law of tithing have been met with multiple experiences of spiritual reaffirmation, as the Lord has fulfilled His promise to "open . . . the windows of heaven, and pour . . . out a blessing." (Malachi 3:10.)

I have often felt the same belief-confirming spiritual response while sharing the talent I believe to be a gift to me from God. At such times—often, but certainly not always—singing has brought spiritual light and enlightenment. The result is a feeling of sweet calmness. But opera singers are famous, or infamous, for living through their feelings. Might not my belief be merely the religious equivalent of artistic affect? My answer is that one of the reasons I believe that God lives and that the teachings of The Church of Jesus Christ of Latter-day Saints are true is that singing has helped me learn to distinguish emotion which is both the product and seal of spiritual influence from mere self-indulgent emotionalism.

The test case for me is singing in church, which is nearly the most intense worship I ever experience. While I sing, I am the actualizer of a worshipful atmosphere for the members of the congregation. In order to perform well in this role, I must control myself, no matter how moved I may be. If I lose control and indulge myself with my own emotions, I will become vocally tied up, physically restricted. Such a self-centered condition results in the inability to express oneself freely, as is required if the singer is to do justice to both the music and the text. The outcome of such self-absorbed subjectivity is emotionalism—emotions are manufactured solely from within. The emotional fruits of the Spirit are for me quite different. In this particular variety of religious experience, feelings of light and calm arrive as a gift from without—almost as if the Spirit, as audience, is applauding a successful performance! A latter-day scripture teaches that when the Lord communicates truth, He "will tell you in your mind and in your heart, by the Holy Ghost." (D&C 8:2.) Perhaps that means that spiritual communication involves our whole being, heart and mind, as our minds provide counterbalance to our emotions.

Membership in the Lord's Church, even righteous living, does not guarantee immunity from pain, but my mind and heart bear witness that a genuine sense of joyful peace results from trying to keep the commandments, from living a life of service—even musical service.

Opera News recently described Ariel Bybee as having been "a prominent Mezzo at the Metropolitan Opera for eighteen seasons." At the Met and elsewhere, she has performed such roles as Carmen, Hansel, Nicklausse, Suzuki, and Jenny in Kurt Weill's *Mahagonny*. Her many concert engagements include performances in *Elektra*, conducted by Lorin Maazel at Carnegie Hall and by James Levine at the Ravinia Festival. Miss Bybee can be heard in Franco Zeffirelli's motion picture of *La Traviata*, singing the role of Flora, and appears on numerous Live at Lincoln Center videos. She is artist-in-residence in the School of Music at the University of Nebraska, Lincoln, where she teaches voice and directs operas. She has held such LDS Church assignments as ward Relief Society president and member of the International Affairs Committee in New York City.

CLAYTON M. CHRISTENSEN

As I have progressed through my life, my commitment to The Church of Jesus Christ of Latter-day Saints has deepened for two reasons. The first is my reason for *belonging* to the church as an organized institution: Because of the way the Church is organized, it puts opportunities to help others in my path every day. It facilitates my efforts—and in some instances almost compels me—to *practice* Christianity, not just believe in it. The second is my reason for *believing* that the doctrines taught in the Church are true. As I have studied the Bible and the Book of Mormon, I have come to know through the power of the Spirit of God that these books contain the fullness of the gospel of Jesus Christ. My conviction has deepened as I have continued to study these books and have tried to do the will of my Father in Heaven.

Why do I choose to belong to The Church of Jesus Christ of Latter-day Saints as an organized religion rather than attempt as an individual to live a good life? It is because the Church helps me understand and practice the essence of Christianity. The mechanism by which the organization achieves this is to have no professional clergy. We don't hire ministers or priests to teach and care for us. This forces us to teach and care for each other—and in my view, this is the core of Christian living as Christ taught it.

Several years ago I read a story in a news magazine about flooding in several western states that resulted from the rapid spring melting of a heavy accumulation of snow. One photo showed thousands of LDS citizens in Salt Lake City who had been mobilized with only a few hours' notice through a call from their local church leaders. They were shown filling sandbags that would channel the flow of run-off water. The article marveled at the command-and-control precision—almost military in character—through which the LDS Church was able to put its people onto the front lines of this civil crisis. Another photo in an article the next week showed a thirty-something resident of a town along a flooding stream in another state, sitting in a lawn chair reading while national guardsmen filled sandbags nearby. The author of the article attributed what he saw to the "organizational efficiency" of the LDS Church, but he completely missed the point. Thousands of people instinctively showed up and went to work *because they do this sort of thing all the time, week after week in over a hundred countries around the world, as part of being Latter-day Saints*. This was not an unusual event—just another week in the life of a typical Church member.

To illustrate, let me review some of the things that I was able to do in the normal course of being a member of the Church in a recent year. Because graduate students and young families move into and out of apartments with regularity in the Boston area, a list gets passed around at church every few weeks, asking for men to show up the next Saturday to help some family load or unload their rented moving truck. My children and I signed up every time and worked shoulder to shoulder with five to fifteen other men and their children for two or three hours, helping each family move. At least once each month and more often when needed, I visited by assignment an elderly Hispanic couple—a woman who was in poor health and whose husband was struggling to overcome his addiction to alcohol. They lived in a dilapidated apartment in a rough part of the city. Over the course of the year, the men in our congregation replastered, rewired, painted and recarpeted their apartment. We contributed money to fly their grown children, who were struggling financially and living in other parts of the country, to a special family reunion we helped them organize in Washington, D.C. Every Sunday for two hours, I cared for about fourteen children aged eighteen to thirty-six months in the church's nursery so that their parents could attend Sunday School class in peace.

My wife, Christine, was similarly engaged. In the assignment she had at that time, when she learned that a mother had a new baby or some-one was otherwise ill, with just a few phone calls she would enlist people to appear on their doorstep for a day, a week, or a month. They would bring meals ready to eat, or hands ready to clean the house and do the family's laundry.

The important point about the prior paragraph is that our experi-ence was *not* unusual. *Everyone* in the congregation was similarly engaged, not just accepting assignments to help but actually seeking opportunities to help. We gave often and received often. For example, a short time later our family had outgrown our small home, so we found a larger one and put the word out that we would appreciate any help in loading and unloading our rented moving truck. Among those who showed up that morning was Mitt Romney, one of the other con-tributors to this volume, who had just completed his unsuccessful campaign for the U.S. Senate in Massachusetts. Mitt had a broken col-larbone, but for two hours he traipsed between our home and the truck, carrying out whatever he could manage with his one good arm. That spirit is just in the air in the Church, week after week, year after year. The strong help the weak, and the weak help the strong. It creates an extraordinary spirit of mutual love, because as we work to help others who are in need, our love and respect for those we help intensifies.

My children have been raised not just by their parents but by an entire community of remarkable people. One of the world's foremost materials scientists, the dean of the Harvard Business School, a podia-trist, and the executive vice president of American Express Corporation were our sons' Scoutmasters. These men of substance and position selflessly taught my sons first aid and citizenship and camped with them in the snow. Each of our children, during their high-school years, went to early-morning seminary—scripture-study classes that were held in the home of a Church member every school-day morning from 6:30 until 7:15. The women who taught these classes had degrees not in religion or theology but in art, law, nursing, and literature. They had spent several hours the day before, preparing and searching for a way to help the sleepy high-school students learn an element of the gospel more deeply and to send them off to school with a firmer resolve to do what is right. Christine and I haven't raised our children. A whole community of selfless Christians has contributed to helping them become faithful, competent adults. Whenever we have thanked these men and women for what they have done for us, without exception they have expressed gratitude for having had the chance to help—because *they* grew as they served.

Because we employ no professional preachers, it means that every sermon or lesson in church is given by a regular member—women and men, children and grandparents. This means that we have the chance to learn from *everyone*—people in all walks of life who are struggling in their own ways to follow God. I have found, in fact, that some of the most profound things I have learned about the gospel of Jesus Christ have come from people from whom, if judged by the standards of the world, you would not have expected such profundities to come. For example, about a decade ago I was serving as the bishop, or lay minister, of the congregation of college students in the Boston area. We had assigned a college sophomore to give a sermon about repentance in our service on a particular Sunday. I still remember his key point: "We often view repentance as a slow process. It isn't. Change is instantaneous. It is *not* changing that takes so much time." I had been struggling to overcome a certain weakness of which I wanted to rid myself, and I resolved that I would change my behavior right then and there—to quit "not changing."

I believe strongly that these Latter-day Saints that I have described are *not* more loving or more selfless or more competent than many,

many individuals in other faiths. What is different, however, is that we live and serve within a context that causes us to *use* those attributes—to serve rather than to be served. And as we use them, they become an even more powerful part of us.

What I appreciate about the Church of Jesus Christ as an infrastructure for Christian living is that it puts me in touch with people I can help. I told a friend once, "If you truly want to live your life as Christ taught, then start coming to the LDS Church. You don't even have to believe what we believe. But if you want to practice Christianity, *this* is where the state-of-the-art is practiced." This is why I choose to *belong* to The Church of Jesus Christ of Latter-day Saints.

The second topic I want to address is why I *believe* in the doctrines of the church. I was born into a wonderful LDS family, and as I grew up I found few reasons to disbelieve the teachings of the Church. My parents had deep faith in its precepts, and their example and encouragement were powerful. I believed in my parents, and I knew that they believed the gospel of Jesus Christ. It was not until I was twenty-four, however, that I came to know these things for myself.

I had been given a Rhodes Scholarship to study at Oxford University in England. After I had lived there for a few weeks, far away from the supportive environment in which I had been raised, it became clear that adhering to my faith in that environment was going to be *very* inconvenient. In fact, doing the sorts of things I described in the first part of this essay within the Latter-day Saint congregation in Oxford would preclude my participation in many of the things that had made Oxford such a rich experience for prior recipients of my scholarship. I decided, as a result, that the time had come for me to learn for certain and for myself whether the Church was true.

I had read the Book of Mormon before—seven times, to be exact. But in each of those instances I had read it by assignment—from my parents or a teacher—and my objective in reading it was to finish the book.

This time, however, my objective was to find out if it was a true book or a fabrication. Accordingly, I reserved the time from 11:00 until midnight, every night, to read the Book of Mormon next to the fireplace in my chilly room at the Queen's College. I began each of those sessions by kneeling in verbal prayer. I told God, every night, that I was reading the book to know if it was His truth. I told Him that I *needed* an answer to this question—because if it was not true I did not want to waste my time with this church and would search for something else. But if it *was* true, then I promised that I would devote my life to following its teachings, and to helping others do the same.

I then would sit in the chair and read a page in the Book of Mormon. I would stop at the bottom of the page and think about it. I would ask myself what the material on that page meant for the way I needed to conduct my life. I would then get on my knees and pray aloud again, asking the Lord to tell me if the book was true. I would then get back in the chair, turn the page, and repeat the process for the remainder of the hour. I did this every evening.

After I had done this for several weeks, one evening in October 1975, as I sat in the chair and opened the book following my prayer, I felt a marvelous spirit come into the room and envelop my body. I had never before felt such an intense feeling of peace and love. I started to cry and did not want to stop. I knew then, from a source of understanding more powerful than anything I had ever felt in my life, that the book I was holding in my hands was true. It was hard to see through the tears. But as I opened it and began again to read, I saw in the words of the book a clarity and magnitude of God's plan for us that I had never conceived before. The spirit stayed with me for that entire hour. And each night thereafter, as I prayed and then sat in that chair with the Book of Mormon, that same spirit returned. It changed my heart and my life forever.

It was as if I had been looking out as far as I could see toward the horizon and had been quite satisfied that I could see everything that there was to see. When I undertook to read the Book of Mormon in that manner, however, it was as if I went out to the horizon of what I previously had been able to see. I discovered that *so* much more beauty and truth about who we are and what God has in store for us lies beyond that old horizon.

I love to go back to Oxford. As the beautiful, historic home of the world's oldest university, the town is filled with students and tourists. To me, however, it is a sacred place. It is there that I learned that the fundamental message of the Book of Mormon is in fact true—that Jesus is the Christ, the Son of the Living God. It is there that I learned that God is indeed my Father in Heaven. I am His son. He loves me and even knows my name. And I learned that Joseph Smith, the man who translated the Book of Mormon and organized The Church of Jesus Christ of Latter-day Saints, was a prophet of God in the same sense that Peter and Moses were prophets. I love to return to Oxford to remember the beautiful, powerful spirit that came to my heart and conveyed these messages to me.

During my adult life I have been blessed to witness many miracles—events that the scriptures term "gifts of the Spirit." (See 1 Corinthians 14:1.) These truly have been gifts, great blessings in my life. But when I assess the collective impact that they have had on my faith, my heart, and my motivation to follow Jesus Christ, they pale in significance and power to those evenings I spent with the Book of Mormon in Oxford.

This happened to me a quarter of a century ago. I am grateful to be able to say that in the years since, I have continued systematically to study the Book of Mormon and the Bible to understand even more deeply what God expects of me and my family while on this earth. I have spent thousands of hours doing my best to share what I am learning with others and to serve others in the way that Christ wants. And I am grateful to say that, from time to time, that same spirit that permeated my heart in Oxford has returned—reconfirming that the path I am trying so hard to follow is in fact the one that God my Father and His Son Jesus Christ want me to pursue. This understanding has brought me deep happiness. This is why I belong, and why I believe. I commend to all this same search for happiness and for the truth.

Clayton M. Christensen is a professor at the Harvard Business School. His research and teaching interests center on the management of technological innovation and finding new markets for new technologies. Prior to joining the NIBS faculty, he served as chairman and president of CPS Corporation, a materials science firm that he co-founded with several MIT professors. He holds a B.A. in economics from Brigham Young University; an M.Phil. in economics from Oxford University, where he studied as a Rhodes Scholar; and MBA and DBA degrees from the Harvard Business School. His publications have received numerous academic awards. His book, *The Innovator's Dilemma*, received the 1998 Global Business Book Award. He serves as a consultant to the management teams of many of the world's leading corporations. He and his wife, Christine, are the parents of five children.

JOE J. CHRISTENSEN

I am sure that among the major reasons I believe is that I grew up in a home where both of my parents were honest, committed, church-attending, active members of The Church of Jesus Christ of Latter-day Saints. We lived in the little farming community of Banida in southeastern Idaho. There were all of 124 residents in the whole town. We were like one big family. The one-room schoolhouse and the chapel across the road were the centers of our community's activities. The educational and religious experiences I had there had a profound impact on my life.

My father was a son of immigrants who had been converted to The Church of Jesus Christ of Latter-day Saints in Denmark. My mother's ancestors had been converts for generations with roots going clear back into early New England. I grew up hearing about "Mormon" pioneer ancestors who had crossed the plains.

All of this brought into my life a positive feeling for the common faith shared by my parents and also our neighbors in that little town. My father served nine years as bishop (pastor) of the little congregation, and my mother was always there playing the organ, leading the singing, and teaching Sunday School classes to the youth. I never had any reason to doubt the validity of their faith, and later experiences anchored my own religious beliefs.

In my parents I witnessed a marvelous congruence between what they taught and how they practiced Christian principles. My earliest memories included helping them load the pickup truck with sacks of flour, bags of vegetables, and boxes of fruit to take to families who were having difficulty. This was not just at Christmastime; it happened on any day or month throughout the year. In addition, I observed their choosing to drive less-expensive cars so they could give the difference in price to those who needed it more; and when clouds were rising and a possible hailstorm was developing, they gave instructions to move our harvesters and trucks to my handicapped uncle's farm to harvest his wheat before doing our own because his family was in greater need.

My parents set an example of solid integrity for me and for others who knew them, as illustrated by this experience: I graduated from high school at age sixteen. Just after turning seventeen, I enrolled in what is now Utah State University in Logan, Utah, just forty miles south of my hometown. Soon after arriving, and needing some money, I vividly remember being nervous as I went to the bank to write my first check. It was personal and from out of state. The teller was not about to hand over cash to someone who looked too young to have a checking account. She ushered me into the bank president's office. For a few moments, from behind his massive desk, he studied me with those piercing eyes and then asked my name and where I was from. Then he asked who my father was. I answered, "Joseph A. Christensen." I'll never forget his response as he relaxed, leaned back in his chair, and said, "I know him. He is an honest and hard-working man. You can cash your check for any amount you need." I knew then that I had inherited much from my parents that I hadn't earned.

Still, growing up under circumstances where belief and practice coalesced harmoniously does not necessarily develop an intellectual commitment to a particular doctrine or theology—what in our faith we often call a personal testimony. We shouldn't always live on the "borrowed light" from our parents. My testimony at a cognitive, intellectual level came to me later as I grew older.

When I was nineteen, I had completed two years of college, and by then I knew that I wanted to share our beliefs with any who would be willing to listen. I accepted a call from the prophet and president of our Church and spent the next two and a half years in Mexico and

Central America as a missionary. I was able to see how the principles of my beliefs affected the lives of such as the Franco, Lopez, Segura, and Santana families. The converts' goals in life were elevated, their marriages and families were strengthened, and many overcame destructive habits that had plagued them for years. For me, it was pragmatic proof that what I had been taught from childhood really made a positive difference in others' lives.

In the early 1950s, I was called into active duty as an officer in the Air Force. After being released, I had a real desire to go on to graduate school and, if possible, obtain a Ph.D. degree. I remember being warned by several that pursuing graduate degrees, particularly in the social sciences and philosophy, could be very destructive to one's faith. Nevertheless, Barbara and I bundled up our three children, hooked the little trailer onto the car, and traveled to Washington State University, where I immersed myself in a variety of studies. Rather than finding the experience to be destructive to what I believe, I found it to be just the opposite. Intellectually, some of the most significant reinforcements to my religious conviction came while attending graduate school.

I remember so well the day when Professor Waterman wrote those words on the chalkboard: *Ontology*, *Epistemology* and *Axiology*. He pointed out that most of the major questions of the philosophers and mankind over the ages could be included in one of these three major categories, which deal with the nature of reality, knowledge, and values, respectively. During the semester, we wrestled with questions like "What is man, and how do we relate to all that we see around us?" "How can we know, and for what can we hope?" "What is the source of evil in the world?" "What is the good, the true, and the beautiful?"

As we went through that semester reading from a variety of the writings of brilliant philosophers of differing persuasions, there washed over me like a flood the deep reassurance that true and very satisfying answers to those pressing questions are found in the teachings and doctrine of The Church of Jesus Christ of Latter-day Saints. That feeling has never left me. It brings warmth and peace of mind. I knew as never before that Joseph Smith was in very deed a true and inspired prophet of the Lord. With his very limited formal elementary education, he tapped into light and revelation that deal with so many of the major questions that have challenged deep thinkers for centuries.

Today, I find it easy to agree with Yale professor Harold Bloom's assessment when he wrote, "I . . . do not find it possible to doubt that Joseph Smith was an authentic prophet" and "an authentic religious genius."[1] Also, my experience in graduate education makes it easy to understand why research studies show that the more education members of my faith receive, the greater their commitment and activity become, because it happened in my own life.

It is very reassuring to be able to look anyone in the eye and sincerely express that I know by the influence of the Spirit that we are literally spirit children of a loving Heavenly Father and not merely creatures brought into existence for some unknown purpose; that Jesus *is* the Christ; and that His Church has been restored to the earth in this era by living prophets.

In summary, my faith assures me of my personal identity. It teaches me that our Father in Heaven lives and that He loves us as His literal spirit sons and daughters. The doctrine includes a moral and health code that enables anyone who complies with it to protect health and increase longevity. It provides me with assurance that the family is central to life and that the love I share with my wife, Barbara, and our children was meant by the Lord to last throughout time and eternity.

---

1. *The American Religion* (New York: Simon & Schuster, 1992), pp. 95, 97.

Finally, it brings to me that promised and comforting peace of mind that is "not as the world giveth." (John 14:27.)

Joe J. Christensen grew up in the little farming community of Banida in southeastern Idaho. He received his undergraduate degree from Brigham Young University and his Ph.D. degree from Washington State University. He fulfilled his military obligation serving as an officer in the United States Air Force. He has served as associate commissioner of the Educational System of The Church of Jesus Christ of Latter-day Saints and was responsible for the administration of worldwide secondary and college-level religious education. He has served as a mission president in Mexico City and at the Missionary Training Center in Provo, Utah. At the time of his call to serve as a General Authority and a member of the First Quorum of the Seventy, he was serving as president of Ricks College (now BYU—Idaho). Currently he serves as president of the Church's temple in San Diego, California. He married Barbara Kohler, and they are the parents of six and the grandparents of twenty-eight.

KIM B. CLARK

My belief in The Church of Jesus Christ of Latter-day Saints is grounded in experience. I believe because the Church and its doctrines give me an eternal perspective that connects deeply to my daily life. The words of truth from ancient and living prophets who guide the Church have touched my heart. They allow me to see beyond the horizon and give me insight and understanding. Through this spirit of revelation, the Church creates a profound sense of purpose and meaning in what I do with my family, my work, my relationships, my commitments, and my service to others. The gospel of Jesus Christ thus engages me as a whole person—heart, mind, and spirit. It teaches me of the great love the Savior has for me, and it brings joy and hope and inspiration into my life.

Nowhere are these great blessings of vision, perspective, wholeness, and truth better illustrated than in the Church's commitment to learning and education. For members of The Church of Jesus Christ of Latter-day Saints, it is a commandment to seek knowledge, to enlarge our understanding, to learn throughout our lives. This certainly includes learning about the scriptures and the gospel, but the reach of this responsibility includes knowledge of all kinds. Coupled with the scriptural mandate to develop and strengthen our faith, this means that the Lord's word to the Latter-day Saints is clear: Be educated and faithful.

This is a challenging mandate. To be educated means more than attending school or acquiring credentials. By "educated" I have in mind something Henry Rosovsky, former dean of the faculty of arts and sciences at Harvard, wrote several years ago:

An educated person must . . . be able to communicate

with precision, cogency and force; should . . . be trained to think critically . . . have a critical appreciation of the ways we gain knowledge . . . an informed acquaintance with the . . . methods of the . . . sciences; the historical and quantitative techniques needed for investigating . . . modern society; with some of the important scholarly, literary and artistic achievement of the past; and with the major religious and philosophic conceptions of mankind; . . . cannot be provincial in the sense of being ignorant of other cultures and other times; . . . have some understanding of . . . moral and ethical problems; . . . should have achieved some depth in some field of knowledge.[1]

To be educated in this sense is much more than knowing facts or having skills. It is also about habits of mind, approaches to problems, and perspective on our lives and the world around us. Likewise, to be faithful is more than attending church and participating in religious worship. For Latter-day Saints it also means being obedient to the commandments, following the counsel of a living prophet, seeking and listening to the Spirit of the Lord in making decisions, devoting priority time and energy to family, being honest, serving others, paying tithing, living the Word of Wisdom (the LDS health code), and in general living the gospel in practice. It is about habits of mind but also heart, about approaches to problems and perspective on our lives and the world around us.

EDUCATION IN LDS HISTORY AND DOCTRINE

The emphasis on education among the Latter-day Saints has roots in both the doctrines of the Church and its history. From the found-

---

1. Henry Rosovsky, *The University: An Owner's Manual* (New York: W.W Norton and Co., 1990), pp. 105–7.

ing of the School of the Prophets by Joseph Smith in 1833, to the creation of the Church Educational System for high-school and college students, to the ongoing support of the three campuses of Brigham Young University, the leaders of the Church have created an institutional history of commitment to learning and education.[2] Moreover, the prophets and apostles have created in their personal lives a living witness of the importance of learning, knowledge, and education. We have, of course, the example of Joseph Smith and Brigham Young, both of whom were largely self-taught and invested in learning throughout their lives. Among the current First Presidency and Quorum of the Twelve Apostles, a college education is common, and many of these leaders have advanced degrees in medicine, engineering, law, education, business, political science, and the humanities. Gordon B. Hinckley, president of the Church, framed this personal commitment this way:

> I love to learn. I relish any opportunity to acquire knowledge. Indeed, I believe in and have vigorously supported, throughout my life, the pursuit of education, for myself and for others. I was able to obtain a University education during the Great Depression and from that time forward I have never been satiated with the pursuit of knowledge. From my point of view, learning is both a practical matter and a spiritual one.[3]

A commitment to learning and education plays an important role in the daily lives of members of the Church. I know this from personal experience. Consider what a bird's-eye view of a fairly typical LDS

2. For a brief review of this history, see David P. Gardner, "Education," in Daniel H. Ludlow, ed., *Encyclopedia of Mormonism* (New York: Macmillan, 1992), pp. 441–46.
3. Gordon B. Hinckley, *Standing for Something* (New York: Times Books, 2000), p. 59.

household (ours) reveals about this commitment to education. As the sun creeps over the horizon, twenty LDS teenagers (sixteen to eighteen years old) show up at the house; it is 6:15 A.M. They are there for early-morning seminary, a fifty-minute class on the scriptures (this year, the New Testament) that meets every school day. Later that day, the family gathers for family home evening, where the lesson is on the plan of salvation. As the week progresses, we see the mother preparing her lesson and activity for her nursery class (two- and three-year-olds) on Sunday, the teenage daughters heading off to a Tuesday-night class on service in the community, and the father preparing for a talk he has to give on Sunday evening at the LDS Institute of Religion that serves multiple college campuses in the area. For the children in the family, this participation in Church classes and lessons comes in the midst of hours spent in college and high school, completing research projects, and working on homework (for parents too!). If we extend the view a bit, we can see a beautiful new LDS temple close to the family's home. The adults in the extended family gather early on Saturday morning to complete an endowment session in the temple. Here, in what for them is the most sacred place on earth, the central activity is learning: about the purpose of life, God's plan for our eternal progression, and the eternal nature of the family.

Indeed, it is precisely in these principles of eternal progression that we find the doctrinal roots for the Church's commitment to education. We are commanded to learn and to gain knowledge because that is an important part of our purpose here on earth and in the eternities. In 1843 Joseph Smith wrote these words, connecting knowledge and our eternal progression:

> Whatever principle of intelligence we attain unto in this life, it will rise with us in the resurrection. And if a person gains more knowledge and intelligence in this life through his diligence and obedience than another, he will

have so much the advantage in the world to come. (D&C 130:18–19.)

In addition to their impact on our personal progression, knowledge and learning allow us to more effectively serve God and His children, including our families. Brigham Young taught that education was important in building the kingdom of God, and that it had the power to improve the lives of people in the world. It should be sought for those purposes. LDS scholar Hugh Nibley makes clear this connection between education and service to the Church and God's children (the words in quotation marks come from Brigham Young):

> "The business of the Elders of this Church (Jesus, their elder brother, being at their head), is to gather up all the truths in the world pertaining to life and salvation, to the Gospel we preach, to mechanisms of every kind, to the sciences, and to philosophy, wherever they may be found in every nation, kindred, tongue and people, and bring it to Zion." The "Gathering" was to be not only a bringing together of people, but of all the treasures surviving in the earth from every age and culture; "Every accomplishment, every polished grace, every useful attainment in mathematics, music, in all science and art belong to the Saints, and they rapidly collect the intelligence that is bestowed upon the nations, for all this intelligence belongs to Zion. All the knowledge, wisdom, power, and glory that have been bestowed upon the nations of the earth, from the days of Adam till now, must be gathered home to Zion." "What is this work? The improvement of the condition of the human family."[4]

4. Hugh Nibley, *Brother Brigham Challenges the Saints*, edited by Don E. Norton and Shirley S. Ricks (Salt Lake City and Provo: Deseret Book Co. and Foundation for Ancient Research and Mormon Studies, 1994), 316–17.

The Lord's Plan for Learning:
Even by Study and Also by Faith

In the Lord's calculus, education and faith are connected: one gains knowledge and intelligence through diligence—digging, seeking, studying—and through obedience—exercising faith by keeping the commandments of the Lord. Indeed, whenever the Lord talks to us about education, He always connects study and faith. Consider, for example, these words from a revelation given to Joseph Smith in 1835 in which the Lord lays out instructions for those who would embark in His service:

> Call a solemn assembly, even of those who are the first laborers in this last kingdom. . . . And I give unto you, who are the first laborers in this last kingdom, a commandment that you assemble yourselves together, and organize yourselves, and prepare yourselves, and sanctify yourselves. . . . And I give unto you a commandment that you shall teach one another the doctrine of the kingdom. Teach ye diligently and my grace shall attend you, that you may be instructed more perfectly in theory, in principle, in doctrine, in the law of the gospel, in all things that pertain unto the kingdom of God, that are expedient for you to understand; of things both in heaven and in the earth, and under the earth; things which have been, things which are, things which must shortly come to pass; things which are at home, things which are abroad; the wars and the perplexities of the nations, and the judgments which are on the land; and a knowledge also of countries and kingdoms—that ye may be prepared in all things when I shall send you again to magnify the calling whereunto I have called you, and the mission with which I have commissioned you. . . . And as all

have not faith, seek ye diligently and teach one another words of wisdom; yea, seek ye out of the best books words of wisdom; seek learning, even by study and also by faith. (D&C 88:70, 74, 77–80, 118.)

Preparation for the work involves the mind and the spirit. It is about building a life of faith and obedience and also a life of learning. Gaining knowledge of all kinds is important (notice the connections between D&C 88 and Rosovsky's description of an educated person above), and that knowledge is to be had through reason (study) and revelation (faith).

Why does the Lord connect study and faith in this way? Why this linking of reason and revelation, of intellect and spirit? It might have been different. He could have said, "Study is study, and that you do in school; faith is faith, and that you do in church." But He didn't. He connected them. Why? Part of the answer is that inspiration from God is a powerful way to gain the kinds of knowledge and intelligence essential to our education here on earth. Latter-day Saints believe in personal revelation, that God can speak to us in many ways to help us in our lives. We believe in the power of prayer and that these times of personal meditation and reflection can yield new understanding and insight. A life of faith can, therefore, create habits of prayerful contemplation and quiet reflection that open our minds and our hearts to revelation and inspiration.

Many times I have sat in Church and listened to faithful Latter-day Saints talk about solving a particularly knotty research problem or finding a way to write something difficult and feeling they had been blessed with insight and understanding beyond their capacity. I have had these experiences myself, and I am confident they would not have happened without a lot of studying and work (this is what I emphasize to my children after listening to a talk in Church like this). But I also

believe that faith plays an important role in what are important learning moments.

So, part of the purpose for connecting faith to study is the Lord's
desire to help us learn through inspiration. But it is also true that using
our minds to actively seek knowledge in the way that the Lord out-
lines helps prepare our minds to receive that inspiration. This principle is at the heart of the following reprimand received by Oliver
Cowdery, who served as scribe to Joseph Smith during the translation
of the Book of Mormon. Oliver had sought permission to try to translate but had not had success:

> Behold, you have not understood; you have supposed
> that I would give it unto you, when you took no thought
> save it was to ask me. But, behold, I say unto you, that you
> must study it out in your mind; then you must ask me if it
> be right, and if it is right I will cause that your bosom shall
> burn within you; therefore, you shall feel that it is right.
> (D&C 9:7–8.)

The Lord promises confirmation but only after hard thought and
study. Joseph Smith taught the same principle and emphasized the
connection between the intellect and the spirit:

> We consider that God has created man with a mind
> capable of instruction, and a faculty which may be enlarged
> in proportion to the heed and diligence given to the light
> communicated from heaven to the intellect.[5]

And again:

> The things of God are of deep import; and time, and

---

5. *Teachings of the Prophet Joseph Smith*, selected by Joseph Fielding Smith (Salt Lake City:
Deseret Book Co., 1976), p. 51.

experience, and careful and ponderous and solemn thought can only find them out. Thy mind, O man! If thou wilt lead a soul unto salvation, must stretch as high as the utmost heavens.[6]

The Prophet thus taught that our intellect receives "light . . . from heaven," that we can expand our capacity to learn from that light if we are diligent, and that our minds are essential to finding out the things of God as we ponder and learn from our experience; but they must be connected to heaven if we are to achieve all that God has in store for us. There is no distinction here between secular and religious knowledge or between the spirit and the intellect.[7] We may have separated the spirit and the intellect into different compartments of our lives, but according to the Prophet, that is not our true nature. In that sense, connecting study and faith is the Lord's plan for learning because it is precisely the best way to learn. The process He gives us for gaining knowledge—study, seek, ponder, pray, keep the commandments—is thus intended to help us integrate the intellect and the spirit.

IN CONCLUSION

Commitment to education among the Latter-day Saints is an important aspect of the faith. It is deeply rooted in both the history and the doctrine of the Church. And it shapes in a powerful way the lives of its members. It has certainly shaped mine. For more than thirty years I have been involved in learning and education. The words of the prophets and the commandments of the Lord have given me an eternal perspective on that personal journey. Revelation and

---

6. Ibid., p. 137.
7. Hugh Nibley, *Approaching Zion*, edited by Don E. Norton (Salt Lake City and Provo: Deseret Book Co. and Foundation for Ancient Research and Mormon Studies, 1989), p. 72.

commandment link this commitment to religious faith: Among the Latter-day Saints the ideal is to be both educated and faithful. Pursuing that ideal in practice is not just a matter of one's habits of mind but also of the practical pattern of activities that define one's life. In this realm in particular, I have learned that being an educated, faithful Latter-day Saint is a way of life. And I know from my own experience that it is the best way to true perspective, to a sense of wholeness, to hope, and to joy. And that is one of the important reasons why I believe.

Kim B. Clark, the George F. Baker Professor of Administration, is dean of the faculty at Harvard Business School. A member of the Harvard faculty since 1978, Professor Clark received the B.A., M.A., and Ph.D. degrees in economics from Harvard University.

Dean Clark's research examines modularity in design and the integration of technology and competition in industry evolution. He and Carliss Baldwin are coauthors of *Design Rules: The Power of Modularity* (MIT Press, 2000). Earlier work has focused on technology, productivity, product development, and operations strategy.

By birth, Kim Clark is a Westerner, having grown up in Washington and Utah. He and his wife, Sue, live in Belmont, Massachusetts, where they are the parents of seven children and three grandchildren. Dean Clark is an avid golfer.

JANE CLAYSON

As a journalist, I feel the honor and the responsibility of watching history unfold firsthand. Some of the stories I cover are heartwarming. Others are heartwrenching. I have witnessed enormous suffering around the world. But in the midst of it, I have also observed faith, hope, and the light of Jesus Christ shining from within people everywhere, illuminating and redeeming and restoring. This is the Good News. It is worth reporting. It changes everything.

I'll never forget slogging through muddy refugee camps in Macedonia, along the Kosovo border. There were thousands of people living in squalor, in the echo of Serbian shelling across the river.

Near the tiny, mountain hamlet of Molina, a wave of about 1,000 refugees washed across the border one night—mostly women and children—whose husbands and fathers had been rounded up and murdered. For three days, they raced from danger. Fumbling through darkness, they were hungry and cold.

Then, slowly, one by one, the lamps inside Molina's small, modest homes came to life. It was three o'clock in the morning when the villagers awoke to welcome their bewildered guests. The village women baked bread until the sun rose, and these poverty-stricken potato farmers turned over their homes, their beds, their clothing—everything they had—to strangers.

It is in moments of incredible suffering and despair that I have repeatedly witnessed the inextinguishable human spirit flare up to push back the darkness. I believe that those sparks of compassion and courage have a divine origin.

I felt it during the fall of a government while standing among thousands of protestors in Jakarta, Indonesia. They marched through the streets waving banners, raising their voices for freedom. With the world, I watched a ruthless dictator bow to a rising generation that refused to live in darkness anymore.

And I felt it with the volunteer doctors and nurses with whom I traveled to China. They had sacrificed much to help hundreds of children with debilitating facial deformities. Baby Li was one of their patients, a child abandoned and left to die simply because of her cleft lip and palate. A sixty-four-year-old grandmother found that baby in a garbage pile near her home. She traveled by train and on foot for three days to find the doctors who would operate and ultimately change the course of Baby Li's life.

I felt indescibable courage and faith from the parents whose children were murdered in the Columbine High School massacre. I felt it from countless families in Oklahoma City after the bombing of the federal building, and from those who lost their loved ones in the horrible crash of TWA flight 800.

And I felt it again—overwhelmingly—in the aftermath of the terrorist attack on New York City, Washington, D. C., and a field in Pennsylvania. Seldom have I witnessed such heroic acts of courage, such faith, and such service and an outpouring of love in the face of tragedy.

As a journalist, I cover and analyze every news story with all the objectivity my profession demands. As a believer in God, I share with you what I have witnessed from our neighbors around the world: that the light of Christ shines forth from those who seek to learn from Him—who seek to emulate Him.

My faith has taught me that each of us has, within us, a source of enormous, benevolent power: "the true Light, which lighteth every man that cometh into the world." (John 1:9.)

I believe we are most alive when we heed the call of Jesus Christ: "Come unto me, all ye that labour and are heavy laden, and I will give you rest. Take my yoke upon you, and learn of me; for I am meek and lowly in heart: and ye shall find rest unto your souls." (Matthew 11:28–29.)

I believe there is a God. I have felt His hand in my life, and I have seen it in the lives of others.

I cannot deny it. That is why I believe.

Since becoming co-anchor of CBS' *The Early Show* in September 1999, Jane Clayson has covered a wide variety of news events along with intriguing feature and lifestyle reporting. She has interviewed President George W. and First Lady Laura Bush, Vice President Dick Cheney and Lynne Cheney, former Vice President Al Gore and Tipper Gore, Senator Joe Lieberman, Secretary of State Colin Powell, former Secretary Madeline Albright, Senator Hillary Rodham Clinton, Senator John McCain, and Ralph Nader, among others.

Before co-anchoring *The Early Show*, Clayson was a correspondent (1997–99) for ABC News in Los Angeles, reporting for *World News Tonight* and other network broadcasts. Between 1990 and 1996 she anchored and reported for KSL-TV in Salt Lake City.

Clayson's work has received numerous awards from the Society of Professional Journalists, as well as an Emmy and The Edward R. Murrow Award from the Radio and Television News Directors Association.

A native of Sacramento, California, she graduated from Brigham Young University in 1990 with a degree in journalism. In 2001 her alma mater honored her as one of its most distinguished alumni at a gala homecoming weekend.

STEPHEN R. COVEY

I believe for six reasons:

First, my parents believed.

Second, I learned the hard way that freedom is born of discipline and wise structure.

Third, the new information in modern revelation answered life's toughest questions for me.

Fourth, I need to believe so that I serve purposes bigger than myself and my abilities.

Fifth, seeing is believing.

Sixth, believing is seeing.

First, *I initially believed because my parents believed*. And they believed because their parents believed. Most of my ancestors were converts from Great Britain and Europe who came across the plains to Utah with Brigham Young. This intergenerational heritage is the foundation of my childhood and faith. In fact, I cannot ever remember doubting either the truth or the supreme importance of the restored gospel of Jesus Christ.

I remember, as a boy, going with my mother into an elevator with the most prominent person in our city. In awe, I asked my mother why she talked to the elevator operator almost the entire time instead of the VIP, whom she knew. She replied that she had never had the privilege of meeting the operator before. "No respecter of persons"—in other words, to respect everyone equally—was a lesson I never forgot.

After hearing me brag to my friends about some of our family adventures, my father taught me another lesson I never forgot: to never brag or drop names, places, or accomplishments but instead to focus on others, to listen to them, and to affirm their worth, potential, and accomplishments.

It was this kind of humility, unconditional love, and integrity of life that gave such force to their faith and teachings.

Second, *true freedom comes from discipline and wise structure*. I remember how disappointed my parents were, particularly my mother, when I didn't take piano lessons seriously. Instead, I took the course of least resistance and played with my friends instead of practicing the piano. Consequently, I am not now free to play the piano. From that and similar experiences, I learned for myself that true freedom comes from discipline. I learned that freedom wasn't the absence of restraint; rather, it was the fruit of having the kind of structure that promotes the growth and empowerment of people.

This became an invaluable lesson for me when, as a young man, I served a two-year mission for the Church in Great Britain. I accepted structure and rules and the strict discipline of getting up every morning at 6:00 A.M., studying the scriptures for two hours, both alone and with my companion, getting out by 9:00 A.M., and proselyting until around 5:30 P.M. with a short break for lunch, and then teaching in the evening from about 6:30 until 9:30 with about an hour's break for dinner and travel. Rather than choosing, I was assigned different companions, and we were to work in unity and harmony through this disciplined process six and a half days a week for two years.

A few years later, I served as a mission president for three years supervising 480 young men and women missionaries. Our motto was "Work, prayer, and love." Again, an amazing thing happened on these missions. From discipline, we literally became "discipled." With few exceptions, discipline consistently produced more belief and faith and a huge repertoire of freedoms. We learned that love is a verb rather than a feeling, and that love, the feeling, was essentially the fruit of love, the verb. We learned to dedicate ourselves completely to the service of others with our whole heart and soul. We learned not to take offense, to love unconditionally, to serve with sincerity and integrity, to repent rapidly when necessary, to forgive as we were forgiven. We learned that to *know* and not to *do* is not to know.

Even though I always acknowledged my ancestral roots on my missions, the spirit of the discipline and the truth of the message we were sharing distilled upon my mind and soul as the dews from heaven. I came to know deeply and independently—for myself—the truth and sacredness of our work, all of which centered on Jesus Christ, the Redeemer of the World and my personal Lord and Savior.

Third, *the new and clarifying information contained in revelation given through modern prophets satisfies life's toughest questions for me*, such as:

1. Really, who are we? Where did we come from?

2. What is the purpose of life?

3. What is our destiny?

4. If God is so loving, why is there so much innocent suffering?

5. If Christ is the "only way," what about those who live and die and never even learn about Him (most of the human race)?

6. If Christ established one church and relatively few join it, where is the justice of God?

7. Can family be eternal? If so, how?

8. What happens to the spirit when the body dies and before its resurrection?

9. How does the resurrection work, anyway?

10. What hope is there for one who has been profoundly abused or for one who has made terrible choices in life?

Frankly, I'm both astounded and humbled to see how the restored gospel satisfactorily answers these and many other significant questions.

Fourth, *I need to believe so that I can serve purposes bigger than myself and my abilities.*

From many experiences as a parent, grandparent, teacher, writer, and entrepreneur, I've come to learn something priceless that may at first seem perplexing: The more you know, the more you know you don't know, and the greater need you have for faith.

To understand this, think of knowledge as a circle. Where is ignorance? It's on the outside edge of the circle of knowledge. Now, as knowledge increases, what happens to ignorance? It has also grown! Now, what if your purpose as a parent or leader lies outside your circle of knowledge? Will you not require more faith, more belief?

I feel, now, that my most important work is with my family, not just with my nine children and, at this writing, more than thirty-five grandchildren but with the extended and intergenerational family as well. Ultimately, this family encompasses the whole human race, the family of God. Obviously, this purpose transcends my puny powers. Acting on my desire to make a difference, slowly and gradually, I have cultivated a global consciousness and an awareness of the immense suffering that much of the human race experiences every day. This requires more *faith* in the unseen God and also more *work* within His incredible plan and structure to serve both temporally and spiritually His other children, both living and dead, respecting every person's freedom to choose.

Fifth, *seeing is believing*. When you see the fruits of belief—that it really works—it strengthens belief

As a professional working extensively with organizations worldwide, I am stunned by the inevitable *upward surge* that happens when leaders are changed at the local or general level of The Church of Jesus Christ of Latter-day Saints. Also, by sheer contrast, I am overwhelmed by the trust and empowerment given to every Church member—by an open pulpit; by extensive, lifelong, lay participation; by an unpaid ministry; by a welfare plan wisely balancing "help out" with "help up"; and by carefully programmed attention to the needs of children and youth and families and single adults. It's truly exceptional and amazing to see an organization institutionalize its values. "Ye shall know them by their fruits." (Matthew 7:16.)

Sixth, *believing is seeing. Believe* is a verb, also. I choose to believe. Then, when I act on my belief, I am truly happy. My family is happy and unified. Belief gives purpose and meaning and order to life. It explains things. Because I believe, I "see." I understand. Connecting with divine roots produces good things, including a deep change in our nature. C. S. Lewis expressed it beautifully:

> When I come to my evening prayers and try to reckon up the sins of the day, nine times out of ten, the most obvious one is some sin against charity, I have sulked or snapped or sneered or snubbed or stormed. And the excuse that immediately springs to mind is that the provocation was so sudden or unexpected. I was caught off my guard, I had not time to collect myself. . . . Surely, what a man does when he is taken off his guard is the best evidence for what sort of man he is. Surely what pops out before the man has time to put on a disguise is the truth. If there are rats in the cellar you are most likely to see them if you go in very suddenly. But the suddenness does not create the rats; it only prevents them from hiding. In the same way, the suddenness of the provocation does not make me an ill-tempered man; it only shows me what an ill-tempered man I am. . . . Now that cellar is out of reach of my conscious will. . . . I cannot, by direct moral effort, give myself new motives. After the first few steps . . . , we realize that everything which really needs to be done in our souls can be done only by God.[1]

---

1. *Mere Christianity* (New York: Macmillan, 1952), pp. 164–65.

I also believe in Mother Teresa's simple path:

The fruit of silence is prayer.
The fruit of prayer is faith.
The fruit of faith is love.
The fruit of love is service.
The fruit of service is peace.

In summary, I believe because of my heritage, my disciplined obedi-ence and repentance, and my need for explanation and for power outside myself, because it works and is so life-changing, and because I choose to.

I feel, as Helen Keller put it, that "the best and the most beautiful things in the world cannot be seen or touched but are felt in the heart."[2] God's spirit has filled my whole heart and soul with belief.

Dr. Stephen R. Covey is co-founder/vice-chairman of Franklin Covey Company, a global professional-services firm. Dr. Covey is perhaps best known as the author of *The 7 Habits of Highly Effective People*, which has sold more than 12 million copies in 33 languages throughout the world.

Dr. Covey earned his undergraduate degree from the University of Utah, his MBA from Harvard, and his doctorate at Brigham Young University. While at Brigham Young University, he served as assistant to the president and was also a professor of business management and organizational behavior.

Dr. Covey is the recipient of the Thomas More College Medallion for con-tinuing service to humanity and has been awarded four honorary doctorate degrees. Other awards include the Sikh's 1998 International Man of Peace Award, the 1994 International Entrepreneur of the Year Award, *Inc.* magazine's Services Entrepreneur of the Year Award, and, in 1996, the National Entrepreneur of the Year Lifetime Achievement Award for Entrepreneurial Leadership. He has also recently been recognized as one of *Time* magazine's twenty-five most influential Americans and one of *Sales and Marketing Management's* top twenty-five power brokers. Dr. Covey currently serves on the board of directors for the Points of Light Foundation.

2. See Mary Ann Glendon, *Abortion and Divorce in Western Law* (Cambridge, Mass.: Harvard University Press, 1987), p. 78.

PAUL ALAN COX

I have devoted my professional career to the study of tropical plants in Africa, Central and South America, Southeast Asia, and the South Pacific. As an ethnobotanist, my work has focused on discovering new medicines from plants. I have spent many months living in small villages studying with traditional healers. I have been greatly blessed in my work, and some of the drugs I have discovered are on their way to clinical trials, including one now being developed by the National Cancer Institute and the Aids Research Alliance as a candidate therapy for AIDS.

My work has been very pleasant. Rain forests are not like the frightening scenes of "jungles" that are sometimes portrayed in the movies. Rainforests are peaceful and beautiful. One rain forest I studied in Samoa has hundreds of small, thin-stemmed *Balaka* palms growing beneath large rain forest canopy trees with their massive buttress roots. *Balaka* produces small, pendulous racemes of white flowers, each with a tiny drop of dew hanging from its stigma. As early light pierces the morning mist, each little stigmatic drop begins to glow, and the entire rain forest becomes magical in appearance.

I usually work alone in the forest, which gives me time to think and even to pray. Walking gently among the large green ferns, hearing the gentle cooing of tropical birds, delighting in the sight of a beautiful orchid peering at me from the foliage, I sometimes feel as if I am in the Garden of Eden. When I look up toward the sunlight filtering through the cathedral-like rain forest canopy high above me, I often feel a holy presence. I believe I have glimpsed what is meant in the second verse of Genesis, which describes the Spirit of God moving throughout the world.

My career path began in my childhood. My father was a conservation officer, and as I saw how he cared for injured birds and animals he brought to our home, I thought that Heavenly Father must be something like my dad—powerful but gentle, caring for the smallest sparrow. How could I not believe in God when I was raised in such an environment? I began to kneel each night by my bed to ask God to protect the plants and animals of the world.

When I was five years old, my mother took me to Primary—the Church's children's program—which in those days was held on Tuesday afternoons. As I entered the chapel, the Primary president stood at the podium with her arms folded. After the children were seated, she smiled and said, "Welcome to Primary. If you are still and reverent here in the chapel, you will feel a warm feeling and know that this is Heavenly Father's house." Her words helped me want to be reverent in the chapel, and soon I came to experience the warm feeling she spoke of.

Three years later, I was baptized. I remember vividly the white clothing I wore into the font and the coolness of the water. As the priest prepared to immerse me, I felt that I was doing what Heavenly Father wanted me to do. I took my baptismal covenants very seriously: to love Jesus, to keep His commandments, and to always remember Him.

When I was ten, my father worked as a ranger in the Grand Teton National Park. Together with my mother and father, I lived in a trail camp high in the mountains. I was puzzled that a young man on my dad's trail crew disappeared early each morning for half an hour or so. To my inquiry he responded, "I like to go out in the forest early each morning and read the Bible." He was not of my faith, but he inspired me to embark on my own personal study of the New Testament.

When I read the Sermon on the Mount, I absolutely knew that no mere human could invent such beautiful doctrine—to love our enemies, to repay evil with good, to turn the other cheek, to be peacemakers, to depend on the Lord for our sustenance—these doctrines were clearly divine. Jesus often used nature in His teaching: "Consider the lilies of the field, how they grow." (Matthew 6:28.) Such teachings and images were particularly vivid for me. My study of the New Testament left me with a deep and abiding belief in the divinity of Jesus Christ. I believed with my whole heart that Jesus is who He said He was—the Son of God—and that He led a perfect life to show us the way back to our Heavenly Father.

A few years later, after a day of backpacking in the Tetons, I gazed up in the evening at the orange alpenglow on the mountains high above. I am not sure why the Lord chose that particular moment to communicate with me, but as I looked at the reflection of the mountains in the lake, I was filled with the Spirit of the Lord. I received a witness that The Church of Jesus Christ of Latter-day Saints is His true church on earth. I later read the Book of Mormon cover to cover and received a witness of its truth. I have since read it many times and still cannot read a single page of the Book of Mormon without feeling the power of God in its pages. The Book of Mormon is true.

I was the first person from my extended family to serve a proselyting mission at age nineteen. When I opened the call from the prophet with my mother and father, I was surprised to read "Samoa." I noticed that my mother was weeping, and I tried to comfort her. Mother told me that her tears were of joy because she knew that the Samoan people would care for me.

As the aircraft descended to land at Pago Pago, I felt the Holy Ghost and knew that I had made the right decision to accept this assignment. Though my repeated reading of the Book of Mormon and the New Testament had helped me to spiritually prepare for my mission, nothing had prepared me for the tremendous impact the rain forest would have on my development as a young scientist. I was also overwhelmed by the love that the Samoan people showed me without reservation. When I completed my mission, I decided to study rain forest biology in the hope that I could somehow help the Polynesian people conserve their rain forests.

I wasn't sure if I was a good enough scholar to get into the right universities for my studies, but after my mission the necessary admissions and the right fellowships to fund my graduate education developed. I always knew deep inside that my opportunities were not due to my own abilities but instead to the Lord.

During my studies I became aware that some people struggle with apparent contradictions between science and religion. Some scientists are suspicious of those with religious convictions, and some religious people regard science as an evil force. While I don't belittle those who agonize over such issues, I must admit that I personally have found few contradictions between faith and science. What I have learned about science has only increased my admiration for Heavenly Father and His creations.

Like the Book of Mormon prophet Alma, "I have all things as a testimony that these things are true." (See Alma 30:40–41.) The overall harmony and beauty of the heavens and of the earth are to my mind a powerful witness of the reality of God. "All things denote there is a God; yea, even the earth, and all things that are upon the face of it, yea, and its motion, yea, and also all the planets which move in their regular form do witness that there is a Supreme Creator." (Alma 30:44.) Extraordinary claims require extraordinary evidence, and to my mind the assertion that there is no God falls into the nature of an extraordinary claim. While I respect those who have no religious beliefs, I have never seen anyone produce one shred of credible evidence that there is no God.

Of all of the sentient beings in the entire universe, surely one is the most intelligent, and it is this Being that I call God. Millions of people can bear the same witness I do: that He lives!

God himself can be discovered only through faith. Were we able to irrefutably prove His existence in an equation or in the results of a test-tube experiment, those performing the experiments or the equations would have an edge on everyone else, and "God is no respecter of persons." (Acts 10:34.)

Fortunately, many good people who do not share our faith demonstrate tolerance and kindness to those of us who believe. I was one of the few students in my Ph.D. program at Harvard who had strong religious convictions. While there I served as a teaching fellow for a famous scientist, Professor E. O. Wilson. One day during a lecture, he told the story of seagulls rescuing the crops of the early Mormon pioneers from a horde of crickets. After the lecture, I asked Professor Wilson if he knew that I was a Latter-day Saint. He replied, "Of course I do, Paul. Why do you think I put that story in?" Later, when I taught sociobiology to the undergraduates and told Professor Wilson I had a religious problem with one of the sections, he was very gracious with me. "You just teach however you feel comfortable, Paul," he told me.

In general, my professors did whatever they could to accommodate my standards, even serving nonalcoholic champagne when I passed my final doctoral exams! That pattern of tolerance has continued throughout my career. Once, after a lecture for the king and queen of Sweden, a formal toast was made to Her Majesty. Seated on the queen's immediate right, I didn't want to pick up a wine glass, so I raised my water glass instead. The crowd of several hundred people gasped in surprise, but as I sat down, Queen Silvia leaned over to me and kindly whispered, "You are very wise."

In the past several decades, the Lord has blessed me in my study of plants and has protected my life and the life of my family during these efforts. Although I do not proselytize the indigenous peoples with whom I work, they are appreciative when they observe that I have my own religious beliefs, for they know that I will respect what they believe to be sacred. I find one fact striking: All of the indigenous groups with whom I have worked believe that this earth is sacred. I share their belief and have devoted much of my life to conservation. If you love the Artist, don't slash His painting.

Why do I believe? Because I can't help believing. My most precious possession is my membership in The Church of Jesus Christ of Latter-day Saints. That membership has allowed me to be married to my beloved Barbara in a temple of God, which means that our marriage vows do not disintegrate with death. It allows me to have access to the priesthood and to partake of the sacrament each week. It allows me to pay my tithing, to attend church services, and to receive counsel from my bishop. I am particularly grateful for a living prophet and for the apostles—how grateful I am that the Lord has sent his servants among us! I study their counsel avidly. I love to attend the temple, and I am grateful beyond measure to know that my family will be mine forever. I know that the Church is true, and I am proud to be a member of it.

I love Jesus with my whole heart—I lack sufficient words to adequately praise Him and His works—and I am amazed at the beauty I find in the little flowers as well as in large geological formations or the stars at night. My dearest hope is that my entire family, including all of my descendants, will share my commitment to the Church, and that my own efforts to understand and protect the plants and animals I study will evidence my love for their Creator.

Paul Alan Cox is director of the National Tropical Botanical Garden and Distinguished Professor of Biology at Brigham Young University—Hawaii. He has previously served as a Miller Fellow at the Miller Institute for Basic Research in Science at Berkeley, a Melbourne University Fellow, a professor and dean at Brigham Young University, and as King Carl XVI Professor of Environmental Biology at the Swedish Biodiversity Center. His numerous scientific articles and three books include *Nafanua: Saving the Samoan Rain Forest* (New York: W. H. Freeman, 1997), which details the work for which he received the Goldman Environmental Prize and *Time* magazine's Hero of Medicine award. Brother Cox serves as Gospel Doctrine teacher in the Kalaheo Ward of the Kauai Hawaii Stake.

LARRY ECHOHAWK

Echo Hawk was the name given to my great-grandfather, a Pawnee Indian, who did not speak English. The name was given to him by elders of his tribe because it told something about him. Among the Pawnee, the hawk is a symbol of a warrior. My great-grandfather, a Pawnee Indian war scout, was known for his bravery. But he was also known as a quiet man. He did not speak of his accomplishments; however, other members of his tribe spoke of his deeds. These laudatory words were "echoed" from one side of the village to the other. Thus, he was named Echo Hawk, the "hawk" whose deeds are "echoed."

The first white men to come into contact with the Pawnee Indians estimated their population to be between fifteen and twenty thousand. The Pawnee Indians owned about 23 million acres of land in what is now the state of Nebraska. In the winter of 1874 the Pawnee Indians were forced to leave their homelands in Nebraska to make room for white settlers. They were marched several hundred miles to the south and placed on a small reservation in the Oklahoma Indian Territory. After relocation to Oklahoma, the Pawnee numbered less than 700.

Echo Hawk was among the few surviving Pawnee Indians.

The Pawnee Indians were not permitted to return to their Nebraska homeland. They could no longer visit their ancestral grave sites; seek religious visions on the high, grassy plains of Nebraska; or pursue the great buffalo herds that had sustained them for many generations. They were confined to the small reservation in Oklahoma, where they had to subsist on government rations. They became a dependent people.

This tragic history deeply influenced the next few generations. My father was removed from his parents at an early age and placed in a government boarding school for Indians. His hair was cut, and he was dressed in a gray uniform. He was physically beaten if he spoke his native language.

As a small boy, I witnessed my father's struggle with alcohol, which I believe was in large part due to the traumatic experiences of his youth. Problems brought on by my father's drinking caused me to wonder if my family would stay together. I also had difficulty establishing a positive self-image in my early school years when I read lessons that described Indians as savage, bloodthirsty, heathen renegades.

In my early childhood I had no expectation of obtaining a higher education. Talking about where we were going to go for college and what we were going to study was not part of our dinnertime conversation. But things began to change when two Latter-day Saint missionaries came into my home and taught my family about the gospel of Jesus Christ. These lessons led me to be baptized and to become a member of The Church of Jesus Christ of Latter-day Saints at age fourteen.

Thirty-two years later, in 1994, while I was serving as the attorney general for the State of Idaho, the missionary who baptized me came to see me at my office in the state capitol building in Boise, Idaho. It was an emotional reunion with many tears shed by both of us. We were both overcome to realize how dramatically the gospel had altered my life.

My opportunity to become the first American Indian to be elected as a state attorney general was in large measure due to the influence of the values I was taught as a member of The Church of Jesus Christ of Latter-day Saints. As a part of my conversion I had read the Book of Mormon. This book taught me about the lineal roots of my people and foretold a promising future for the American Indian. The message of the Book of Mormon helped me develop a positive attitude about my heritage and a belief that a great destiny lay ahead for me person-ally if I would be obedient to the teachings of Jesus Christ.

My opportunity to be fully exposed to the positive principles of the restored gospel came in 1966, when I was awarded a full scholarship to play football at Brigham Young University. At BYU I not only devel-oped my athletic ability; I also strengthened my spiritual values.

After graduating from BYU and law school, I went into the world to serve my people. I became a tribal attorney for one of the largest Indian tribes in the United States, the Shoshone and Bannock tribes of the Fort Hall Indian Reservation in Idaho. My work in behalf of Indian people in Idaho gave me great satisfaction in my career in law. Eventually, my vision of what I had to offer was broadened, and I entered politics. Again, my twelve years serving in state elective offices brought me an opportunity to serve others.

In 1994 I lost the race for governor of Idaho. I led in the polls from the beginning of my campaign until election day. The day before the election I was sure I would be the next governor of Idaho. However, in a surprise finish I lost a close election. In defeat I learned something about myself and the true meaning of life. I was disappointed I would not have the opportunity to do the things for people that I could have done as governor of Idaho. But in giving what should have been a dif-ficult concession speech on election night, I found myself filled with a great sense of peace and calm. I knew that we can never really fail if we put our trust in the Lord and make a sincere effort to do His work. The important thing is to live a life of integrity, honesty, and service to others as the Lord would have us do. Even in our failures we will be sustained and uplifted.

I believe in the gospel of Jesus Christ because my heart tells me it is true. Christ lives and is the Savior of all mankind. I believe in The Church of Jesus Christ of Latter-day Saints because I know it to be an organization designed to show us the way to live according to the teachings and commandments of Jesus Christ.

As a Native American, I have seen what was, but I see very clearly the beauty of what we can all become by following the example of Jesus Christ.

Larry EchoHawk, a law professor at Brigham Young University, previously served as attorney general for the State of Idaho (1991–1995), the first American Indian elected to that office. He also served as a member of the Idaho House of Representatives (1983–1986) and as Bannock County prosecuting attorney (1986–1991). In 1999 he was appointed by President Bill Clinton to serve on the Coordinating Council for Juvenile Justice and Delinquency Prevention.

EchoHawk graduated from Brigham Young University in 1970 and earned a juris doctorate from the University of Utah in 1973. In 1991 EchoHawk was awarded George Washington University's Martin Luther King Medal for his contributions to human rights. In 1992 he was honored as a speaker at the Democratic National Convention in New York City. As Idaho's delegation chair, he became the first American Indian to lead a state delegation to a national political convention.

EchoHawk is a member of the Pawnee Indian Tribe, and he served honorably in the United States Marine Corps. He and his wife, Terry, are the parents of six children.

LaVell Edwards

I believe that Jesus Christ is our Savior, that He was the center point of God's plan for the salvation of His children, and that I, along with everyone on this earth, agreed to the terms of that plan. I believe that He came to earth to show us the way and taught and performed miracles during His ministry. I believe that He willingly took upon Himself our sins, through intense suffering in the Garden of Gethsemane, and on the cross as He gave His life to His Father in Heaven on our behalf.

I believe that Jesus Christ has restored the true gospel, in its fullness, to the earth through His servant and prophet Joseph Smith. I believe that it is embodied in The Church of Jesus Christ of Latter-day Saints.

I believe that through the priesthood, families can be sealed together for eternity. I believe that we can live again with the Savior and our loved ones and enjoy many of the associations we have had here on earth.

I believe that our testimonies and the skills, talents, and leadership abilities that we gain through church service should influence everything else in our lives.

I couldn't always state these beliefs with such conviction. As a young man, I would hear people bear testimony of signs, events, and other specific experiences they had had that helped them gain a testimony. I had never had what I recognized as an outward sign of the divinity of the gospel, and for many years I worried about it. I finally came to understand that I indeed did have a testimony and had had it much longer than I realized. It had been instilled in me by my parents and had grown slowly and steadily with each experience I enjoyed and service I rendered in the church. The gospel of Jesus Christ is of a very personal nature, and I finally understood that the person I am is a combination of influences from my parents, my wife and family, and especially the gospel. I am part and parcel of all three.

My family situation and that of my wife couldn't have been more different as we were growing up. I was one of fourteen children, and our family was very active in the Church. My father, a man with only an eighth-grade education, served as a bishop, stake president, and leader in the community. Patti, on the other hand, was an only child. Her family lived in a very small Wyoming town, and her father wasn't a member of the Church, although he was very supportive of the rest of his family who were. Many Sundays, it was just Patti and her mother and one other family at the services. Her father did eventually join the Church, and he and Patti's mother served two missions together.

Early in our marriage, Patti became pregnant with our first child, Ann. It was then that the importance of our family responsibilities hit us, and we decided to reevaluate our life together. Although we had been going to church, we were mainly just going through the motions. We discussed what kind of home life we wanted for our family and how much the Church would be a part of that. The two things we had in common as we started our own family was that we came from "goodly parents" (see 1 Nephi 1:1) and that we were members of The Church of Jesus Christ of Latter-day Saints. We decided right then that we wanted a Christ- and church-centered family life. We've since held a wide variety of callings in the Church and have grown personally and spiritually because of our decision.

Two months after I was hired as an assistant coach at Brigham Young University, I was called to be a bishop in a student ward on campus. I had observed my father in his role as bishop as well as the bishop I served under as counselor in Salt Lake City, but I was grateful for the Church guidelines for a bishop around which to build my "game plan" for the ward. I found that my experiences in this capacity greatly influenced my role as a head football coach.

After serving as an assistant at BYU for ten years, I was hired in 1972 to be the new head football coach. When it came time to put the coaching staff together, I wanted to surround myself with people who were far more qualified in their specific areas than I was. Drawing on my experience as a bishop, I delegated a lot of responsibility to them within their individual areas. I felt that one of my major responsibilities was to create an environment that would help them be successful. Of course, we had staff meetings often to evaluate, plan, and discuss our "flock" (our 120 players), their individual progress and problems, and how we could best help them. Two of the things I learned from my father that helped me both as a bishop and as a coach were to not be afraid of being creative in my approach and to be consistent in my attitudes and actions.

My approach with the players was to begin with the individual. As with each member of a ward, I wanted each player to realize who he was, what he could achieve, and what he needed to do to reach his potential on the field and in all facets of life. I met with my players one-on-one and talked about their personal lives, their schoolwork, their mission plans, and their families, along with how they were doing athletically.

One of the players who has achieved the most on the football field is also one who was well-grounded in his religious beliefs and lifestyle. Steve Young came to BYU having thrown only four or five passes a game in high school. We considered playing him at defensive back, but he envisioned himself as a quarterback, a BYU quarterback!

He worked hard to develop the passing skills needed for our offensive schemes. In one of his first games as a starter, against the University of Georgia, he threw five interceptions in the first half. Worried about him, I tried to reassure him. He just looked at me and said, "Coach, there's no problem. We're going to win this game." And that was his philosophy of life—on the field, in class, and in his spiritual development: Keep picking yourself up, keep trying, keep progressing, and you'll be a winner. This perspective helped keep him grounded even as a pro. From the time he became the "$40 million man," Steve Young had to depend on his spiritual base to help him keep his priorities straight and set proper goals for himself.

One young man who didn't achieve the fame that some other quarterbacks did, but who made just as strong an impact on my life, was Sean Covey. A two-year starter, Sean lost the starting job his senior year to Ty Detmer. When I called him into the office, I explained to him our decision to go with Ty. Although disappointed and hurt, he looked me in the eye and said, "Coach, I don't agree with the decision, but I just want you to know one thing. I will be ready if you ever need me." And he was a man of his word. Sean never missed a practice or a meeting and was totally ready emotionally, physically, and mentally to play each week, never complaining, completely supportive of Ty and the program. Who could ask for a finer player and leader than that? He has always been ready for whatever life offered him and has found success in business, as a family man, in his church callings, and in his community service.

The Church and football, for me, were inextricably connected. Just as in my personal family, I exulted with my football family in their growth, their strengths, their heartaches and mistakes, and their triumphs. I witnessed the fruits of our labors and theirs at baptisms, weddings, and baby blessings. I saw young LDS players without testimonies gain them, serve missions, and leave BYU to become meaningful contributors to society. I saw active LDS players come into the program and be a tremendous influence on their peers, infusing in them the desire to learn and gain their own testimonies. I saw players who weren't members come, feel the Spirit, and join the Church. I saw some players of other faiths come, leave, and then return years later to tell me they had joined the Church, married in the temple, and been in service to their Lord. Such events and associations were what made my time at BYU so memorable and worthwhile to me and my family.

I've faced many challenges as a person and as a coach, but that's why we're here on earth—to learn and grow through our struggles. I love this statement by President Gordon B. Hinckley: "My life is rich because of problems to solve and relationships to savor." I have seen the growth in myself, my family, my ward members, and my players through facing adversities, and I know that the Lord was wise in giving us challenges and loving in giving us the tools to triumph.

I know that The Church of Jesus Christ of Latter-day Saints is the Lord's church. I know that Jesus Christ is my Savior and that He lived, died, and lives again for me. I know that He loves me. This knowledge has brought balance and perspective to my life. In the coaching profession, priorities tend to get skewed, and my testimony helps keep me focused on what is truly important in life. I am eternally grateful to the Lord for His blessings upon me and my family.

LaVell Edwards is a legend in collegiate football. After twenty-nine years as head coach of the Brigham Young University football team, he ranked third among active coaches and seven in the all-time wins list, with a record of 257 wins, 101 losses, and 3 ties. Under his direction, the Cougars won a national championship, nineteen conference championships, a Heisman Trophy, two Outland Trophies, and four Davey O'Brien Awards, and appeared in twenty-one bowl games. He has twice been honored as the national coach of the year, has received many conference and district accolades, and has been feted by a myriad of state and national organizations, not just for his accomplishments on the field but also for the integrity and distinction he brought to the profession.

LaVell and his wife, Patti, have three accomplished children: John, an orthopedic surgeon; Jim, an attorney; and Ann (Cannon), a writer and columnist for the *Deseret News*. LaVell earned his bachelor's degree from Utah State, his master's degree from the University of Utah, and his doctorate from Brigham Young University.

RICHARD PAUL EVANS

I was being interviewed on a radio station about the success of my first book, *The Christmas Box*, when the interviewer expressed her joy that a number-one *New York Times* best-seller testified of Jesus Christ. She said, "I think it's wonderful that this international phenomenon started with the Christian bookstores."

"Actually, that's not true," I replied.

She was surprised by my response. "What do you mean?"

"Initially I was banned by Christian bookstores."

"Why on earth would they ban your book?"

"Because I'm a member of The Church of Jesus Christ of Latter-day Saints. And there are those who erroneously believe that we aren't Christians."

She said that she was truly sorrowful that such bigotry still existed.

I was twenty-one before I first heard the accusation that I was not really a Christian. At the time, I thought it was a joke. I was raised to believe that Jesus Christ was the Son of God and that through Him and His atoning blood, I might be saved. I was taught from the same passages of the Bible that my Protestant and Catholic friends learned from. I wondered in awe at the same Bible stories and, like them, was taught to try to emulate the life of Jesus in word and deed.

Then why does there remain the misconception that "Mormons," as we are sometimes called, aren't Christian? Having recently read a statement from a major Protestant denomination denouncing my faith, I concluded that it was, in part, because of our use of "non-traditional" scripture—specifically the Book of Mormon.

"Jesus is God," a reader once wrote to me, "and the Book of Mormon is not true." I agreed with her on the first point and disagreed on the second. This woman had never read the Book of Mormon. In fact, she had not the slightest notion of what the Book of Mormon was about. She would likely be surprised to learn that the Book of Mormon was not about Mormon any more than the book of John is about John or the book of James is about James. Rather, all of these writings are testimonies to the divinity of Jesus as Christ, the risen Savior of the world. The Book of Mormon is a powerful testimony of Jesus Christ and, on a personal level, was the key to my belief in and subsequent conversion to Christianity.

As a writer, I find the Book of Mormon, and the man who brought it forth, Joseph Smith, fascinating. Whenever one of my novels is released, I am sure to hear within a few days about the errors in it. In spite of my seemingly endless hours of research and rewrites, and the fact that I work with some of the most respected and relentless editors in America, errors are still made by me and missed by my editors. This is a common complaint of every writer I know. Even the great writer J.R.R. Tolkien wrote that he was weary of being reminded of the errors in his books, as he asked his readers to just keep them to themselves. Writing anything of a historic nature compounds the chance for errors. A casual mention of what the character might be wearing, eating, or even driving may be inaccurate and requires careful research. I do not believe that Joseph Smith, even if he had been schooled (he was not), could have invented so complex a work as the Book of Mormon. It would have been so fraught with error that today's readers would have found the book absurd. In fact, the greatest errors made would have been those that Joseph Smith would not have known he was committing. In writing a novel, we write through the paradigm of our own experiences—perspectives that are subtly influenced by our particular time and place in culture. Dickens's *Christmas Carol* could not have been written in eighteenth-century Peru or China. Interwoven through Dickens's work are the influences of English industrialism and poverty, which Dickens experienced firsthand. In writing the Book of Mormon, Joseph Smith would have made references that this century's readers would recognize today from his culture and era. But they are not there. Nor are the errors. Were the Book of Mormon not true, it would not have withstood the test of time. But that is not why I believe the Book of Mormon to be true. I believe it to be true because of a spiritual experience I once had.

When I was nineteen, I served a mission for my church for a year and a half in the Republic of China, Taiwan. I did not go blindly. Deciding whether or not to serve was a difficult decision for me. When I was sixteen, I believed that the teachings of my church were true, and I believed in my parents' testimony. But I did not have a spiritual witness or even the deep, abiding belief that comes from personal conviction. It was at this time that I came across a passage in the Book of Mormon: "When ye shall receive these things, I would exhort you that ye would ask God, the Eternal Father, in the name of Christ, if these things are not true; and if ye shall ask with a sincere heart, with real intent, having faith in Christ, he will manifest the truth of it unto you, by the power of the Holy Ghost." (Moroni 10:4.) The Bible contains similar promises, as recorded in James 1:5: "If any of you lack wisdom, let him ask of God, that giveth to all men liberally, and upbraideth not; and it shall be given him." I asked myself this question: If a sixteen-year-old young man, truly seeking God's will, reads the book and then prays in the name of Jesus Christ to know the truth of it, would a loving and just Heavenly Father, as we must believe Him to be, allow that young man to be deceived? It would defy logic and scripture. For Jesus said, "For every one that asketh receiveth; and he that seeketh findeth; and to him that knocketh it shall be opened. Or what man is there of you, whom if his son ask bread, will he give him a stone? Or if he ask a fish, will he give him a serpent?" (Matthew 7:8–10.) So I set forth on my quest for truth. I read ten pages in the

Book of Mormon every day. No matter how late I got home at night, I read, and each night I knelt and prayed, reminding my Heavenly Father how important it was that I receive His guidance. During this time I was amazed at the spiritual insight and power I received from reading the book. I began to believe that the book was clearly from God and that it was a true testament of Jesus Christ. Still, I was not willing to trust or rely solely on my own reasoning. This was a question for a higher power, I decided. Several weeks later, when I finished reading the book, I knelt by the side of my bed and asked God, in the name of Jesus Christ, if it was true. At that moment something happened that I can only describe as the divine blessing of the Holy Ghost. A beautiful, serene, yet powerful feeling came over me. I was filled with not only an assurance of the truth of the book but with pure peace and pure love—a powerful compassion for all of God's children. My thoughts were not on myself but on others.

This experience has served as the cornerstone of my belief. It was the first of many to come. Of course, it did not answer all my questions about God and religion, and my search for spiritual truth will require more than this lifetime. I admit that there were even times of my life, times of darkness, when some wayward part of my psyche wished that I had not had such a powerful and undeniable experience, as other lifestyles or desires seemed more appealing. But I knew that I had had that experience, and I feared to deny it, fearing to face a just God, for we both knew that I had been given an answer to my prayer.

I am not surprised that bigotry and misunderstanding continues in these "enlightened" times. It is understandably difficult for us to believe in something so radical as new scripture or a living prophet. Declaring that God, through a prophet, has reestablished His church of old is a radical concept—as radical, perhaps, as Jesus, in His day, declaring himself the Christ. But all religious thought is, initially, radical. That is why Christians were fed to the lions. When it comes to religion, we are simply not comfortable with "new." This is not a condition unique to our generation. Jesus Himself reprimanded the scribes and Pharisees for such hypocrisy: "Ye build the sepulchres of the prophets, and your fathers killed them." (Luke 11:47.) In modern jargon, prophets don't have last names. An expert, as they say in the business world, is someone who lives a thousand miles away. Similarly, history sadly demonstrates that in a religious context, a prophet is someone who lived a thousand years ago. In the quest for spiritual truth, I am grateful that the heavens are not sealed and that God continues to bless the lives of His children. Through the years, as a father and husband, I have seen the gospel's effect on the lives of those I love most, filling them with faith, hope, and a desire for the things of God. "By their fruits ye shall know them," the scriptures counsel us. (Matthew 7:20.) My family and I have tasted the fruit of this religion and found that it is good. I am grateful for its blessings in my life. I am grateful to God for allowing me personal inspiration and guidance. But, most of all, I am grateful to my Savior, in whose atonement I have hope in someday returning to my Heavenly Father.

Best-selling author Richard Paul Evans first came into international recognition in 1995 when he self-published his book *The Christmas Box* and set the publishing world on fire, outselling every major publisher and author in the world at that time. He has since written seven consecutive *New York Times* best-sellers and sold more than 11 million copies of his books worldwide. He was awarded the 1998 American Mothers Book Award for his first children's book.

Evans is director and founder of The Christmas Box House International, a shelter and assessment facility for abused and neglected children. The Washington Times Foundation awarded Evans the American Century Award for his service to humanity.

LINDA J. EYRE

The obnoxious beeping of the alarm clock pierced my soul after a night of fitful sleep, and my consciousness told me that it had arrived—the day I love to dread. At about two-thirty A.M., Noah, our nineteen-year-old, brown-eyed, six-foot-seven-inch son, had finished packing all that he would need for two years in Santiago, Chile: dark suit, ten new white shirts, six ties, eight pairs of socks, three pairs of shoes, three pairs of thermal underwear, two sweaters, gym clothes, an alarm clock, a first-aid kit, toiletries, a laundry bag, and, most important, his scriptures.

No matter how much I reminded myself that this was the day we had excitedly talked about and looked forward to since the day Noah was born, I still felt as if someone was squeezing my heart—a lump of dread and joy, all wrapped up in one mother's heart. Visions of the parade of friends who had left our house just after midnight a few hours before wafted through my mind. Pretty girls and loyal guys who had screamed for him and played with him at high-school basketball games, stayed up with him until the wee hours of the morning making posters and badges for his campaign for student-body president, and shown up dressed "fit to kill" on Junior Prom nights had come to say their good-byes, promising a plethora of letters. They knew that life would be very different for all of them when they saw each other again after two long years. Many were preparing for their own mission departures within weeks. I especially loved seeing that kids who were left out or excluded in high school were part of the farewell crowd. Noah's special friendship with them reminded my heart that he would be a great missionary.

So why was this unmistakable feeling of gloom still pressing against the joy inside me? It wasn't that I knew he would be cooking for himself. He can scramble up an egg and make macaroni and cheese with his eyes closed, and I knew that rice and beans would be a pretty good filler-upper for one who eats like a vacuum cleaner. It wasn't that I knew he would be assigned to a "companion," someone he'd live and work with twenty-four hours a day, who would probably be a native of South America who spoke not one word of English. "Hard is good" is one of our family mottoes.

The apprehension wasn't that I knew that we would be corresponding with him only by mail and talking to him on the phone only twice a year, at Christmas and on Mother's Day. It wasn't that I had heard horror stories of missionaries being yelled at, spat on, met at the door by shotguns, sworn at, and even mugged and killed by gang members in Russia or hit in the head with bottles in Bulgaria. (Well, I guess maybe that had a *little* to do with my uneasiness.) I knew that he would have doors slammed in his face every day. But I also knew that with Noah's sense of humor, he would have the presence of mind, after a long string of rejections at the door, to say, "Here, let me slam that door for you!"

I guess my rare combination of sadness and yet perfect joy came from realizing that Noah was making the rite of passage from being a carefree youth to becoming a full-time ambassador for our Savior Jesus Christ. He was saying good-bye to the life of the boy who had previously worried about girls, grades, and games to gladly immerse himself in a life of service and love. He would bring struggling brothers and sisters he hadn't yet met to a joyous understanding of the life and mission of Jesus Christ, whom he loves so dearly. He would have the privilege of telling them about the gospel of Jesus Christ restored to the earth and of a modern-day prophet who guides the Church and gives us an anchor in this uncertain world. And in the process, Noah would become a man—one who stands for what he believes so strongly that he is willing to give his life for it.

This interesting combination of trepidation and joy is not new to me. Noah is the seventh child, four sons and three daughters, that we have sent on missions for The Church of Jesus Christ of Latter-day Saints, with two teenagers still waiting "in the wings." In addition, we've sent out our semi-adopted Bulgarian daughter and Ukrainian son (whom our children met on their missions and brought home to live with us) on missions of their own to New York City and Chicago. Young men who go on missions usually go at age nineteen and serve for two years. Young women who choose to go leave at about twenty-one and serve for eighteen months. Our oldest daughters went to Bulgaria and Romania, where they had opportunities not only to teach the gospel and lead people to baptism but also to work in the desolate orphanages there. Two sons have served in England, another daughter in Spain, and our most recent missionary son just returned from Brazil.

They leave their battered cars for their next younger sibling and instead walk countless miles on battered feet. They leave the comforts of home for bare apartments, often complete with courageous cockroaches. Analyzing movies is replaced with two hours of analyzing the richness of the life-changing wisdom found in the scriptures at 6:30 A.M. each morning. They lock up their hearts to feelings for the opposite sex and pour out their love unceasingly to those who are seeking for truth and light. They quit thinking about what they want to *have* and concentrate on what they want to *give*. In the process, they discover the depth of their abilities to pray, to yearn, and to love.

Noah joins an army of some sixty thousand young men and women as well as thousands of retired couples who are currently serving as missionaries all over the world. They do not choose where they will serve. Instead, each one has amazing faith that they have been called by inspiration to serve where they are needed, at their own expense of time and money, to stand for what they believe.

The letters we receive from these great missionaries while they are in the full-time service of the Lord are priceless! Our oldest daughter,

Saren, on her mission in Bulgaria, wrote, "I love the orphanages. The babies with birth defects need so much love and have so little. They light up at a gentle touch after initial shock and fear. I want them to know that at sometime in their short lives someone loved them and held them close and made them feel like a precious, real person. Maybe someday, if I'm really, really good, I can be friends with these special spirits in heaven."

At the same time in Romania, Shawni wrote, "The other day we saw three of the ladies we've been teaching the gospel coming toward us in the distance. These three beautiful women, glowing with happiness with their little four-year-old Alexander in tow, were walking along the street with sunlight shining through their hair. It was so beautiful. They've made such progress! I don't think I've ever been that purely happy before. I couldn't stop smiling the whole day."

"Missions are such an adventure!" wrote one of our sons. "When you wake up in the morning, you just have no idea what will happen to you by the end of the day. It's so exciting!" (It's not that our children have lacked for adventure in their lives. We have done crazy things with them through the years, ranging from building a log cabin together in Oregon; to spending a summer in the Philippines; to building a cistern in a remote village in Africa. But through the years, I have realized that there is nothing quite like the amazing adventure of serving a mission.)

From Saydi in Spain we read, "The mission is the hardest thing I've ever done in my whole life. Yet it somehow produces a more exquisite joy than I could ever have imagined: You overcome challenges that you thought you could never surmount, you have deep feelings of love that surpass what you thought you could feel, you see lives and hearts fill with glorious light as people find the answers and truths that their souls have yearned for. I'm learning that only through hard work, deep feelings, and the trial of faith is true strength and joy found."

And from a son in Brazil came this: "The joy of witnessing the change in this wonderful family all together is something indescribable. I have watched the spirit of God in them through their eyes. We were so full of joy after our discussion that when we left, my companion and I just had to jump over a few bushes. Plus, I taught him how to say, 'That was awesome!' in English."

Seeing the miraculous changes that missions have made, not only in the lives of those people our children have touched but also by the touch of the Master's hand in their own lives, is one of the major pillars of why I believe! These valiant missionaries take the message of my heart and theirs—that Jesus Christ lived and atoned for our sins so that we could rise again in a glorious resurrection and that He established His church again in these latter days, complete with all that is needed for our eternal joy. Only through this knowledge as Noah walks through the doors at the Missionary Training Center today can the tears of sadness that we won't see him for two years be replaced by tears of joy for the person he'll become and the lives he'll touch. Besides, I must remember that when it comes to standing for something you believe, "Hard is good!"

Linda and Richard Eyre write and lecture on parenting, life balance, and values-based planning. (Richard's essay follows Linda's in this book.) Their latest efforts are their new books *The Happy Family: Restoring the 11 Essential Elements That Make Families Work* (St. Martins Press, 2001) and *Empty Nest Parenting* (Shadow Mountain, 2002).

One of the Eyres' best-selling books, *Teaching Your Children Values*, became the first parenting book in fifty years (since Dr. Spock's) to reach the number-one spot on the *New York Times* best-seller list. They have also advocated strong families and balanced lifestyles on major network shows, ranging from *Oprah* and *Prime Time Live* to CBS *This Morning*, *The Early Show*, and *The Today*

Show, and in national print media from the *New York Times* to *USA Today.* For several years they hosted the national weekly cable TV show *Families Are Forever* and two national satellite TV shows, *Lifebalance* and *Teaching Children Values.* They founded (and run) the international parents' cooperative organization HOMEBASE with a membership of more than 100,000 parents throughout the world, and they were named by President Ronald Reagan to direct the '80s White House Conference on Children and Parents. Richard and Linda have nine children.

RICHARD EYRE

I believe in families! My wife, Linda, and I have basically devoted our lives to that belief. In addition to raising nine children of our own (a work in process), we have been writing books and doing various kinds of media aimed at family and parenting for more than twenty-five years. Our commitment stems from our conviction that family is the most important purpose of mortality.

Subconsciously at least, we all recognize this importance. After all, we all entered this life through family. And family will surround our exit. In between, family provides us with our greatest joys and deepest sorrows. Family has always been our main societal reference point and the basis for much of our terminology and metaphors. In history, the past is best understood and connected through extended families. In economics, markets and enterprise are driven by family needs, attitudes, and perceptions. In education, family support is the key variable, and parents are the most influential teachers. In sociology and anthropology, society doesn't form families; families form society. In politics, all issues reduce down to how public policy affects private family. Public opinion polls reveal that family commitments exceed all other commitments. In ethics or morality, family commitments teach the highest form of selfless and empathetic values, and lack of those commitments promotes selfish and antisocial behavior. In media, the things that touch us most deeply or offend us most dramatically generally involve family. In nature, everything that grows is in a family.

Our semantics, our similes, our symbols, indeed our whole frame of reference is family. In my own private frame of reference, family is the first priority, both personally and professionally.

How does all this tie to my belief in The Church of Jesus Christ of

Latter-day Saints? In virtually every imaginable way. The theology of the Church centers on the family, and the programs of the Church are designed to support and strengthen the family. Let me devote the balance of this essay to an elaboration of each of those two statements and to a summation of why I believe.

The theology of the Church is powerfully family centered. We believe that God is literally the Father of our spirits and that we lived with Him as His spirit children in a premortal existence. He created this earth and this mortal phase of our eternal lives to enable us to have the profound learning experiences of family. It is within families that we encounter the highest levels of sacrifice, of stewardship, and of unconditional love—not to mention patience and self-control.

We believe that family relationships and bonds continue after death, and when marriages are performed within our temples, the ceremony's wording is not "till death do you part" but "for time and all eternity." For Linda and me, one of the most memorable (and deeply spiritual) experiences in our lives was kneeling across an altar during our own marriage ceremony, looking into each other's eyes, and saying yes to commitments that we believe last forever. Each decision to have a child has had a similar spirituality as we have prayed to God that He would, according to His will, send to us a spirit whom we could both teach and learn from.

With this eternal perspective, welcoming each child at birth has felt to us almost like a spiritual reunion. It has also, we believe, given us a profound respect for our children and caused us to think of them not as our possessions but as our stewardships. When one of our boys was born nine and a half weeks early at three pounds in a tiny rural hospital in the south of England, and when it was unclear whether he would survive, we were able to pray and receive a confirmation that he was sent from God and was intended to grow up in our family. That answer, by the way, led to a spiritual prompting to transfer him immediately to the finest hospital in London, where procedures were taken that ultimately saved his life. (That little three-pounder, by the way, now stands a healthy 6'6" and weighs in at two hundred and twenty pounds.)

During our entire parenting career—the twenty-five years spent raising our children—we have felt that our deepest, truest prayers (and our clearest answers) have come when we were praying about our children. These answers and the spirit they have come with are a big part of why I believe.

The programs of the Church also center on and around families. In fact, a fundamental principle of the Church is to support families and individuals in growing to a level where they can return to Heavenly Father.

Amid the complexities, amorality, and peer pressure of today's world, I have often wondered how we could even approach the challenges of raising children without the help and support of the Church. When they are small, children attend Primary and Sunday School and learn the fundamental faith and basic values that shield them from much of the danger thrown at them by the media and by society at large. As they approach adolescence, the Church sponsors Scouting, athletic, and cultural involvements in addition to the Sunday programs. Teenagers can attend a daily seminary class while they are in high school. The best-qualified adults in each ward or congregation are called as youth leaders, teachers, and mentors to help kids make the most of their teenage years. Parents receive manuals and materials to help them hold a "family home evening" once a week to unify their families and to help kids with their problems.

In our own case, the Church has enabled our children to be somewhat protected from the world without being removed from it. While they have been leaders and student-body officers at large, diverse public high schools and have gone on to college at Harvard, Wellesley,

Columbia, and Boston University, they've managed to attend and participate in church and to live by their personal values and commitments. And though they've been involved in media and politics and in plenty of secular causes and issues, they have been able to keep their own priorities and perspectives. We like to call it "being in the world but not of the world." (See John 17:11, 14–16, 18.) This simply would not be possible without the Church, and it is another very practical reason why I believe.

For me, the bottom line is that the "most spiritual" and the "most practical" have always proven to be synonymous. The theology of the Church has given our family the perspectives and joys that allow us to set correct priorities, and the programs of the Church have given us indispensable help in keeping our family together. I have found, in my life, that the truest things work best, and that the things that work best are the truest. The Church works, and the Church is true.

BRUCE C. HAFEN

⤳

Hollywood has recently found a theme the public loves: happy-ending stories about life, and love, after death. In one hit movie, the lead character dies in an accident, then finds his family in a colorful "heaven"—but only after going through an ugly "hell" to save his wife and children. The film's message is that love can outlast death—a theme that seems to resonate within the hearts of many people today.

Yet this resonance occurs in spite of (or is it because of?) this being the age of the dysfunctional family. In the U.S. now, a full third of new babies are born outside of marriage, and over half of all marriages will likely end in divorce. Indeed, we are living through the biggest change in attitudes about family life in five centuries.[1] An *Atlantic Monthly* writer believes that today's massive family disintegration is a central part of "the Great Disruption," a wave of history as big as the shift from the age of agriculture to the Industrial Revolution in the 1800s.[2]

No wonder the public hopes that Hollywood will find a few happy endings.

In this climate, the hope-filled teachings of the LDS Church about families are unusual—but they're not going unnoticed. Consider how some thoughtful people view the LDS family across three dimensions: Family Future, Family Past, and Family Present. That may sound like something out of Charles Dickens, but the three perspectives must be seen together.

Let's begin with Family Future. When I was a law professor at BYU a few years ago, I received a phone call from Kenneth Woodward, the

---

1. See Mary Ann Glendon, *Abortion and Divorce in Western Law* (Cambridge, Mass.: Harvard University Press, 1987), p. 78.
2. Francis Fukuyama, "The Great Disruption," *Atlantic Monthly*, May 1999, p. 55.

religion editor of *Newsweek*. After talking about family law issues, he asked if I was a Mormon. When I said yes, he said, "I see where the Mormons got some pretty good play in the new book on heaven out of Yale."

Not knowing that Yale was into books about heaven, I asked him to tell me more. He said that the book *Heaven: A History* was written by two non-Mormon scholars and published by Yale University Press.[3] It traces the history of beliefs about heaven in Western culture. It concludes by reporting how people, and religions, think of heaven today. The public feels a widespread hunger for heaven—and families in heaven. Most Americans still believe in life after death *and* in "the eternal nature of love and the hope for heavenly reunion" with their families. Yet most Christian churches offer little response to this public yearning. Rather, today's "ideas about what happens after death are only popular sentiments and are not integrated into Protestant and Catholic theological systems."[4]

Then the authors describe one "major exception" to this religious vacuum about heaven—"the theology of the Church of Jesus Christ of Latter-day Saints." They describe our teachings about temples and eternal marriage, concluding that "the understanding of life after death in the LDS church" offers the most complete concept of heaven in our day.[5] So ordinary people feel a longing to belong after death, and the Restoration fulfills this yearning to a surprising degree. This welcome vision of Family Future is captured in a favorite LDS children's song: "Families can be together forever, through Heavenly Father's Plan. . . . I always want to be with my own family, and the Lord has shown me how I can."[6]

---

3. Colleen McDannell and Bernhard Lang, *Heaven: A History* (New Haven: Yale University Press, 1988).
4. Ibid., pp. 308, 309, 312.
5. Ibid., pp. 308, 320.
6. *Children's Songbook* (Salt Lake City: The Church of Jesus Christ of Latter-day Saints, 1989), no. 188.

Next consider Family Past. Most people know of our Church's deep commitment to family history. I was present when the Church gave a two-volume personal family history to the prime minister of Australia, John Howard. The PM, as the Aussies call him, was delighted to learn about his ancestry. Then he asked, "Do I correctly understand that your Church has the largest collection of family history records in the world?" We were glad to say yes.

The Church has now made many of those family records freely accessible on the Internet. People everywhere feel a growing hunger to understand themselves better by understanding their ancestral roots. Church members pursue these roots and records partly to know their ancestors better but also to help fulfill the dream that "families can be together forever" by building eternal bonds across the generations.

The spirit of Family Past in LDS teaching also includes our appreciation for Adam and Eve, our first mortal parents. Our understanding of Family Past reaches even further back, prior to Eden, prior to the earth's creation—to our family relationship with God Himself. We believe that each human being lived in a pre-earth life with God, the literal father of our individual spirits. Thus we pray to Him as "Heavenly Father," and we may refer to one another as "brother" and "sister." He gave us the opportunity of coming to earth to gain a body and to have the experiences required to teach us the skills and attributes needed to live permanently with Him. The atonement of Jesus Christ then makes it possible for us, if we are faithful, to live eternally "at-one" with our Heavenly Father and with our mortal families. Christ's mission and atonement are therefore centrally connected to our vision of eternal love in families.

The most beloved of all LDS children's songs captures this idea in childlike clarity: "I am a child of God. / And He has sent me here; / Has given me an earthly home, / With parents kind and dear. / Lead me, guide me, walk beside me, / Help me find the way. / Teach me all that I must do / To live with Him someday."[7]

I once visited a small congregation of the Church in Australia's Northern Territory. All of the members there are Aboriginals. Because these people were so isolated—500 miles from other members—I wanted to know what the families there were learning about Church teachings. On impulse, I asked the children if they could sing, unrehearsed, "I Am a Child of God." I can still feel the joyous assurance I felt as they stood and sang every word with earnest smiles, their faces full of light. I sensed they were on the homeward spiritual path.

As the song teaches, our earthly home is an extension in both purpose and pattern of our pre-earth home. And it prepares us for our eternal home. This "great plan of happiness" (Alma 42:8) is all about life in families. As stated by Elder Dallin H. Oaks of the Quorum of the Twelve Apostles, "The fulness of eternal salvation is a family affair. . . . The gospel plan originated in the council of an eternal family, it is implemented through our earthly families, and it has its destiny in our eternal families. The mission of our Church can be expressed in terms of the mission of the family."[8]

This understanding places the Family Present—our mortal family—within the *eternal* perspective of a Family Past and a Family Future. This context makes the LDS understanding of our mortal families like the second act in a three-act play. Without the vision gained from acts one and three, the second act could seem either too short, too long, too hard, or too confusing. When we do know about all three acts, act two acquires an infinite significance.

I've sometimes been asked why so many LDS families seem to

---

7. Ibid., no. 2.
8. Dallin H. Oaks, "Why We Must Act to Preserve the Families of the World," unpublished manuscript, World Family Policy Forum, Brigham Young University, January 15, 1999.

thrive, even in this age of family decline. We clearly have our share of troubled homes. But I'm still asked, "How do you explain the remarkable degree of confidence in marriage and family life that I see in the Mormons I know?" A law professor from Tokyo visited the U.S. to explore his concerns about the corrosive effect of self-oriented American law on Japanese family attitudes. After being on the BYU campus several days, mixing in the dorms with students, he said, "You must tell me about these students and their families. This feels like an island of hope in the time of the apocalypse. What is the secret behind all the shining eyes?"

Questions like these can't be fully answered in social or behavioral terms, because Act One and Act Three of a Latter-day Saint's family understanding make Act Two—Family Present—a matter of theology, not sociology. Thus, when we consider LDS attitudes toward marriage and children, we are talking primarily about religious doctrine. Only at this level do the resilient attitudes and commitments of LDS families find both motivation and meaning.

Those who lack eternity's perspective on time can too easily cave in to the pessimistic assumptions of believing "there's no tomorrow." King Macbeth's chilling speech upon hearing of Lady Macbeth's death captures the attitude that sees Act Two as the entire play: "Tomorrow, and tomorrow, and tomorrow, / Creeps in this petty pace from day to day,! . . . / And all our yesterdays have lighted fools / The way to dusty death. / Out, out, brief candle. / Life's but a walking shadow, a poor player, / that struts and frets his hour upon the stage, / and then is heard no more. / It is a tale told by an idiot, / full of sound and fury, signifying nothing."

Yet because *there is tomorrow* after death, true love is never wasted, and our sacrifices for children and spouses signify everything. We do not strut and fret for but an hour on life's stage, and our candles do not go out by darkness. "Death is not an extinguishing of the light. It is a putting out the lamp because the dawn has come."[9]

With this background, each sentence of the Church's inspired 1995 Proclamation on the Family is rich with religious meaning. It begins with, " . . . the family is central to the Creator's plan for the eternal destiny of His children."[10] The family is the basic unit of both society and the Church, and it is the only element of the Church organization that will continue in eternity. The Church's activities consciously support parents and their families. The First Presidency has said, "The home is the basis of a righteous life, and no other instrumentality [including the Church] can take its place nor fulfill its essential functions."[11] The temple and the home are the two most sacred buildings in the Church. Therefore, LDS parents try to teach their children to know and love God, in "example . . . , in word, in conversation" (1 Timothy 4:12), "when thou sittest in thine house, and when thou walkest by the way, when thou liest down, and when thou risest up" (Deuteronomy 11:19).

Harold B. Lee, president of the Church from 1971 to 1973, said, "The greatest of the Lord's work you . . . will ever do . . . will be within the walls of your own home."[12] President Gordon B. Hinckley said, "Our problems, almost every one, arise out of the homes of the people. If there is to be reformation, . . . it must begin in the home."[13]

It isn't easy to translate these principles into a tidy, daily reality, because family life is by nature a continual struggle between the ideal and the real. But if our homes often know the warm feelings of love

9. Hugh B. Brown, in *Improvement Era*, June 1967, p. 26.
10. "The Family: A Proclamation to the World," September 23, 1995, in *Ensign*, November 1995, p. 102.
11. First Presidency letter to members of the Church, February 11, 1999.
12. Conference Report, April 1973, p. 130.
13. *Ensign*, November 1998, p. 97.

and laughter, if needed discipline is accompanied by loving affection, and if the family is trying—even most of the time—to have regular family prayer and honest gospel conversations, our children are likely to develop a love for God and for each other.

As our children grew up, we tried to work together, pray and play together, and hold weekly family home evenings, as encouraged by the Church. Often, however, I found myself remembering the early words of our ward bishop. He would smile at our little brood trying to hold still on a Church bench and say, "The Hafen children—curtain climbers, rug rats, and house apes!" I also once said in frustration to my wife, Marie, "God placed Adam and Eve on the earth as full-grown people. Why couldn't he have done that with this child of ours?" Marie replied wisely, "He gave us that child to make Christians out of us."

We can't help seeing each other at our worst, and our best, in the closeness of family life. In the worst moments, we may wonder how we can keep living with each other. But in the best moments, we can't really imagine living without each other.

The night before our oldest son left for his Church mission, we put together "the family slide show," the best and funniest pictures of our family over twenty years. At the end of the show, we knelt in prayer together, and spontaneous tears flowed. No more curtain climbers and rug rats—just imperfect young men and women, and their imperfect parents, who felt an honest love for each other. And those feelings keep growing as the constant striving from family reality toward family ideals gives each of us the desire to be more Christian.

Regarding marriage, the Family Proclamation states that "Marriage is ordained of God," that fathers are to "preside over their families in love and righteousness" and to "provide the necessities of life and protection" for them. "Mothers are primarily responsible for the nurture of their children. . . . Fathers and mothers are obligated to help each other as equal partners."

Ideally, Latter-day Saints will marry in the temple, because only there can a couple be joined in eternal marriage. Temple marriage requires a degree of personal commitment to Church teachings for which every person may not feel ready. In or out of the temple, the Church teaches that marriage is by nature a religious *covenant*, not just a private *contract* one may cancel at will. Nourishing that marriage covenant is among our highest religious obligations.

When troubles come, the parties to a "contractual" marriage often seek happiness by walking away. They marry to obtain benefits, so they stay only as long as they're receiving what they bargained for. But when troubles come to a "covenant" marriage, the husband and wife work them through. They marry to give and to grow, bound by covenants to each other, to the community, and to God. Contract companions each give 50 percent to the marriage. Covenant companions each give 100 percent.

Jesus taught about contractual attitudes when He described the "hireling," who performs his conditional promise of care only when he receives something in return. When the hireling "seeth the wolf coming," he "leaveth the sheep, and fleeth . . . because he . . . careth not for the sheep." By contrast, the Savior said, "I am the good shepherd, . . . and I lay down my life for the sheep." (John 10:14–15.) Many people today marry as hirelings. And when the wolf of adversity comes, they flee. This shallow sense of commitment is a major factor in today's widespread "collapse of marriage," the primary social institution that holds the bricks of society together.

The doctrine of eternal covenant marriage helps one resist the urge to run when the wolf comes. Our perspective changes when we view an Act Two marriage with the eternal perspective of Acts One and Three. Then we discover why the demands of marriage and family life are an important part of the Lord's curriculum for the earth school. As one friend said in a time of family turmoil, "I simply made up my mind that I couldn't, and wouldn't, leave him." This conviction sustained her until she discovered remarkable inner wellsprings of compassion and discipline—a discovery so powerful that she concluded, "I didn't know I had it in me."

In practice, the divorce rate among all Church members is lower than the national average, and far lower among couples married in the temple. One study of LDS marriages showed that divorce occurs among 5.4 to 6.5 percent of temple-married people, compared to a range of 28 to 33 percent among Church members married outside the temple.[14]

The LDS concept of marriage regards the husband and wife as equal partners. In this complete togetherness, the man and the woman each make a unique and crucial contribution. Some versions of the Victorian model of motherhood viewed women as excessively *dependent* on their husbands. But today's liberationist model goes too far the other way, stereotyping women as excessively *independent* of their families. The modern prophets teach that husbands and wives are *interdependent* with each other—not two solos, but the interactive parts of a duet.

Regarding childbearing and intimacy, the Proclamation states that "children are an heritage of the Lord," that "God's commandment . . . to multiply and replenish the earth remains in force," and that "the sacred powers of procreation" are reserved only for husband and wife.

In the light of these teachings, a higher fraction of Latter-day Saints marry than is typical of the general population. Similarly, LDS fertility rates are higher than national averages. Church doctrine does not prohibit contraception per se; rather, it urges couples to have

---

14. Heaton and Goodman study, reported in Darwin Thomas, "Family Life," in Daniel H. Ludlow, ed., *Encyclopedia of Mormonism* (New York: Macmillan 1992), p. 489.

children, leaving personal decisions with each couple. Rates of teen pregnancy and sex outside marriage are significantly lower among Church members than national average rates.[15]

The Church refrains from entering political debates, issuing formal statements only when grave moral issues are involved. Thus the Church has taken public positions against homosexual marriage and, except in the rarest circumstances, abortion. The Church's opposition to same-sex marriage is based on its commitment to the sanctity of marriage as an institution.

The Church has also taken a serious interest in preventing, and encouraging thorough treatment from, spouse and child abuse. In President Hinckley's words, "We condemn most strongly abusive behavior in any form" and "We are doing all we know how to do to stamp out this terrible evil." (Gordon B. Hinckley, "What Are People Asking About Us?" *Ensign*, November 1998, p. 72.)

As with other practical applications of family-related issues, the Church's position on these matters of deep moral gravity is grounded in its doctrine about all three acts of the human drama. For example, the Family Proclamation regards gender as "an essential characteristic of individual premortal, mortal, and eternal identity and purpose." It also affirms "the sanctity of life," because "the means by which mortal life is created" is "divinely appointed." And it offers words of sober warning to those "who violate covenants of chastity, who abuse spouse or offspring, or fail to fulfill family responsibilities."

The Church's doctrines about the family offer eternal hope and promise. However, many Church members are not now living in homes that fully reflect these ideals. Many adult members are single. Numerous Church members, especially among new converts, are

---

15. For a summary of relevant research studies, see Thomas, Ibid. In 1990, Utah had the fewest births to unmarried women per capita in the U.S.—135/1000 live births. The national average is 300/1000.

married to spouses who are not active Church members. Some converts from troubled family backgrounds are attracted by the Church's doctrine and its reputation for family solidarity—which they hope, with good reason, will bless their own lives with better circumstances.

The local and general leaders of the Church wholeheartedly accept and support their brothers and sisters whose family lives fall short of the ideal—in no small part because every family since Adam and Eve has known its share of discouragement.

President Gordon B. Hinckley wrote this to the parents of wayward children: "Our children are never lost until we give up on them! Love, more than any other thing, will bring them back into the family fold. Punishment is not likely to do it. Reprimands without love will not accomplish it. Patience, expressions of appreciation, and that strange and remarkable power that comes with love and prayer will eventually win through."[16]

In the musical *Les Miserables*, Fantine sings of her childhood dream "that love would never die." Then she cries, "But the tigers come at night, and tear your [dreams] apart." I have seen the tigers tear at people's dreams. I also know many valiant Latter-day Saints who, literally empowered by their religious faith, have absorbed and transformed the pain of past family trauma rather than passing it on. Emulating—and aided by—Christ, who is afflicted in our afflictions (see Isaiah 63:9), they give healing in exchange for wounding. They "renounce [family] war and proclaim [family] peace, and seek diligently to turn the hearts of the children to their fathers." (D&C 98:16.)

Whatever our circumstances, nearly all of us feel the longing to belong in eternal unity with a loving family. I know the power of hanging on to that feeling as a personal, yet divinely sanctioned, vision. I once saw Mt. Cook, New Zealand's highest peak, rising majestically against a

---

16. Gordon B. Hinckley, *Standing for Something* (New York: Times Books, 2000), p. 157.

clear blue sky. For the next few days, the mountain was enshrouded by dense clouds. Some visitors came thousands of miles to see the mountain but never did. I shared their disappointment, but I knew the mountain was there. I had seen the vision of the mountain's reality. I feel that same assurance about my vision of family love—past, present, and future. And these assurances form part of the reason that I believe.

Sometimes our dreams of joyful marriage and family life are obscured by dark clouds. But we must not give up on those dreams. The spiritual longing of the heart for this fulness is a source of great power, even—especially—on those cloudy days, or years, when the dreams seem impossible. The longing to belong forever to a loving family will be fulfilled by the Father of our spirits: "For he satisfieth the longing soul, and filleth the hungry soul with goodness." (Psalm 107:9.) We can live happily ever after, if we are true and faithful, for the Lord God has spoken it.

Bruce C. Hafen has been a member of the Church's First Quorum of Seventy since 1996. In that capacity, he was most recently president of the Australia/New Zealand Area of the Church. Earlier he was provost of Brigham Young University (1989–1996), dean of the BYU Law School (1985–89), and professor of law (1973–96) at that school. From 1978 to 1985 he was president of Ricks College (now BYU—Idaho). His publications on family law and education law have appeared in such journals as *Harvard Law Review*, *Michigan Law Review*, *Duke Law Journal*, *Ohio State Law Review*, *American Bar Association Journal*, and *Harvard International Law Journal*. He and his wife, Marie, are the parents of seven children.

ORRIN G. HATCH

From the beginning of time, there have been many arguments for and against the existence of God. The greatest philosophers have debated whether or not a higher power exists as the Supreme Being governing our universe.

I was raised as a member of The Church of Jesus Christ of Latter-day Saints and have been inspired by the scriptures, and my faith in our Father in Heaven has become an integral part of my life. My faith has become so much a reality that I can testify not only to the existence of a great and all-powerful God, our eternal Father, but also to the divinity of His Son, Jesus Christ, as the Savior of the world.

I was not always in a position to testify to the divinity of Jesus Christ. But at the age of seventeen, I read the holy scriptures from beginning to end. I prayed for assurance every day. Upon finishing, I got on my knees and, after much supplication, received a tremendously spiritual manifestation of God's power through the Holy Ghost. This feeling was so strong that now I could never deny the existence of God or the divinity of Jesus Christ. I have loved and studied the scriptures ever since.

Throughout the ages, there have been many philosophical arguments for the existence of God. St. Anselm, the medieval priest, ontologically taught, "God is that, the greater than which cannot be perceived."

St. Thomas Aquinas, the great religious philosopher of the Roman Catholic faith, believed God to be the great "Prime Mover," the beginning of all things. He formulated the cosmological argument for the existence of God, believing that all things have a cause, God being the cause of all things.

Knowing that God exists is one of the greatest blessings of our lives. A belief in God helps us endure the vicissitudes and challenges, pains and sufferings, and everyday difficulties of this life. Assurances of a loving God warm our souls and help to make life worthwhile.

Rufus Jones, the Quaker mystic, taught that searching for the Spirit, reading the scriptures, fasting, praying, living Christ's teachings, and doing good for others will lead to a mystical assurance that God exists. He argued that if we pay the price he did, we will also know that God exists. Immanuel Kant, the great philosopher, in articulating his Kantian argument, believed that virtue, for the most part, is not rewarded in this life. Therefore, he reasoned, there must be a life hereafter where virtue will be rewarded, and the great rewarder will be God. These arguments are profound and compelling. Naturally, I have briefly stated them. I have found that there are four simple arguments for the existence of God that arise out of the question "What evidence have ye that there is no God, or that Christ cometh not?" (Alma 30:40.)

1. We have the testimony of countless numbers of people filled with faith, truthfulness, generosity, and love, that God exists and that God has played a role in their lives.

2. We have the testimony of all the holy prophets who have gone on before.

3. The scriptures themselves are laid before us, and I believe that you cannot sincerely read them without knowing they were written through the inspiration and power of our Father in Heaven.

4. The teleological argument makes a lot of sense because not only do we have the testimonies of others, the testimonies of the holy prophets, and the scriptures that testify of God and Christ, but we also have the teleological argument that confirms our belief. We have the earth and all things that are upon the face of it, including its motion; all the planets that move in their regular form; the balance of nature;

and so many other teleological reasons for assuring us that all of this order drawn from chaos is a result of our Supreme Creator.

I have written lyrics to various inspirational music renditions. One of the first songs that I wrote with Janice Kapp Perry, who is one of Utah's greatest composers, is "My God is Love":

> My God is love,
>> He lifts me from the depths,
> He gives me hope,
>> He grants me daily breath.
> My God is love,
>> He rules with tenderness,
> And when I pray,
>> He hears and loves to bless.
>
> *Chorus*
>> My very soul
> Requires His daily love.
>> In darkest hours
> His spirit bears me up.
>> My love for Him,
> Is built upon the rock
>> Of perfect trust,
> For this I know:
>> My God is love.
>
> My God is love,
>> He walks with me each day.
> His love and light
>> Illuminate my way.
> My God is love,
>> And in this world of sin,
> He helps me see
>> That I am safe with Him.

My God is love,
　　As constant as the sun.
Each gift of nature
　　Testifies of Him.
My God is love,
　　Who died that I might live—
His perfect life
　　The purest, sweetest gift.

For this I know,
　　My God is love

Also with Janice Kapp Perry, imagining a sinner dreaming, I wrote a song titled "At the Foot of the Cross":

Once I was lost,
　　Never counting the cost
Of a life filled with
　　Darkness and sin.
But one tearful night
　　I prayed for God's light,
And an answer came
　　From Him.

I dreamed I was there,
　　At the foot of the cross,
As He hung there on Calvary's tree.
　　As I looked in His eyes,
My broken heart cried,
　　To see Him in such agony.
And I wondered what was
　　This marvelous love

That caused Him to die willingly.
    I wept as I watched
At the foot of the cross
    As He suffered and died for me.

I dreamed I was there,
    At the foot of the cross,
When the elements raged at His death.
    There was fear in the air
And deepest despair
    As thick darkness covered the earth.
How I sorrowed that day
    As they laid Him away,
Saying truly He was God's own son.
    Then humanity cried
And the universe sighed,
    For Jesus, the Lord, was gone.

I dreamed I was there,
    At the foot of the cross,
When a messenger brought the glad news
    That the Savior of men
Was alive once again
    And risen from His earthy tomb.
Then in wonder I went
    To the place where they said
He appeared to disciples that day,
    Felt His wounds, kissed His feet,
Then my joy was complete,
    With His victory over the grave.

Once I was lost,
    But I learned at the cross

> I am part of an infinite plan.
> For I know Jesus Christ
> Saved my soul, bought my life,
> And will bring me to heaven again.

I have a personal testimony through music, reading the scriptures, prayer, experience, fasting, observation, and inspiration from others that God lives; that Jesus is the Christ, the Savior of the world; and that God has risen up and will raise up prophets to guide us and to help us understand the needs of our modern age. John 7:16–17 shows us the way to a faith and knowledge of God and Christ: "Jesus answered them, and said, My doctrine is not mine, but his that sent me. If any man will do his will, he shall know of the doctrine, whether it be of God, or whether I speak of myself."

It is this testimony that has given me the solace and determination to do the very best I can for my fellow beings.

May God be with you always.

Orrin G. Hatch has been a United States senator (R-Utah) since 1976. He received his juris doctorate in 1962 from the University of Pittsburgh Law School and has been awarded honorary doctorate degrees from the University of Maryland, Pepperdine University, Southern Utah State University, and Samford University.

Noted for his commitment to principles of limited government, tax restraint, and integrity in public service, Senator Hatch has passed legislation covering everything from tough criminal laws to AIDS research, from reducing the cost of drugs to child care. He is most proud of his Religious Freedom Restoration Act, which brought together a coalition of religious faiths from liberal to conservative. He has participated in confirming the appointments of 1,000 federal judges and all but one of the current Supreme Court justices.

In addition to his public service, Senator Hatch has served eight missions for The Church of Jesus Christ of Latter-day Saints, one a full-time mission to Ohio, Indiana, and Michigan. He has also served as a bishop. Senator Hatch and his wife, Elaine, have six children and nineteen grandchildren.

SHARLENE HAWKES

When autumn falls on Buenos Aires, it's a time to breathe deeply again after wading through several months of typical, muggy summers. My family had come to look forward to this breather since living in Argentina some three and a half years while my father served as an ecclesiastical leader in The Church of Jesus Christ of Latter-day Saints.

As a sophomore at the American High School where I attended with my two younger sisters, I was as eager to begin the fall track and field season as I was to check out my new classes. During the summer break, I had spent some time working on my technique in the hurdles, and thanks to a little growth spurt, I could finally get it down to the three-step rhythm in between leaps.

My coach was pleased with my progress, and it was a good thing, since she didn't waste any time announcing that our team would soon be competing in a rather prestigious event—a track meet claiming to be the largest high-school track meet in the world, with roughly 20,000 competitors coming in from all surrounding provinces. The event would be held at Colegio Militar—the West Point of Argentina.

It was a three-day meet, Friday through Sunday, with all the finals held on Sunday. The moment we arrived I was in awe and intimidated by the sheer number of other teenagers, all with numbers on their backs. I held no grand illusions that I would do well—my main goal was simply to keep from tripping over a hurdle in front of all those people. I honestly expected to be eliminated on Friday, so I gave no thought to Saturday's races, and certainly not Sunday's. I just focused on Friday's series.

But I was surprised on Friday when I not only remained upright during my series but actually won it. That meant I got to run in the semifinals on Saturday. I was excited but again never even imagined that I would do well enough to qualify for the finals. So then on Saturday, after I crossed the finish line first, I instantly knew I had a problem. I had always been taught to keep the Sabbath day holy, and though something like this—what to do if a sporting event fell on Sunday—had not exactly been a regular topic of gospel discussion at home, I felt that running in a track meet didn't fit my family's interpretation of appropriate Sunday activities. And yet, I wondered if it wouldn't be okay because, hey, this was *important*. There should be exceptions to all rules, right?

I thought all of that in the few seconds after I won and before my coach came running up to hug me. "Felicitaciones!" she fairly shouted in my ear as she hugged me. "Congratulations! You're the only one of the girls to make it to the finals!"

And before I knew what I was saying, I blurted out almost apologetically that I couldn't run in the finals because they were on Sunday. I surprised myself more than anyone that my decision had been made.

She looked at me almost as if she didn't understand my Spanish. Then, realizing she had heard me right, she said, "Oh, come on! This is too important! Your parents will understand. They'll let you this time. We'll talk them into it when we get back."

For some reason, that made me mad. *She thinks I'm just a puppet! She thinks I just do whatever my parents tell me to do and I don't make any of my own decisions! She thinks my beliefs are stupid!*

My beliefs. Yes, they were my beliefs, and she thought so little of something that was my very foundation that, well, I'm afraid I wasn't very nice as I told my coach this decision had nothing to do with my parents. I could speak for myself and my beliefs, and I would not run that race on Sunday. She had no idea she had just goaded me into that quick answer.

For the first time I was aware of, I knew I didn't need to ask my parents. It was entirely my decision.

On the way back to the city as I sat alone and in the back of a bus full of quiet, exhausted athletes, feeling a bit ostracized, I wondered why I was so quick with my answer. Was I really that sure of my beliefs? Or was it such a part of my life—having been taught since I was born— that I simply couldn't imagine reacting any other way? Did I believe in the truth of the gospel doctrine of my church, or was I hanging onto my parent's testimony? Or . . . did I believe *just in case* it was all true?

I decided to analyze exactly what I believed and why—beyond just my Sabbath Day activities—in a logical, sequential pattern. I didn't trust just *feeling* something when I was fifteen—I had to have a reasonable explanation for everything. In all other areas of my life, after all, I was never satisfied to just "take someone's word for it." Shouldn't my religious beliefs be the same? My parents, my Sunday school teachers, and my church leaders had always encouraged us to find out for ourselves, to ask questions and seek the answers. Up until then I had never really needed to ask. Now was a perfect time.

My first question began right at the top. Did I really believe in God? I looked out the window at the tall, golden pampas grass filling the fields like stately soldiers in dress uniform, the farmers still tediously working with plows and plodding horses (we had not yet entered the Buenos Aires city limits), and I thought again, *Does God exist?* I remembered reading somewhere that the likelihood of our world and all of its beauties "just happening" is about the same likelihood that a dictionary was produced as a result of an explosion in a printing shop. I concluded rather quickly and decidedly that yes indeed, I knew there had to be God, a Creator.

Okay then, what kind of a God? One who views His creations as cosmic playthings, to toy with while they live and then destroy at His pleasure, never to exist again? Or one who is loving, is deeply concerned about His creations, and wants them to become someone *great,* to fulfill their potential—just as any parent would desire for a child. The latter made much more sense to me.

Then since I believed in a caring Creator, would it not stand to follow that He would have a purpose in creating life? And if a purpose, then it must be grander than just earning a living. And if it is so grand, no doubt He would offer some means of assistance. He would, of course, have a *plan.* What father would stand by and not give their children aid?

I thought of my own parents and how much they were always trying to give advice, but as a quite knowledgeable teenager, naturally I already knew everything! I laughed to myself as I thought of the same relationship that exists between God and His children. We think we know so much, but only when we humble ourselves and turn to Him do we learn and then realize how little we do know.

No parent, not even God, can force advice on a child. But He can provide a way to return to Him.

God's plan, which I had learned about as a child, centered on the sacrifice of His Son, Jesus Christ. Somehow, in a way I couldn't understand in my finite and juvenile reasoning, His death on the cross meant that I could rise above my sins and weaknesses to live beyond death. It made sense to me that justice—the consequence for disobeying God's laws—had to be carried out, yet I was in awe at the incredible measure of mercy that was extended despite our constant disobedience and rejection.

So if my loving Heavenly Father wants me to reach my highest potential, wouldn't He have a way to offer specific instruction about His rules? Something that would keep me headed in that direction? Of course, and that must be our scriptures, and a living prophet. Isn't that the way God says He works? "Surely the Lord God will do nothing, but he revealeth his secret unto his servants the prophets." (Amos 3:7.)

By the time we reached the school, I was sure of my reasons for standing by my beliefs. Of course, I was tremendously disappointed about missing the finals. My coach told me as I left what time the bus would be leaving in the morning just in case I changed my mind.

All day Sunday I thought about the events going on fifty miles away, but I was pleased to find that I no longer felt disappointed. I felt strangely okay about everything, mostly because I had done something tangible to define myself, if that makes sense. While most teenagers didn't have a clue about who they were, I was becoming surer by the moment. And interestingly enough, it didn't have as much to do with my mind as it did with my heart. "God is not the author of confusion, but of peace." (1 Corinthians 14:33.)

On Monday morning my coach couldn't wait to tell me that the girl I had beaten in the semifinals on Saturday took first place on Sunday.

I was never emotional as a kid. I didn't cry like a lot of other girls over broken dolls, skinned knees, or hurt feelings. I was a tomboy. I thought I would go through life just analyzing everything rationally as I had on that bus ride home. But about a year after staying home on that Sunday, I decided one morning to pick up my copy of the Book of Mormon and read it for the second time. It had been awhile since I had last read this lengthy account of one family's journey out of Jerusalem, their trek across the ocean to the Americas, and the troubled history of their posterity spanning a thousand years. Most important though, I had been taught that this book was another testament, a witness, of Jesus Christ as He visited those people in the Americas. It really is a fascinating saga. But this particular morning, I wasn't looking for a good story as much as I was interested in truth.

Just two pages into it, I was quite surprised to find the words becoming blurry. My eyes were filling with *tears*, of all things! *What a strange reaction to a story*, I thought. And as I wiped my eyes, one distinctive thought replaced the previous one: *This is a true story. These people were real.*

That was it. And in that moment I knew that I had experienced a peace "which passeth all understanding . . . the peace of God" (Philippians 4:7)—a peace that speaks of truth.

About four years later, I stood in fear before a group of 400 or so members of the press just minutes after being named Miss America 1985 in front of a record television audience of more than 100 million viewers. I had won on the heels of the scandalous resignation of the previous Miss America as a result of pictures that had been published of her in *Penthouse* magazine. There were many in the press who were critical of the program for demanding her resignation, and I feared that their criticisms would now be aimed at me. I should have been bursting with confidence, but instead I felt fear as they shouted questions at me.

Then, in the time it took for me to approach the podium, I did one of the smartest things I could ever take credit for. I thought about my "absolutes"—those things that absolutely do not change regardless of all the craziness going on around me—and I suddenly didn't care what they thought or what they asked. I cared about the love of my Heavenly Father and my trust in Him, the love and support of my family, my definition of self-worth (which had nothing to do with trophies), and my knowledge that Christ lives and stands at the head of this church that bears His name.

The fear was shoved aside and immediately replaced with courage and confidence, peace and purpose. It is amazing how much comfort and power my beliefs offer when I allow them to be my defining pillars.

Today, some seventeen years later, I haven't changed much—on the inside! But I am more easily moved by things I can't really explain—like the unwavering love of my husband, the unbelievable births of my children, the untimely passing of a loved one, and the undeniable confirmation of truth.

In a world of immediate gratification yet never-lasting satisfaction, I believe in the gospel of Jesus Christ—The Church of Jesus Christ of Latter-day Saints—because it is truth right here and now that gives me courage and joy, *and* lasts forever.

"Peace I leave with you, my peace I give unto you: not as the world giveth, give I unto you. Let not your heart be troubled, neither let it be afraid." (John 14:27.)

In the midst of constant social chaos and change, I believe in the gospel of Jesus Christ because it is in that belief that I always, always find peace and purpose.

"Did I not speak peace to your mind concerning the matter? What greater witness can you have than from God?" (D&C 6:23.)

Born in Asuncion, Paraguay, the fifth of seven children, Sharlene Wells Hawkes spent twelve years of her youth in South America. In 1984 Sharlene played the Paraguayan harp and sang in Spanish for her talent presentation at the Miss America pageant. Traveling nearly 250,000 miles that year, she often relied on her fluent Spanish as Miss America 1985.

She later graduated magna cum laude from BYU and received the Earl J. Glade Award as the outstanding senior in broadcasting. Immediately after graduation in 1988, she signed a contract with ESPN, and since then Sharlene has covered such world-class events as World Cup Soccer, World Cup Skiing, and the Kentucky Derby. Her work has earned her national recognition, including an Emmy nomination and the Women's Sports Journalism Award.

In 1995 Sharlene changed from full-time to free-lance to allow for her growing popularity as a professional speaker—a flexible career pursuit for a full-time mother of four. She is a member of the National Speakers Association and on the boards of the University of Utah Music Department, "Children First Utah," and the Utah Tip-Off Club. She is currently president of Hawkes Communications, a volunteer for the Salt Lake Winter Olympics 2002, and spokesperson for the Intermountain Donor Services.

Sharlene and her husband, Bob, have four children.

GLADYS KNIGHT

I was blessed to have a mom, dad, family, and friends who taught me and nourished my faith in God from birth. My mom, in particular, instilled a firm trust of God in my soul. I have always believed in Jesus Christ. As a little girl I tried my best to keep His light by doing what is right. But then came the day when, even though I still believed, I took that faith for granted. Life took over, and I forgot that our greatest responsibility is to live in a manner that pleases God, not man. Little by little the gospel's influence in my life gave way to social doctrines and worldly ways. But despite this confession, I share my abiding gratitude to the Lord for His kindness and mercy in my life, even before I became a Latter-day Saint. During the most difficult periods of my life He delivered and preserved me, not only from physical dangers but, as I sought His aid, from many of my own weaknesses.

I am also deeply grateful for the mustard seed of faith we read about in the Bible that my mom worked so hard to instill in me. Its force remained strong enough in my heart to keep me searching for truth. It has been a long road. I looked in many places. And now, at last, I have found the fulness of the gospel of Jesus Christ. To me, this is a miracle greater and more significant than moving a mountain.

Let me share why I feel so strong. In my quest over the years to obtain greater light, I attended many churches. I met wonderful people whom I will always love. Along the way I learned important doctrines: God's creation of this earth; the placing of Adam and Eve in the Garden of Eden and their fall; the birth, life, teachings, and atonement of Jesus Christ; and that if we believe in Him we can go to heaven. I know and appreciate these vital truths. But my mind went further. I had one more question. It was simply: "Then what?" I wanted to know what happens after our initial orientation to heaven. Our stay there will be for more than just a week or two. We will reside there for millions and billions of earth years—for eternity! The only answer anyone could give was that God created the earth, Adam and Eve fell from the garden, and Jesus will save those who believe in Him. But again I would ask, "And then what?" The answer would be the same—just a loop of limited information. I was left to wonder, *For what purpose were we created? What happens in the eons of time after people achieve salvation?*

At one point in my search, several years ago, my son Jimmy was baptized a member of The Church of Jesus Christ of Latter-day Saints. Initially, the rest of our family was unaware of his decision. But finally one day while he and my daughter, Kenya, were sitting together on a plane, she looked over and asked, "What are you reading?"

"The scriptures," he said.

Kenya looked closer and asked, "1 Nephi? I can't remember seeing that book in my scriptures!"

Jimmy then explained to her a little about the Book of Mormon, where 1 Nephi is found. As time passed, she learned about the important role the Book of Mormon plays as another testament of Jesus Christ. On another occasion Jimmy's wife, Michelene, invited Kenya to attend what was called a homemaking meeting, where women in the Church gathered together to learn and serve. Kenya felt right at home. When the visitors were asked to introduce themselves, Kenya looked around and thought, *Yeah, who are the visitors today?*—not realizing that she was one of them. That's how at home she felt. Eventually she began to attend more than just the homemaking meetings. She started learning about the Church's teachings, and in time, as she took what she had learned to God, she obtained a witness from the Holy Spirit that the Book of Mormon and the restored gospel is the work of our Savior, Jesus Christ.

She wanted the whole world to know about her baptism. She even made sure that my brother, Bubba (one of the Pips), attended. But I arrived late, after Kenya had been baptized. When I returned home later, I cried the rest of the day. On one hand I thought I had disappointed Kenya; on the other, I didn't really know why. She told me that one day I would see the baptism, which at the time I didn't understand.

After the passing of more time, I found myself in the hospital with an adult form of meningitis that settled in my knee. It was agonizing. Kenya spent a lot of time with me in the hospital. For two weeks she read to me from a book published by the Church called *Gospel Principles*. I learned many new things. One of them dealt with our lives beyond death and the final judgment. Since we are all so different, there is more diversity to our eternal destiny than just heaven or hell. In God's mercy, He provides more variety in our eternal rewards. I also learned that God has a wonderful plan of happiness for us to embrace and follow. Thus, our time on this earth is very important because it is given to provide the way for each of us to achieve the highest potential we are willing to receive. The more we yield to God and His loving counsel, the greater our eternal opportunity. As I listened, I knew that what I heard was true.

In the meantime, my mother, though not a member, regularly watched the general conferences of the Church on television. She was very familiar with both the names of the leaders and their teachings. She would always say to us, "Be sure to watch general conference." She would even call each of us during the broadcasts to remind us to watch, saying, "These are wise men. Listen!" Without giving the rest of us any explanation, she somehow knew the Church is true. I remember her saying, "I am more Mormon than you know." My mother, however, never joined the Church before she passed away. She felt too far along in years to take that step. She stood, nevertheless, as a stalwart beacon pointing the way for the rest of us.

More years passed—years loaded with their share of weighty difficulties. Yet I also enjoyed attending special occasions as Kenya's and Jimmy's families grew in the gospel—blessings of my grandchildren, baptisms, and priesthood ordinations. Eventually Kenya saw that the time was right for me to seriously investigate the Church. She extended the invitation, I accepted, and before I knew it I was meeting with the full-time missionaries. I listened, I learned, and to my amazement I was filled with great joy. The Spirit testified to me again and again that their testimonies of Jesus Christ were true. I knew that the doctrines they taught were of God. I knew that their message, so unique in today's world, is true: Christ's gospel, as taught nearly two thousand years ago, and His priesthood authority has now been restored through prophets in our time. God's greatest blessings await those who love Him so much that they are willing to receive and follow His ongoing revelations of higher truths. As I learned, lifelong questions were finally answered, and I clearly saw my life in the perspective of God's eternal plan. There was no doubt in my mind: I wanted to be baptized.

It was at that point that opposition raised its head. I found myself hindered, not knowing how or at what time I could proceed. I did not know what to do. To my utter amazement, however, the delivering power of God reached into my life and removed that resistance, almost in a single moment. Suddenly the way was open. I knew the right path, and I knew the next step. On August 11, 1997, I was baptized a member of The Church of Jesus Christ of Latter-day Saints. Why had I waited so long?

In all of this, I did not have to disregard a single previously known truth. Instead, the knowledge given in this dispensation through God's prophets only expands my understanding like a rose blossoming in beautiful splendor on a clear day. His words through His servants in our time help us plainly perceive the true meaning of biblical passages recorded so long ago. I now clearly see the difference between God's words and the man-made concepts born during years when prophets were not upon the earth—interpretations and philosophies derived not from God's revelations but from limited knowledge and the traditions of men.

I started reading the Book of Mormon, which is another wonderful witness of our Savior, Jesus Christ. I called Kenya constantly to talk about the things I read. I marveled at the words and testimonies of Christ recorded by ancient prophets who lived in the Americas long before Columbus arrived. I now know that Joseph Smith, who translated that great work by the gift and power of God, was the Lord's chosen prophet to begin the gospel restoration, as we find prophesied in the Bible, in these latter days.

Among the many things I have come to know from God's revelations to His prophets today, I have learned that we are literally children of God. Before we were born on this earth, we lived with Him. That is why Jesus, in His prayer given during the Sermon on the Mount, addressed God as "Our Father which art in heaven." (Matthew 6:9.) The Lord was not speaking figuratively. God's link to us is an actual Father-child relationship. We all are literally brothers and sisters.

This alone expands my understanding about His love for us, about the love we should have for Him, and about the love we should have for each other. It also paves the way to finally learn about the eternal blessings He seeks to give His children after they return to His presence. As I have acquired this greater knowledge, my question of *Then what?* has been answered. God's love for His children exceeds all the bounds of my previous understanding. As the apostle Paul said: "Eye hath not seen, nor ear heard, neither have entered into the heart of man, the things which God hath prepared for them that love him. . . . Now we have received, not the spirit of the world, but the spirit which is of God; that we might know the things that are freely given to us of God." (1 Corinthians 2:9, 12.)

The plan of God, our Eternal Father, is surely the plan of happiness. Why do people resist? I know, I know—it took me a long time to find this Church. But now that I see what my brothers and sisters are missing, I want them to find it faster than I did.

Why? Well, for one thing, the restored gospel of Jesus Christ bears wonderful fruit for families—most especially my own. I closely watched Kenya after she joined the Church. Following her baptism she married a man who was not a member. After two children, her marriage failed. Then came a time of reassessment. Through that difficult trial she resolved to serve God and to walk in His counsels as never before. Over time we watched the hand of the Lord lead her to a wonderful man who eventually joined the Church and to whom she was later married, or sealed, by the power of God's holy priesthood in His sacred temple, not only for time but for all eternity. Her husband's name is Jimmy, just like my first son. Both Kenya and my son-in-law, Jimmy, lead their family to pray, attend church, and learn the scriptures together. I see Jimmy grow in his role as a faithful husband and father who presides in love over his home and family. This is the result of measuring up to the priesthood he holds. In their family I see the fruits of faith, love, and joy, coupled with the presence of the Lord's Spirit. Even in the midst of their challenges they look up to God with trust, knowing that He is merely schooling and refining them to one day receive His greater blessings. They strive to follow the divine formula of happiness. As they do so, their family carries a light I love being around. I know that only the hand of God could give them the blessings they now enjoy. For me, those blessings bear witness of God's restored truths. They bolster my resolve to settle for nothing less than the eternal marriage covenant in my own life. Through that little family, I taste God's fruits, and they are good.

Since I joined the Church, I desire to be more and more obedient to God. As I do so, many people say to me, "I see a light in you more than ever before. What is it?" And you know I want to tell them. During one performance at Disney World, for example, the audience was allowed to write down questions for me. During the first part of the show, the director of Disney World pulled several of the questions out of a container and read them while I did my best to answer. Most asked about my career and my hits. But one question went something like this: "I have been a fan of yours for many years. Yet lately you have had a greater light about you. Could you please share with us how this happened?"

Now, we had a very mixed audience that night—many different ages, races, and religious backgrounds. Attempting to be diplomatic, I answered something like this: "I have learned more about God's standards or commandments that, if obeyed, bring greater peace and happiness. It's not enough to just talk about them, as so many people do. I am now striving more than ever to live them."

Afterward, several other career-oriented questions came up. Then the director said, "We have two roving microphones in the audience. We'll take just a few more moments for those who would like to ask some more questions."

One of the first people to stand up was a tall, beautiful African-American woman sitting near the front. After receiving a microphone she said, "I am the one who asked about the light you now have. Could you please tell us more specifically how you got that light?"

The question was direct. So I gave a direct answer: "I have become a member of The Church of Jesus Christ of Latter-day Saints." To the surprise of some of my friends watching the show, the audience suddenly burst into applause.

Another person sitting in a side row stood up and asked, "If you could have any wish, what would it be?" I said, "To be a missionary and share the wonderful things I now know are true." I really meant what I said. I am seeking more and more whenever and wherever I can to share my testimony of the truths revealed in our time by Jesus Christ.

I would like to share an additional two reasons why the restored gospel is such a great treasure in my life. Not long ago my dear mother passed away. Her health had steadily declined during her final years, so her death was somewhat expected. Still, I miss her deeply. But some time later, to everyone's surprise, my oldest son, Jimmy, also died. Nothing I had previously experienced ever penetrated so deep into the recesses of my soul. Never had I felt such pain. Yet in the midst of these two extreme trials came the profoundly assuring truths found in the scriptures given in these latter days and in the teachings of the Lord's living prophets. So much has been revealed. How comforting, how strengthening is this greater knowledge for those dealing with the death of a loved one! Yes, as long as I remain in mortality, I will greatly miss my mother and my son. Yet I now have a firm hope and faith that not only will I see them again but that through the power of God's restored priesthood we can continue to enjoy each other as a family in the eternities to come. I now understand, by the Lord's Spirit, that our mortal experience is only a minuscule moment in the vast expanse of time.

I am so happy to report that recently Kenya, her husband Jimmy, along with some of our friends, and I attended the Lord's holy temple, where we, by proxy and by those holding the proper authority, performed my mother's baptism. I am hopeful that she, in the spirit world, has taken advantage of this opportunity to accept the baptismal covenant and the blessings it provides. We also performed the work for my father and other deceased members of my family. We then participated in the sealing of my mother and father to be united as husband and wife for all eternity. As they embrace this wonderful gift, we will have the privilege of remaining together as a family forever. At last we are able to receive the blessing of the power promised by the Lord to Peter when He told him, "I will give unto thee the keys of the kingdom of heaven: and whatsoever thou shalt bind on earth shall be bound in heaven." (Matthew 16:19.) We can now remain together as a family with the highest of heavenly blessings, with those we love most, beyond the grave and for all eternity. Other than the atonement of Jesus Christ, what other manifestation of God's love could be more wonderful? This power is available to all who are willing to receive.

With the assurance I have in these loving gifts from God, I can spend the rest of this life pressing forward accomplishing good things with a calm heart and deep-felt joy. Since I joined the Church, my knowledge and understanding of the amazing gifts Jesus Christ offers to the faithful continue to grow. And, above all, my love for Him is greater than I have ever known.

Now, to share one more thought from my heart. I have always wanted to live while a prophet was upon the earth to enjoy God's revelations just as the people did in biblical times. With the unique challenges in today's world, we certainly need divine guidance as much as the ancients did. And since the apostle Paul taught that "Jesus Christ [is] the same yesterday, and to day, and for ever" (Hebrews 13:8), the Lord would certainly call prophets today as He did in the past. As the prophet Amos declared, "Surely the Lord God will do nothing, but he revealeth his secret unto his servants the prophets." (Amos 3:7.) As I learned more about the LDS faith, I realized that Paul's words are true! God does call prophets today. He still loves His children and seeks to guide them to His path of happiness. With all the disparity in doctrine over the Bible's teachings among the Christian churches today, this is the greatest message since the resurrection of Jesus Christ. At last, a sure beacon, a place where God's words through His chosen servants again manifest themselves with eternal certainty far greater than the mere scriptural interpretations of men.

Recently, the testimony of today's living prophet, Gordon B. Hinckley, and the testimonies of the members of the Quorum of the Twelve Apostles were recorded on a video called *Special Witnesses of Christ*. As I watch, I look into their eyes. As I listen to their words, I know, from the Lord's Spirit, that they speak the truth. They need no showmanship or theatrics to deliver their message. Their unified witness stands on its own. They are, in fact, special witnesses of Jesus Christ. They know and testify of His living reality, His divinity, His Messiahship, His love, and His guidance given to us today. I am thrilled to not only live during a time when God again calls His prophets but also when I can hear and accept the messages He gives through them. To their special witness I add my simple confirmation that those men are the Lord's chosen and that our Savior, Jesus Christ, again directs His properly appointed leaders today as He did in the past.

To all who love God, come and listen to the words given to us especially for our day. Seek in your prayers to know if they are true. We certainly would not discard a letter from one we love without reading it. If we really love God, we will not dismiss His words but read and treasure them as a pearl of great price all the rest of our days.

Gladys Knight began performing gospel music at age four in her Mount Mariah Baptist Church and as a special guest soloist with the Morris Brown College Choir. At age seven, she won the grand prize on *Ted Mack's Amateur Hour*. At age eight, she, brother Bubba, sister Brenda, and cousins William and Elenor Guest formed a "little group" called *The Pips* after their manager, cousin Edward "Pip" Woods. After some personnel changes, Gladys Knight & The Pips' first album made its debut in 1960 when Gladys was just sixteen. Four decades of hits followed, including their signature song, *Midnight Train to Georgia*. After thirty-four albums with the Pips, Gladys made her world premier as a solo artist on March, 30, 1989, at Bally's in Las Vegas.

Gladys received a star on the "Hollywood Walk of Fame" in 1995. In 1996 Gladys Knight & The Pips were inducted into the Rock 'n Roll Hall of Fame; in 1998 they were inducted into the Rhythm 'n Blues Hall of Fame.

Gladys has been featured in such leading publications as *Essence*, *Ebony*, and *Redbook* for her philanthropic efforts, which include work with the American Cancer Society, the Minority AIDS Project, the American Foundation for AIDS Research, and programs that help with homelessness, hunger prevention, crisis intervention, battered women, and abused children. Numerous other honors include the NAACP Legal Defense Fund's Black Women of Achievement Award, the Congress of Racial Equality's Creative Achievement Award, an honorary doctorate from Shaw University, and the B'Nai B'Rith Humanitarian Award.

WON YONG KO

One of the reasons I believe in The Church of Jesus Christ is because I have seen the universality of gospel principles and how the Church adapts to and succeeds in varying cultures. I myself am a typical example. As an ordinary man from one small country, I have the privilege of participating in this great work to introduce the Church to the people of the world by testifying how the gospel has been and is being adapted to the country of Korea and to Asian countries nearby.

Through my business experiences, I have had quite a number of chances to visit with people in many countries. Wherever I go and meet with members of the Church, I find the same principles of the gospel. The beginning of the Church in my country has also proved, or more precisely has been proving, the universality of gospel principles for around fifty years.

Korea is a part of Oriental culture, of which Confucianism is at the center. When Christianity was introduced to Korea in the late eighteenth century, it was not accepted well by Korean society. Rather, people who believed in Christianity suffered great persecution because of their beliefs. They were put into jail and lost their social status, and many of them were killed.

The government thought that the principles of Christianity were against the Orientalism that was the ruling principle of Korea at that time. One of the reasons they thought that way was that Christian leaders taught people not to have sacrificial rites for their ancestors. One of the most important social values for Korean people is respect for their ancestors, so we have a sacrificial rite on the anniversary night when each of our ancestors, mostly up to three generations, passed away. We also do this at the beginning of the year and at Korean thanksgiving day in the fall. This is a very serious practice for the family, and all of the family members get together on the ceremony day.

However, most Christians in those early days forbade this sacrificial rite because they believed it to be against the Ten Commandments, especially the first and second. They considered this rite to be idol worship. This has become a serious issue in Korean society, and the government took it as a serious threat to the public order. They thought that Christianity was teaching their members not to respect their ancestors and later not to obey their government. Then the government engaged in cruel persecution, even including death, of those who believed in Christianity.

When The Church of Jesus Christ of Latter-day Saints was introduced to Korea, we had similar challenges. Then a few more challenges were added by other Christian churches.

Before going into that discussion, I would like to tell you how the Church came into Korea. It was introduced during the Korean War.

To help South Korea fight against the communists of North Korea, supported by Russia and China, many countries of the United Nations, including the United States, sent military troops to Korea. Among U.S. military troops there were members of the Church. As they gathered together to worship on Sunday, some Koreans began to join.

However, the first officially recorded Korean member of the Church is Dr. Ho-Jik Kim, who joined the Church in the United States. He was sent by the Korean government to study how to improve nutrition for the Korean people, and he studied at Cornell University.

During his study he was very much impressed with his roommate, who did not drink alcohol, was very kind, and was diligent in studying—but not on Sunday. Dr. Kim learned that his roommate was a member of The Church of Jesus Christ of Latter-day Saints. Dr. Kim studied the Book of Mormon because of his roommate, came to believe in it, and was baptized on July 29, 1951. After earning a Ph.D. in nutrition, he came back to Korea to improve the physical health of the Korean people, but he also brought back a way to improve their mental and spiritual health—the gospel of Jesus Christ.

Korean people appreciated the great effort made by the United States in fighting against communists and helping us rebuild the nation from the disaster of war. This gave Koreans a warm feeling about the American people. Because of this feeling, the Church and the missionaries began to be accepted by the Korean people, although many had misconceptions about the Church.

The first area conference in Korea, with Spencer W. Kimball, president of the Church, was held in the summer of 1975 at one of the public gymnasiums in Seoul. The Korean Saints were very excited about the fact that we could hold the meeting in a public place. However, two weeks after that conference, we planned to have a stake conference at another public place, a concert hall run by the high school. I was serving as executive secretary to the stake presidency and had procured an official contract to use the hall. On Monday of the week before the stake conference, I got a call from the person with whom I had made the contract. He said he must cancel the contract because he could not get approval for the meeting from his superiors. They were upset about allowing a "heretical" church to use their concert hall, which belonged to the Methodist Church.

He almost pleaded with me to cancel the contract. Otherwise, he would be fired. But I could not do that because we did not have time to inform the members of the change, and I could not disappoint more than two thousand people. I reported the problem to the stake president. He and his counselor visited the principal of the school, and I accompanied them. After listening to the facts, the principal approved our use of the hall because the contract was made officially between two organizations and should be honored. She added that she had learned about our church when she studied in the United States and did not think it was heretical as the ministers said. She noted that the Latter-day Saints are good people respected by many people in the United States. "I might have some serious complaints from my foundation," she said, "but I think I should respect this official contract."

As people in Korea have begun to understand the Church, they have seen many similarities between gospel principles and our Korean traditions. For instance, we say, "What is learned at the age of three is carried to the age of eighty." This is similar to an Old Testament saying, "Train up a child in the way he should go: and when he is old, he will not depart from it." (Proverbs 22:6.)

And the Lord teaches us, "All things whatsoever ye would that men should do to you, do ye even so to them: for this is the law and the prophets." (Matthew 7:12.) This is quite similar to the teaching in Confucianism about decorum.

So when the missionaries and the Church members introduce gospel principles to Korean people, they see the similarity between the principles and appreciate that the Church also teaches people how to implement those principles. Many young people think that our traditional value system is out of date, but the Church shows a more effective way to implement our value system, and it even helps us keep our traditions in our daily lives.

In the Orient we believe in five essential virtues: loyalty, filial piety, trust, courage, and benevolence.

The virtue of loyalty emphasizes that people should be true to the nation and its leaders. This is the fundamental virtue in establishing the nation, and it is very important to our leaders. We may need this virtue more than ever before because many people now focus on their own lives and interests and do not care for the public interest. In ancient times, whenever the nation was in danger, not only military forces but also ordinary people stood up and fought because they were dedicated to the nation. Even in a democratic society this virtue is still vital, and we should be good citizens to keep the nation and our society in order. The Church clearly emphasizes the importance of good citizenship and supports this virtue in its twelfth Article of Faith: "We believe in being subject to kings, presidents, rulers, and magistrates, in obeying, honoring, and sustaining the law."

The virtue of filial piety is very special to people in Oriental cultures. People say that filial piety is the source of all virtues, and it is the most important virtue in Korean society. Most Korean families keep a family record from the very first father of their family. Some families are proud that they have records going back more than sixty generations. Korean culture teaches that the spirits of our ancestors are still alive and have some influence on the lives of their family. That is why we have a rite on the anniversary day of an ancestor. But the Church does more than that, teaching that the deceased have a chance to listen to the gospel in the world of spirits, and that we should do temple work to give them a chance to be saved by accepting the gospel even after they die.

The Church emphasizes the importance of the family and the home, which have been crucial components of Korean society. But the Church is teaching more effective and practical ways to strengthen the family. Our Korean family system used to be an extended family system, with three generations living together. However, actual communication among family members was not well established. For example, when family members got together to have a meal, they had to be quiet and concentrate on eating, not talking to other members, except the head of the family, who can say something.

But the Church is introducing more desirable ways to communicate between father, mother, and children through priesthood interviews, family home evenings, and the family council. These days a lot of service organizations specializing on the family have urged people to have more two-way and free communication among family members to avoid youth problems and family issues. The practices implemented in the Church are far ahead of these efforts and are more properly implementing the real aspects of Korean values regarding the family.

Trust, courage, and benevolence are the virtues that people should exercise in daily life. Trust is the fundamental virtue in interpersonal relationships. If you can't give trust to other people, you feel shame and cannot be a part of the community. In order to get trust from other people, you must be sincere in dealing with them. This is a sort of honor code. Anciently the highest class of people were the classical scholars, whose attributes were trust, courage, and benevolence. In dealing with other people, they gave trust and took the courage to say no to what is wrong without worrying about anything, even sacrificing their own lives.

We can find many similar things in the teachings of Jesus Christ. Our Church has more specific principles in helping people execute these virtues.

We are taught to be honest in dealing with other people. We are taught to be Good Samaritans in showing Christlike love to other people who need our help and are less fortunate.

We want to be good neighbors so that people feel comfortable in getting along with us. The reputation we are getting from people in Korean society is that Latter-day Saints are industrious, sincere, and honest, and they refrain from drinking alcohol and smoking.

Still, we are the minority in Korean society, and we are viewed as somewhat strange. However, that attitude is being changed as people come to understand the Church and the things it stands for.

I firmly believe that the principles of the gospel can be applied and accepted in any society because the value system is basically the same in making people more virtuous and happy.

I have a simple confidence that this world was created by the Lord. Even though we live under different cultures and different value systems, the origin of true principles is the same, for they come from our Creator.

That is why we believe in the universality of gospel principles, and The Church of Jesus Christ of Latter-day Saints is working to prove this in more than 130 countries around the world. I am so grateful for this opportunity to share my testimony that this is true, and that we can find true and eternal happiness in the gospel of our Savior, Jesus Christ.

Won Yong Ko is managing director of IBM Korea and currently works for IBM Asia Pacific Headquarters in charge of e-commerce software sales. He studied electrical engineering at Seoul National University.

In The Church of Jesus Christ of Latter-day Saints, he has served as an area authority seventy since April 1997. He was born in Pusan, Korea, on October 15, 1945, and is married to Eun Hee Kim. They are the parents of one daughter and one son.

GERALD N. LUND

❧

It wasn't a great and grand miracle—not like dividing the Red Sea or healing a leper. It happened quietly, unnoticed by any outside of the circle of family.

Julie, our second daughter, was thirteen months old at the time. Off the corner of our kitchen was a shallow stairwell—two steps down, then a landing that led outside. We had been wise enough to block it off with a board about two feet wide—chest high for Julie at that time. We assumed that would be sufficient.

But one day there was a loud crash, and then a piercing scream. Somehow she had gone up and over the top and fallen into the stairwell. In an instant we were both to her. Her mouth was filled with blood, and as I looked to see where she was hurt, I saw two tiny white teeth sitting on her tongue. Then she gasped for breath and swallowed, and they were gone.

Fortunately, there was no other serious damage. We took her to a dentist the next morning. Without the teeth to examine, he couldn't tell if she had broken them off or knocked them out, roots and all. He recommended a children's orthodontist who could take X rays to show whether the root buds had been destroyed. "And if they were?" I asked. He shook his head. A person's baby teeth and permanent teeth are both present, deep within the jaws at birth, in small swellings called buds. If the buds were not damaged, then at six she would get her permanent teeth. If the buds had been lost, then Julie would never have her own front teeth. He explained what that would mean. Without her bottom teeth, she would use a reverse tongue thrust to stop from drooling through the gap in her mouth. This would create a "bucktooth" effect. She would need braces early and for an extended period to correct that. She would also require a dental bridge in her mouth for the rest of her life.

Sick at heart, we made an appointment and began to pray. The orthodontist brought in the X rays, shaking his head gravely. The damage was total. Nothing was left of the tiny buds. He told us to return in about five years so that he could begin the long process of correction.

Knowing how cruel some children can be to those who are "different," my wife and I decided to turn to the Lord with even greater fervency and ask for His help. Our prayers intensified. We added fasting to our pleadings that perhaps the X rays hadn't shown the whole picture, that perhaps at age six her permanent teeth would appear after all.

It was several months later. The baby was laughing up at her mother. "Come here!" my wife called. When I knelt down beside them, she pointed, tears in her eyes. "Look!" And there they were— the first edge of two new little baby teeth just poking through the bottom gum.

The next day, that same orthodontist once again shook his head, only this time in astonishment. "If this were five years from now and you showed me she was getting permanent teeth, I would be amazed. But to get a second set of baby teeth? And when there was not even the hint of any root buds left? I don't understand it. I can't explain it. But you've had a little miracle here."

That single event, though sweetly tender and wonderful, is not *the* answer to why I believe. It is only one example of the countless number of times I have felt the richness of God's love and seen dramatic evidence of the intimate way in which He watches over His children.

Think of the sea for a moment. Deep snows fall through the winter, then thaw in the spring to reappear as mountain springs. Rain falls from the sky and creates tiny rivulets. Springs and rivulets join to become brooks. Brooks and creeks and streams form rivers. Rivers combine to become a mighty Mississippi flowing into the sea. How many raindrops are in a sea? Who could ever tell? How many separate elements have added to this thing I call my faith? The answer is the same. It is not possible to count them all. Here are but a few of the reasons.

Growing up in rural western America was pretty normal for me. And yet in one way, my childhood was different from many. My father always characterized himself as an "uneducated" man. The Great Depression cut off any hopes for a college education. He spent his life as a pipe fitter at a copper smelter. Yet he had an insatiable hunger for knowledge and was relentless in his pursuit of learning and truth. He constantly pushed himself and his family to seek the truth and not just accept things because someone said they were so. My father deeply believed that real faith—the faith that brings actual spiritual power into one's life—is based on personal knowledge and not just on blind acceptance of what others teach.

I say this because I have had people say to me, "Well, you were raised as a Latter-day Saint. It's only natural that you would accept your theology without question." I just smile. That may be true in some homes, but it was not in mine.

That legacy from my father influenced the direction I took in life. I spent thirty-five years as a full-time teacher and administrator in religious education for The Church of Jesus Christ of Latter-day Saints. For more than half that time, I actively pursued the avocation of research and writing. My life as a teacher and writer allowed me to explore my religion—extensively and intensively—and compare it with the faith and value system of others. I have been privileged to travel to more than forty countries across the world. I have friends and associates from numerous cultures—Christians of many persuasions, Jews, Moslems, Buddhists, and even a skeptic or two. After completing a master's degree in sociology at Brigham Young University, I completed the equivalent of a second master's degree in New Testament studies at Pepperdine University in California, a school run by the Church of Christ. I studied the Bible in great detail. I studied ancient history, culture, and archeology. I learned Greek and Hebrew so I could study the meaning of the biblical text in the original language.

I say all of this only to show that my feelings about The Church of Jesus Christ of Latter-day Saints do not come from a provincial or limited view of the world. My experience has led me to understand an important truth: Whether it is along the banks of the Nile, in the shadows of Guatemalan volcanos, or in the rice paddies of China, there is a great sameness among us. Most people are searching for peace and happiness for themselves and their families. Much of that searching leads people to religion. I have found much to respect and admire in those religions and especially in the sincerity and commitment of those who follow them. I would not want to suggest that the Latter-day Saints have an exclusive lock on truth and values and faith.

But I can say this: In this quest for truth, in my lifetime of study, examination, teaching, and research, I have found in the Church a greater fullness and a deeper richness of truth than anything else I have examined. It has a miraculous consistency of theology and religion that brings to individuals and the family quiet joy and true peace. Through those things restored to the earth through the Prophet Joseph Smith, our knowledge of God and of His Son Jesus Christ and their workings is greatly enriched. The ordinances that lead to salvation, and the power and authority to perform them, lost for so many centuries, are once again on the earth.

My faith is not just a way of life; *it is life!* It provides a haven, a beacon, a compass. It is not restricting but liberating. It is not a burden but a joy. I now more fully understand what our Savior meant when

He said, "I am come that they might have life, and that they might have it more abundantly." (John 10:10.)

As a boy of twelve, one day while collecting subscriptions on my paper route, I lost a check for twenty dollars (a full month's wages for me). Sick to my stomach, I got off my bike and walked back and forth half a dozen times across the route I had traveled since I had received the check. I checked every bush, picked up every scrap of paper. After almost two hours of desperate and meticulous searching, I finally stopped. I stood there in place, holding my bike, and bowed my head. "O God," I cried in my heart, "help me to find that check." When I opened my eyes, there, stuck in a bush not five feet from where I stood—a bush I am sure I had previously examined more than once— was the lost check! The astonishing reality of that day, and all that it implies about a loving Father, is as vivid to me today as it was nearly fifty years ago.

I have felt God's hand in my life and in the lives of those close to me so many times and in so many ways that to try to enumerate them would be like trying to calculate the number of raindrops in the sea. They have come in so many different forms: Answers to prayers. An unseen nudge onto a different path in life. Flashes of insight and understanding in moments of questioning. Unseen but evident protection in times of danger. The comforting influence of the Spirit during tragedy and trial. A gentle call to repentance. The sweet sense of forgiveness that came when I answered that call. The quiet but powerful witness that Jesus Christ is my personal Savior who made it possible for me and those I love to return to live with God forever.

Why do I believe? The answer for me is simple. The sea is evidence of rain and snow. My life is a sea of evidence. I *know* that God is there. I *know* that He loves us and wishes for nothing other than our joy. I *know* that His great love moved Him to offer to His children the greatest of all sacrifices, that of Jesus Christ, His Beloved Son. I *know* that the Father and the Son are not stern and vengeful deities but are filled with mercy and compassion and show forth their love to us in count- less ways. I know that Joseph Smith became an instrument in God's hand to carry forth His work in these, the latter days.

This is what a lifetime of seeking has brought me to know. And because I know, I believe.

Gerald N. Lund received his B.A. and M.S. degrees from Brigham Young University and did additional graduate work in New Testament studies at Pepperdine University. He was a religious educator for thirty-five years, serving as a teacher, curriculum writer, teacher trainer, and administrator.

He has written eighteen books which have won several honors, including twice winning the Independent Booksellers "Book of the Year" award. His love for the Bible and its peoples have taken him to Europe and the Holy Land more than a dozen times as tour director and lecturer.

He and his wife, Lynn, have seven children and seventeen grandchildren and currently reside in Alpine, Utah.

ANN N. MADSEN

My father's mother was my favorite grandmother. She was the only one of my two grandmothers whose life overlapped mine. My Grandma Nicholls looked exactly the way a grandmother should look. She was short, stout, and always immaculately clean from her shiny white hair to her sensible black walking shoes. And she always smelled of a sweet sachet her husband had brought her from his Church mission in England forty years before. I knew her well.

It was easy to love Grandma Nicholls because she was so kind to me. She patiently taught me to cook, knit, crochet, tat, and darn socks. She was the child of pioneer parents who had walked across a continent. Darning socks was only one of the unspoken frugalities in her life. She never wasted anything. I remember the carefully cro-cheted rugs she fashioned of fabric from old dresses; each fabric piece included a memory. Today such scraps would be discarded in our dis-posable culture. She is the one who is constantly spoken of in my family when a bit of food is perfectly good but left over. We must eat or recycle it. "What would Grandma say?" She never seems far away.

Grandma had many stories to tell, and I loved to hear them. Her mother had come to Utah from Sweden after joining the Church with her sister, Amelia, and had walked eleven hundred miles across this rugged country. Amelia was frail and ill during much of the journey. They did not have a team and wagon, but someone had offered to transport their belongings so they could walk unencumbered. My grandmother described the journey in a matter-of-fact way:

> [My aunt] Amelia was so slight that when she became
> too tired to walk further, my mother would put her on her
> back, Amelia's arms around her neck and her legs over her

hips, and Mother would thus carry her. It took one hundred days to cross the plains, and on November 8, 1865, they arrived safely in Salt Lake City, six months and fourteen days since they embarked from Sweden.

The stories were part of Grandma and became part of me. Her personal favorite and mine was about her courtship with our grandfather, Frederick William Nicholls:

When I was fifteen I went to live with a prominent family named Sharp at 111 South Temple Street. It was here that I learned the art of cooking under the supervision of a very able and proficient cook. It was while in this home that my romance with my future husband commenced. He was the handsome young man who called for the orders for meat. He was courteous and always had a smile on his face. Once, after greeting him at the door he asked if I would like to go to the theater. I thought he was joking but to prove he was serious he said he would bring the tickets to me and I could keep them. My first date with him was to see the opera, "Faust." We attended many social functions in the old Social Hall, as well as plays and operas in the Salt Lake Theater. . . . We had wonderful times in the "Gay Nineties." He was a wonderful sweetheart and our courtship lasted a little over two years. He made arrangements for a local florist to send flowers to me every Saturday night.

Our marriage took place in the Logan LDS Temple on the 23rd of April, 1890. Three children had been born to us when my husband was called on a mission [for the Church] to Great Britain in April, 1895. He returned home in 1897.[1]

---

1. Personal History of Anna Johnson Nicholls, in author's possession.

My grandfather died in May 1901, when my father was nearly three years old. My father never really knew his father. Of course, I never knew him either until I came upon the two journals Frederick William Nicholls kept on his mission to England. I was so elated to touch the pages of the book he had touched. This was his own handwriting. I tried to conjure his voice reading the words to me. I remember the moment when I realized that if I could hear him saying these words, it would be with an English accent. I read each Sunday afternoon until I had read every word. Finally I knew him. I was so sad that my own father had never touched these precious pages.

On one page my grandfather had drawn the outline of a large apple he had been given, writing:

> Just before leaving the Ashbrooke's Estate I was presented with a couple of very large apples. The smallest was just the size of this circle. I also received a large bunch of double violets, also some white ones, some primroses and daffodils. The whole making a handsome bouquet. I've pressed some and others I have given away.

A few of those pressed blossoms fell into my lap that day. I found such tender clues to my own DNA page after page. Along with the references to fruits and flowers, I discovered his solid devotion to a cause that has become precious to me. Once in a lonely moment, he cried from the page, "I could not stay here one moment, so far away from my sweet Annie and our three beloved children, if I did not know that what I am teaching is the truth!"[2] What pathos I felt when I read those words! I knew, but he didn't, that in a scant six years he would be dead;

---

2. Frederick William Nicholls, Missionary Journal 1895, in my possession.

in that tiny slice of history before his death, my father would be born and my Uncle Bill barely conceived.

My grandfather's journal makes regular references to his Uncle John and Aunt Sarah and his cousins Percy and Edith Pearson. I decided to search the records to see if they had ever been baptized. They had not. In harmony with our belief in proxy ordinances, this was soon done by our family. My journal records how it was accomplished:

> Our family shared a tender experience as we went up to the [Provo] Temple to perform the baptisms for the family of my Grandfather's Uncle John Pearson. Before our grandchildren went, I read to them from my grandfather's missionary journal where he wrote how he loved the Pearsons and longed to bring them into the Church. We assigned each grandchild a name from these entries; they saw each person for whom they would be baptized through my grandfather's eyes.

That sunny morning, when we went to the temple in their behalf, was almost exactly one hundred years since my grandfather had written these entries. I told our grandchildren that Grandfather Nicholls had learned to be an effective missionary but that he had died shortly after he returned home from England. Surely a hundred years was plenty of time (in the spirit world)[3] to complete the teaching begun in 1894.

Thus, our children's children were able to turn their hearts to their fathers in a profound way and know them, too. Our fourteen-year-old grandson, Max, later described his feelings in the temple baptismal font:

---

3. We believe that all who die go to the spirit world to await resurrection.

The water feels warm when you step into the font, and it feels really good to think about the people who never were baptized who are just leaping for joy because now they are members of the Church. And you made that possible! That's a really good feeling.

There is a bond we discover when we find members of our family whom we have never known, whether living or dead. I had heard from my mother about my cousin David Weeks, her sister's son. I thought I remembered meeting him when I was a tiny girl. My vague image was of a handsome, dark-haired boy in a sailor suit, but I wasn't even certain if it was my memory or a learned memory from my mother, who adored the little boy but after her sister's premature death had somehow lost track of him.

Eventually, as an adult, I became curious. Was there really a David Weeks, and was he alive? I began the search, and soon it became very important to me to find him. I used the Family History Library in Salt Lake City combined with several Internet search engines, including FamilySearch. I pieced together the puzzle from many sources, and late one evening, after a day of searching, I found myself speaking to his wife, Betty. He was, indeed, very much alive and in New York City on business. She gave me his number, and the next morning I nervously called, reaching a secretary who asked my name. Then I heard a voice, which seemed so familiar, on the other end of the phone saying my name: "Ann?" And I heard myself saying simply, "David?" He quickly went on, "The last time I saw you was when you were a pretty little girl with blond ringlets."[4] I heard myself mumble something about the boy in the sailor suit, and we promised to meet.

Just a few weeks later, we did. My husband and I flew up to Oregon

---

4. More than sixty years before.

to David and Betty's home. Their view of a range of gorgeous, snow-capped mountains I will remember, but more than that, I treasure the family feeling, the tangible bond that is so real. I was apprehensive as I arrived but was loath to leave this newfound, bona fide member of my own family. I came home cherishing the times he took my hand as we four walked by the river. I didn't ever want to let go.

If there is something remarkable about Latter-day Saint families, I think it is linked to this attitude toward the extended family.

We learn to honor our ancestors. These good folk chose to bear children—us. We understand clearly that their legacy is our opportunity. They are who we are. We search to find them; then we bind ourselves to them in temples built and dedicated to that very purpose. Our hearts turn to them in love and gratitude for their legacy.

In a disjointed world where being disconnected is becoming the norm, in The Church of Jesus Christ of Latter-day Saints we are connecting families, forging eternal links between husbands, wives, parents, children, grandparents, aunts, uncles, and cousins.

In a world that is saturated with technology, many log on to chat groups to counterfeit a family feeling rather than tapping into their own family. We are using technology to gather and write our authentic family stories, moving back through time and using this amazing, swift access to the past to link ourselves to our ancestors. Our family histories become our personal scripture filled with important values and lessons once learned that need not be repeated.

We own our ancestors, complete with their foibles and sins. Our hearts turn to them with a kind of tolerance that transcends here-and-now relationships. We can manage a deepened understanding, having seen their struggle at a distance with the perspective of a generation or two. Given that hindsight we can learn to improve our own here and now. For these insights we are filled with love for them. Providing them the ordinances of the temple is the means by which we can express that love.

When that perspective finds a place in our hearts, we work at building lasting relationships now: husband, wife, brother, sister, father, mother, children. We know we will live together forever so we resolve differences. We forgive. We forget. We help redeem one another. We see life as a test, and we're all in it together. Those of us who are here now can become transition figures. We can learn from those who have preceded us and love them for letting us profit from their lives, thereby blessing those who come after us. A wonderful line from the Book of Mormon, written by the last writer in what in many ways is a remarkable family history,[5] conveys this idea precisely: "Condemn me not because of mine imperfection, neither my father, because of his imperfection, neither them who have written before him; but rather give thanks unto God that he hath made manifest unto you our imperfections, that ye may learn to be more wise than we have been." (Mormon 9:31.)

A tree is a wonderful metaphor for a family. Solid roots nurture the newest twigs. Branches grow stronger having withstood wind and rain. But for the tree to remain alive and thriving, it must draw on its roots constantly.

Having families "sealed," or tied together in bonds that we believe transcend this earthly life, is the crowning ordinance in the temple. Family history research is essential to the task. To connect our families, we have to find them. We begin with our parents and work back through the lives that have produced ours. Then the temple becomes a bridge of love between this world and the next. In the temple we feel the closeness of our eternal family, here and just beyond a thin veil.

---

5. The Book of Mormon includes the history of a family in Jerusalem—Lehi and his wife, Sariah, and their children.

We have complete trust in a life after this. Temples are our affirmation of that trust. Families are meant to be together forever. This remarkable and transcendent facet of Latter-day Saint doctrine is just one reason why I believe.

Ann N. Madsen is the mother of three (plus an Indian foster son), a grandmother of sixteen, and great-grandmother of one adorable little girl. Her hobbies include swimming, cooking, writing poetry, researching family history, and photography.

Ann received her B.S. degree from the University of Utah and her M.A. degree from BYU in ancient studies with a minor in Hebrew.

She began teaching at BYU in 1976 when her family was grown. She also taught biblical courses, including Isaiah, at the Jerusalem Center for Near Eastern Studies. She has recently completed a book titled *Making Their Own Peace: Women of Jerusalem*, which tells of twelve modern women who live or have lived in Jerusalem.

She served with her husband, Truman G. Madsen, who was president of the New England Mission. She has been Jerusalem Branch Relief Society president as well as a stake Relief Society president at BYU. She presently teaches the sixteen- and seventeen-year-olds in Sunday School.

TRUMAN G. MADSEN

A renowned sociologist cornered me in the Harvard library stacks one day. "I can't account for it," he said, "and I probably wouldn't trust your explanation. But I find more spiritual vitality per square inch among the Latter-day Saints than any other group I've studied. And I've covered the waterfront."

I didn't ask him to define his terms, and he didn't wait around for my "explanation." Here, I am invited to give one in brief and totally subjective terms.

For nearly half a century I have had an absorbing academic but also sympathetic role: to study and interrelate world religions and philosophies and to lecture and write about them. Five of those years I have lived in or near Jerusalem.

Over these decades I have often ascended the Mount of Olives from the east with clusters of visitors, most of them here for the first time. Whatever their origins and backgrounds, whatever their faiths or unfaiths, they, like me, typically gaze in awe at the golden vista of Jerusalem. In the heavy silence I wave my arm and say, "There is our past, present, and future."

But I see and feel and revel in something few of them can yet see.

Cranes loom on the horizon to testify that Jerusalem is being rebuilt. My mind's eye sees a related rebuilding. In my own life, in my very nerve endings, so to speak, I have vindicated the audacious and unique affirmation of the Latter-day Saints.

It is this: The original religion of Jesus and His first-generation church and community have, in fact, been twice-born; once in Jerusalem and once in a newer Jerusalem in America. The splendor of Christ's past and much of the splendor of His future has become embodied and realized in a community that is a nucleus of the eventually all-inclusive kingdom of God. This new beginning, this fresh start with all of its fire and fervor, is in the process of transforming lives in the pattern of the earliest disciples of Jesus. The book of Acts is being rewritten in the lives of flesh-and-blood people in the world today. It will lead to a full-scale messianic and millennial age.

How all this came about is chronicled elsewhere. But there is nothing sectarian about it. The vision, traceable to Christ himself, is of a near-nation, a people, a culture, a civilization that encompasses everything this-worldly and everything other-worldly and aspires to make them one in the beauty of holiness.

Colleagues of other faiths who have done their homework on the heart of this restoration theology find in it all the traces of Jewish-Christianity. When I studied under Paul Tillich, he called it "neo-primitivism." The label helps a little if taken as a glimpse of what the Latter-day Saints mean by the "restoration of all things." "Primitivism" points to the testimony that the covenant made with and by Abraham is forever binding and will eventually reach to the whole human family, that the major and minor prophets were prophets in the fullest sense. It points also to the Latter-day Saint recapitulation of the history of Israel, including their exodus into a new Zion—also to the merger of laws and ordinances in people-hood. Above all it points to the centrality of temples as the sanctuaries of full access to Christ's most pervasive life-giving powers. All this is clearly in continuity with the Jewish heritage.

The term *neo* suggests the unblinking witness that men and women of God have beheld the living Christ in this generation as did Paul on the road to Damascus, and that traveling the world today are apostles and prophets and charismatic men and women whose credentials are identical to those of old. Under the sanctions of a royal priesthood, they are empowered and mantled as "servants of all." (See

Mark 10:44.) Young and old, all laypersons, are promised anew all the spiritual gifts of the biblical record. From the day of their conversion, youth as well as aged are called to be a combination rabbi-priest-minister. All teach, all serve, all occupy the pulpit, all perform functions of priestly ministration. More startling still is the insistence on the need and the reality of individual continual revelation. When it comes through the leadership and is upheld by the common consent of the membership, the result is modern scripture, some of which mirrors biblical teaching, some of which clarifies and supplements it. Newly discovered ancient writings confirm the essential thesis that the role of the Messiah has been anticipated in every generation. All this increases the resonance and relevance of biblical scholarship in my life. Doctrinally speaking, it can be put in five sentences:

Christ is like God and God is like Christ.

If we are not Christlike we are not Christian.

There is only one way to become Christlike

That is the way He became what He was.

He submitted to the will of the Father and to all of His laws and sacraments.

These are required of us: they begin but do not end with faith and trust in Christ's atonement. He who was full of grace was also full of truth—and is therefore a Revelator. The process requires enlightenment and growth in knowledge. We are saved through His mission, which is to overcome ignorance and sinfulness, and, beyond both deaths in the body and of the body, to bring us forth in resurrection.

Focus on these precepts as precepts may miss their dynamism, their power in life. In me, and in many others, the movement has created—not just fostered and encouraged, but created—new levels of openness in conscious imitation of the Jesus of history. I call it "Christianity in the present tense." If we follow Him, it means we are:

1. Open upward, to inspirational and creative guidance from on high.

2. Open inward, to the deepest impulses and insights of our own vibrant spirit and those of every man, woman, and child.

3. Open outward, to all the good and true principles in the world, regardless of their source—and to their beauty.

4. Open, if need be, downward, to the wounded and staggering and addicted.

As a biographer I have worked with the whole history of notables from ancient times to now. In this context I have studied line by line and day by day the teachings and life of Joseph Smith. Harold Bloom, prolific literary critic, has lately written that by almost any measure, Joseph Smith stands with the greatest and most influential of American religious figures, including Thoreau, Emerson, and William James. But intriguing and impressive as he is becoming in world thought, his prime impact for those who knew him was to point beyond hearsay and secondhand assent.

Joseph Smith taught after his own encounters firsthand that all could come unto Christ in this way and eventually receive and give what Jesus called a "fulness." (D&C 93:19.) With the advantage of recency and of trustworthy witnesses who shared and duplicated his experience, he stood for the opposite of what many supposed was the role of a prophet. Instead of "take my word for it," his life and teachings say, "Find your own sacred grove and come to your own individual and independent awareness." The one secure way to comprehend a prophet as a prophet, ancient or modern, is both humbling and terrifying. It is to become yourself endowed with the spirit of prophecy, which we are told in the Apocalypse is "the testimony of Jesus." (Revelation 19:10.) My people know as well as we know anything what this means in heartfelt prayer and submission.

Privileges follow that are laden with intimate personal effects, or in the word of Jesus, "fruits." (Matthew 7:20.) Among them are His vitalizing love, joy, and peace that endure and even intensify in the midst of affliction and tragedy. I have tested and been tested by these realities through every critical wringer I know. They hold up.

My life has overlapped the decline and fall of many -isms and institutions. Some around me have despaired of religion and then made a religion of despair. When they cry out, "How can you know?" they are often saying to themselves, "None of these alleged experiences and spiritual outpourings occur today, so how can we believe they ever did?" My response: "Exactly backward." The cumulative witness of the Latter-day Saints is that all of these things are happening today so one may be assured they could have happened before. Much that distinguishes the movement is public, shareable, and repeatable.

In philosophical terms it could be said that the restoration movement is at once rational, for Christ who was and is the truth dissolves contradictions. It is empirical, for the senses were and will be involved in the invitation of the resurrected Christ, "Handle me, and see." (Luke 24:39.) It is existential, for it is whole-souled. And it is pragmatic, for it works at all levels of human need. In these ways, what appears to some to be the least verifiable religion has turned out to be the most.

It is said that we cannot choose three things: our parents, our birth, and, because they are thrust upon us in tender years, our attitudes toward religion. That is as it may be. But in another sense I, and many like me, have chosen all three. I have been reawakened to and reclaimed my Divine parentage and have come to realize that it is as inescapable as my DNA. By submitting to what our people call "the first principles and ordinances of the Gospel" (fourth Article of Faith), I have chosen the time and extent of my rebirth. And with my family I choose regularly to seek out environments charged with light and godliness: among them the sacrament table and the temple. And I choose to bring them into the daily din and into my home. In short I, with my children—a family, we are assured, that can be as immortal as any individual—have embraced to our depths the religion of Jesus the Christ, which transforms all of our loves and all of our lives.

Truman G. Madsen has an A.M. and Ph.D. from Harvard in philosophy and philosophy of religion. He has been a guest professor at Northeastern University, the Graduate Theological Union at Berkeley, and Haifa University in Israel. At Brigham Young University, he was for two decades Richard L. Evans Distinguished Professor of Religious Understanding and was named both professor of the year and honors professor of the year. He was director of the Jerusalem Center for Near Eastern Studies and is a member of the Jerusalem-based Dead Sea Scrolls Foundation. He has written and lectured widely on comparative religion and has sponsored many symposia with Jewish, Christian, and Moslem scholars. Among those published are *Reflections on Mormonism*, *The Temple in Antiquity*, *Covenant and Choseness in Judaism and Mormonism*, and (forthcoming) *The Search for Human Nature*.

J. W. MARRIOTT, JR.

⟨⟩

When I was very young, my father and I left our home in Washington, D.C., to visit his boyhood home on a small farm west of Ogden, Utah. As we walked over the dry and barren fields, we visited the old brick farmhouse where he lived and the irrigation ditch where he learned to swim. He told me about growing up on this little farm and about his parents' hard work as they struggled to raise eight children with few resources. Then he told me about his grandmother, Elizabeth Stewart, who had sailed from Liverpool, England, to America in 1851. He said she was only nineteen years old when she arrived here. She had no money and hardly any clothing, but she went to work in St. Louis and saved enough money to buy provisions for her journey west. She joined a Mormon handcart company and pulled her handcart across the plains and over the mountains to the Valley of the Great Salt Lake. When she arrived, she had no place to live. She had no job, and no hope of finding one. She went from door to door looking for work. Finally, someone took her in and offered to feed and house her if she would take care of the children and do the housework. Later she met John Marriott. They were married and raised nine children. When I asked my father why she left England and came to America to endure such hardships and suffering, he said it was because she had joined our church and had a firm conviction that it was true. She wanted to be with other Church members where she could worship without persecution.

As I grew up attending an eastern prep school, I was often called upon to defend my religion to those classmates who made fun of it. I often thought about Elizabeth Stewart and her sacrifice for her beliefs. As I defended my church, I too came to believe it was true. To strengthen my convictions, I studied and tried to learn more about our teachings and doctrines. The more I learned and prayed about them, the more convinced I was that the church into which I had been born was indeed the church of Jesus Christ.

When I graduated from prep school, I did not follow my classmates to the Ivy League but returned to my roots and attended the University of Utah. There I met and married a beautiful LDS girl, Donna Garff. We were married in the Salt Lake Temple and were promised that we would be together for eternity if we lived righteously.

After serving for two years in the U.S. Navy (I was unable to serve a mission for our church as the Korean War was in progress and no missionaries were being called), I returned to Washington and went to work in the family business. Soon our first child, Debbie, was born, and within a few weeks the doctors advised us that she had a serious congenital heart defect. It was 1957, and the doctors at the Mayo Clinic were just beginning to work with a new heart-lung machine. We were told that someday, perhaps, Debbie could be healed through open-heart surgery but that we should wait for the surgery as long as possible. Finally, in 1962, Debbie became quite weak; she could not walk very far, and her lips were blue from lack of oxygen. The doctors said it was time to operate. We took Debbie to Mayo. She was given a priesthood blessing of healing that she would survive the operation and her heart would be healed. Two days following the surgery, her little heart began to fail. As the doctors worked on her through the night, Donna and I stayed on our knees in prayer. When we called the nurse's station at 4:00 A.M., we learned that she had been close to death but somehow had rallied, and her heart was beating strongly and with a normal rhythm. We knew that our prayers had been answered and that the special blessing she had received had provided the needed power to heal her. This experience continued to prove to me that God lives and answers prayers.

In 1972 I was made chief executive officer of our company, and Donna and I were busy raising our children. In June of 1974 I was called to serve as the bishop of the Chevy Chase Ward in Washington. I would serve as an unpaid minister tending my flock of several hundred souls. My previous church positions had been far less demanding, and I felt inadequate for this new calling. However, my primary concern was where I would find the time to carry out my new assignment. I was working eighty hours a week, and any time left was for the family and a small church assignment. But I accepted my new position and somehow found what typically amounted to an additional thirty hours per week to carry out my responsibilities. It was, perhaps, the most faith-promoting experience of my life. I performed marriages, conducted funerals, helped struggling families, and counseled teenagers with problems. I also worked to help an impoverished group of Hispanic members who were living at the poverty level and yet managed to pay a full tithing (10 percent of their income). Often, when they would make their $5.00 weekly contribution, I had difficulty holding back the tears. I soon realized that I was able to find the time to fulfill my calling because my Heavenly Father opened the way for me.

Through the example of many righteous people and through my own study and church service, I have learned that God lives and Jesus is the Christ. I have learned that prayers are answered—perhaps not always in the way we would prefer, but they are answered. My membership and activity in our church has provided me with balance and stability. It has been an anchor in a busy and sometimes overwhelming life. Above all, I know that life does not end with mortal death and that obedient Latter-day Saints married in the holy temple of the Lord will enjoy eternal life with their families.

Because of our family's membership, activity, and commitment to our church, we have enjoyed happiness beyond measure. The Church of Jesus Christ of Latter-day Saints has been the greatest blessing in my life.

J. W. Marriott, Jr., son of Marriott Corporation founder J. Willard Marriott, was born in Washington, D.C., in 1932. He graduated from the University of Utah in 1954 with a B.S. degree in banking and finance and spent two years as a ship's supply officer on the aircraft carrier USS Randolph. He joined his father's Hot Shoppes restaurant chain full time in 1956.

Elected executive vice president of Marriott Corporation and a member of the board of directors in January 1964, he became president in November 1964. In November 1972 he succeeded his father as chief executive officer. He was elected chairman of the board in October 1985, following his father's death two months earlier. Under his leadership, the company has grown from one hotel to more than 2,200 hotels in sixty countries and all fifty states.

Mr. Marriott is a director of Host Marriott Corporation, General Motors Corporation, the Naval Academy Endowment Trust, and the National Geographic Society. He is a member of the Executive Committee of the World Travel & Tourism Council and a member of the Business Council.

He and his wife, Donna, have four children and eleven grandchildren.

KIETH W. MERRILL

The question of why I believe has prompted a profound exploration of my heart, mind, and experience. In some ways the answers are endlessly complex. In other ways they are remarkably simple.

I believe because my whole life is a manifestation of the reality of God, the atonement of Jesus Christ, the restoration of the gospel, and the great plan of happiness. We have been blessed with joy in accordance with our desire for righteousness. The divine order of the universe has never seemed obscure.

We know that "faith is not to have a perfect knowledge of things" but is rather a "hope for things which are not seen, which are true." (Alma 32:21.) God's promise of salvation, reiterated by inspired prophets since time began, has given me great hope.

I believe because I have desired to believe. That desire was instilled by goodly parents in my earliest days. I learned as a youngster to give place for the word of God. I have endeavored to submit to the Spirit of the Lord. I have planted the gospel in my heart. I have felt the swelling within my breast. I have recognized that the word is good. It has sprouted and grown within me. It has enlarged my soul. It has enlightened my understanding. It has expanded my mind. It is delicious to me.

The ultimate basis of why I believe comes from spiritual experience. But my "hope in things not seen which are true" is firmly grounded in the abundance of temporal experience and tangible evidence.

WHY I BELIEVE IN GOD

I have experienced the power and influence of God in small and personal ways. He has answered my prayers. I have watched my children born into the world and felt the divine connection to our great Father-God in Heaven. I have felt His power and heard His still, small voice. Beyond the intimate touch of God's hand, the universe proclaims His majesty. The evidence of God is in all things.

God is the creator of all things. I believe in Him because I find that alternative explanations—that life is an accident of self-organization and that the universe erupted from a tiny and infinitely dense glob of matter without cause—unreasonable, incomprehensible, improbable, and ultimately impossible.

I believe in God because I am unwilling to trust the finite minds of other men. In every age "the truth" is redefined with arrogant confidence. Theories of the past are pompously replaced by "new enlightenment." There is a limit to what humans can know, but they do not seem to know it. As Brigham Young, the second president of the Church, said, "Could we live to the age of Methuselah and spend our lives in searching after the principles of eternal life, we would find, when one eternity had passed to us, that we had been but children thus far, babies just commencing to learn the things which pertain to the eternities of the Gods."[1]

I believe in God because the most enlightened minds of science seem unwilling to exclude Him from their quest. Stephen Hawking, considered the most brilliant theoretical physicist since Einstein, has said of scientific theory, "It exists only in our minds and does not have any other reality. Any physical theory is always provisional, in the sense that it is only a hypothesis; you can never prove it. No matter how many times the results of experiments agree with some theory, you can never be sure that the next time the result will not contradict the theory."[2]

---

1. *Journal of Discourses*, 3:202–3.
2. *A Brief History of Time* (New York: Bantam Books, 1988), p. 9.

Science describes the universe in terms of two partial theories. Curiously, these two basic theories, the general theory of relativity and quantum mechanics, are inconsistent with one another. One of them has to be wrong. The goal of science, Hawking states, is "to provide a single theory that describes the whole universe." He continues, "Today we yearn to know why we are here and where we came from. Humanity's deepest desire for knowledge is justification enough for our continuing quest. And our goal is nothing less than a complete description of the universe we live in."[3]

At the end of his marvelous treatise *A Brief History of Time*, Hawking concludes, "If we do discover a complete theory, it should in time be understandable in broad principle by everyone, not just a few scientists. Then we shall all, philosophers, scientists, and just ordinary people, be able to take part in the discussion of the question of why it is that we and the universe exist. If we find the answer to that, it would be the ultimate triumph of human reason—for then we would know the mind of God."[4]

WHY I BELIEVE IN JESUS CHRIST

I believe in Jesus Christ because I have felt the unmistakable prompting of the Spirit of God. I believe that He is the Savior and Redeemer of mankind because I have witnessed and experienced the power of His atonement.

But I am twice blessed, for I have been given the gift to believe on the words of those to whom it is given by the Holy Ghost to know that Jesus Christ is the Son of God and that He was crucified for the sins of the world.

From my earliest childhood I have experienced the testimony of

3. Ibid., pp. 10, 13.
4. Ibid., p. 175.

Christ, flowing from the mouths, minds, and hearts of prophets and apostles. The Spirit of God has burned the truth of their words into my heart.

The second witness is that of my father. He was a remarkable man. He wrote his testimony of the Savior to his posterity shortly before he died: "Through my own experiences, through earnest prayer and through study of the scriptures, I know that God lives and that Jesus is the Christ, the Son of God, the Savior of the world."[5]

My faith in the Savior grew in unexpected ways during the filming of The Testament of One Fold and One Shepherd. I was privileged to write and direct this epic 70mm motion picture for The Church of Jesus Christ of Latter-day Saints in 1998–99. Recreating scenes and events from the life and times of Christ was a remarkable experience. It allowed me to enter the world of Jesus in a way not otherwise possible. It was as if I walked where He walked, watched spellbound as He healed the leper, and stood near when He raised Lazarus from the tomb.

The day we filmed the Crucifixion, I saw the actor who portrayed Jesus weeping. He sat alone on the crude pallet constructed near the place of execution. I was concerned that we had injured him. I sat beside him. I put my arm around his blood-stained shoulders and looked into the face painstakingly worked over to depict the suffering Savior of the world. The crown of thorns was on his head. I asked him if he was all right. We wept together as he shared with me the profound realization that had come to him in that remarkable circumstance. "I had always thought of the pain," the actor said, "but trying to understand what He suffered, I realized the humiliation He endured. He was ridiculed, mocked, scourged, and spat upon."

I shall never forget the powerful few moments I sat weeping with

5. David M. Merrill, personal letter, December 1996.

this faithful actor whose own profound belief in Jesus Christ had prepared him to portray the Savior. I shall never forget the feelings or the heightened perception of what happened there. For a moment I was at the cross and caught a glimpse of what our Lord must have suffered.

I have believed in Jesus Christ all of my life. In our vain attempt to dramatize His death in the making of the film, I seemed to enter an altered reality, and those events became very real to me. My faith in Jesus Christ expanded in ways I cannot easily explain. It swelled within me as if to make room for a fuller love and a deeper gratitude. It grew to embrace a more profound understanding of those terrible and marvelous events. I believe in Jesus Christ; I have been blessed with a deep and profound assurance that He is the Savior and Redeemer of the world.

WHY I BELIEVE IN A DIVINE PLAN OF SALVATION

I believe in a divinely appointed plan of salvation because it answers the most fundamental questions of our existence. Who am I? Why am I here? What is the purpose of my life?

I believe there is a "great plan of happiness" (Alma 42:8) for each of us because the quintessential elements, the process, the rules of engagement, are not only abundantly evident in the world around us, but they are also the crucible, crux, and heart of every aspect of our individual lives.

We are engaged in a great battle between good and evil. We give the opposing forces many names, but in the end it is a clear struggle between righteousness and wickedness. It is a continuation of the war in heaven between Jehovah, who is Jesus Christ, and Lucifer, who was cast down to become the devil.

Belief in the devil is a target of ridicule by an "enlightened" society. But he is the master of deception and the father of lies. The horrific manifestation of evil in the world is overwhelming evidence that the power of Satan is real. The great battle for the souls of humanity continues. It is not fantasy or folklore. It is a glaring reality conveniently explained away. I believe that the positive and negative influences in our lives are clear indications of a grand design. Light and darkness, hope and despair, joy and sorrow, life and death all witness a divine plan with its laws of opposites and agency to choose.

My experience with good and my encounters with evil have convinced me there is much more to our existence than happenstance and coincidence. Good brings joy, satisfaction, and ultimate happiness. Evil leads to sadness, misery, and eventual destruction. Evil and wickedness are not a coincidence of nature. They emanate from the influence of Satan in his determination to destroy the children of God. We are not toying with the playful fantasies of Darth Vader battling "the Force." Everything in my life convinces me that we are part of God's great plan. The continuing revelations of God to men have allowed a clear understanding of my precise role and purpose in it.

I believe in the plan of happiness because happiness is the cherished goal of life. Righteousness brings happiness. Wickedness never does. If there were no God, no plan, no law, and no divine order, there would be no reason wickedness would not bring happiness. But it never does. The history of civilization is a testament that hedonism, perversion, brutality, corruption, and wickedness sow seeds of misery, sorrow, and destruction. It is not a quirk of evolution. It is evidence of a divinely appointed plan.

I believe in the great plan of God because it considers the salvation and happiness of every man, woman, and child who ever lived, is now living, or will live upon the earth. No other theology, dogma, plan, or proposition I have ever discovered can spread such wondrous wings and gather all of the children of God.

WHY I BELIEVE THAT JOSEPH SMITH WAS A PROPHET

I believe that Joseph Smith was a prophet, and I believe beyond doubt that the Book of Mormon is true. Unlike many tenets of faith and "things hoped for" (Hebrews 11:1), the Book of Mormon is a tangible artifact available for scrutiny and study. Exhaustive analysis of the book by scholars and critics has provided extensive and persuasive evidences of authenticity.

History documents that the ancient record was translated in a period of sixty days. I have seen a copy of the manuscript, transcribed by quill and ink. It is astounding. It flows without punctuation or substantial correction for 521 pages.

I make movies. I write many of the films I make. I have a fertile imagination and a good education. I have a state-of-the-art computer, word-processing software, writer's programs, a thesaurus, a spell checker, a grammar checker, and high-speed access to the Internet. I have written films demanding significant research. In one instance I had the assistance of forty Ph.D. historians.

I believe that Joseph Smith was a prophet of God because I can substantiate from personal experience the unthinkable difficulty—yes, the impossibility—of composing that elaborately complex document in so little time and yet in perfect form, with primitive instruments, in unfavorable circumstances, and with no education, by any other means than the gift and power of God.

This is but one of hundreds of irrefutable evidences that convince me beyond doubt. With no specific opinion on the veracity of each of the hundreds of other fascinating claims and proofs, I do find the collective body of evidence and probability too overwhelming to ignore. I find the external evidences—so called—too persuasive to come to any conclusion other than one confirming authenticity.

As in all things pertaining to faith, my belief is ultimately based on spiritual confirmations. God's words to His prophets in ancient

America were preserved for the purpose of "the convincing of the Jew and Gentile that Jesus is the Christ, the Eternal God, manifesting himself unto all nations." (Book of Mormon, title page.) It is given with a promise: "When ye shall receive these things, I would exhort you that ye would ask God, the Eternal Father, in the name of Christ, if these things are not true; and if ye shall ask with a sincere heart, with real intent, having faith in Christ, he will manifest the truth of it unto you, by the power of the Holy Ghost." (Moroni 10:4.)

It is by the power of the Holy Ghost that I know the book is precisely what Joseph Smith described it to be, "the most correct of any book on earth, and the keystone to our religion." I have learned from my own exhaustive study of the Book of Mormon the truth of the Prophet's further word, that we would get "nearer to God by abiding by its precepts, than by any other book."[6]

I believe that Joseph Smith was a prophet of God because I was privileged to know him in a most unusual way. In 1990–91 I wrote, directed, and co-produced a 70mm film for The Church of Jesus Christ of Latter-day Saints called *Legacy*. It told the story of faithful Saints and early struggles in the opening decades of the restoration of the gospel. Creating the world of Joseph Smith, casting an actor to walk where he walked, and writing a script with the words that he spoke, allowed me to know him in ways not otherwise possible. In the research, the writing, and the filming, I came to a profound realization that this enigmatic man was indeed a prophet of God—a Moses, an Abraham, a Jacob in our own time.

I believe that Joseph Smith was a prophet because I have experienced the fruit of his ministry and work. Matthew assured us, "Ye shall know them by their fruits." (Matthew 7:16.)

---

6. *History of The Church of Jesus Christ of Latter-day Saints*, 7 vols., 2d ed. rev., edited by B. H. Roberts (Salt Lake City: The Church of Jesus Christ of Latter-day Saints, 1932–51), 4:461.

At times of greatest blessing, our faith seems less about what and why we believe and more about who we are and the joyous acceptance of the true purpose of our lives. I am deeply grateful to God for the fullness of the gospel of Jesus Christ in my life and the life of my family.

I believe in God and in His Son, Jesus Christ. I believe that our lives are part of a great and divine plan of salvation. I believe that God speaks to His children, that Joseph Smith was a prophet, and that the fullness of the gospel has been restored to the earth. I believe that by the power of the Holy Ghost we may know the truth of all things.

Kieth W. Merrill is a motion-picture director, writer, and producer who has created an impressive assortment of motion pictures, television programs, and commercials in a wide variety of formats. His diverse body of work includes numerous award-winning productions. A member of the Academy of Motion Picture Arts and Sciences and the Director's Guild of America, he is a two-time Academy Award nominee and an Academy Award winner for his feature documentary *Great American Cowboy*.

Kieth is the writer and director of *The Testaments of One Fold and One Shepherd* and writer, director, and co-producer of *Legacy*. These landmark 70mm motion pictures were created for The Church of Jesus Christ of Latter-day Saints and continue their play to maximum audiences in selected venues.

Kieth grew up in Farmington, Utah, served an LDS mission to Denmark, and graduated with honors from Brigham Young University. He served six years on BYU's Alumni Board and a term as president of the Alumni Association. He is a recipient of the university's Distinguished Alumnus Award.

Kieth is married to the former Dagny Johnson. They have eight children and twenty grandchildren and reside in the Sierra foothills in California's gold country.

ROBERT L. MILLET

I have always believed there is a God. My earliest memories of childhood contain familiar words spoken beside my bed each night: "Now I lay me down to sleep . . ." It felt right to say my prayers, and I sincerely believed that I was being heard by someone far wiser, greater, and more powerful and loving than anyone here on earth. Further, having grown up in the Southern States, with most of my friends being Baptists, Methodists, and Roman Catholics, I sang songs with them like "Jesus Loves Me, This I Know" and "Jesus Wants Me for a Sunbeam" with gusto and feeling. It seems that I have always believed in the living reality of Jesus Christ as the Savior and Redeemer of mankind.

My grandfather joined The Church of Jesus Christ of Latter-day Saints in the 1930s near New Orleans, Louisiana. When he did so, leaving the faith of his fathers, he was basically asked to leave the home. Later he and my grandmother raised their four sons as Latter-day Saints. By the time I was born, my father and mother were not extremely active church attenders, but in time they felt the need to raise their children in the Church. I recall being asked to speak in church when I was about nine years old. My father did not feel at that early stage of his spiritual development that he was in a position to help me much, and so my Uncle Joseph essentially wrote my talk for me. I memorized it. It was a simple recitation of Joseph Smith's first vision—the story of how young Joseph wrestled in 1820 with which church to join, how he encountered varying and conflicting views on religious questions, and how he chose to follow the scriptural admonition to ask God for wisdom. (See James 1:5.)

It has now been almost fifty years since I looked out at that rather frightening congregation, delivered those brief, halting words, and then sat down with a feeling of overwhelming relief. I also remember something else about that occasion—namely, how I felt at the time I spoke about God the Father and His Son Jesus Christ appearing to a fourteen-year-old boy in upstate New York. Although I was, as one might expect, nervous and fidgety behind the pulpit, I began on that occasion to feel the stirrings of testimony, the beginnings of a spiritual witness that what I was speaking about was true and that it had actually happened. That is, the relief I felt was not simply the flood of emotion associated with having completed a daunting task but also the quiet but poignant assurance that I had spoken the truth. I knew something when I sat down that I had not known before I stood up to speak.

As a young missionary in the Eastern States, my companion and I had moved into a small town in New Jersey, only to find that the local ministers had prepared their parishioners for our coming. At almost every door we approached, we were met by a smiling face and the words, "Oh, you must be the Mormons. This is for you." They would then hand us an anti-Mormon tract. We saved the pamphlets, stacked them in the corner of the living room of the apartment, and soon had a rather substantial pile of material. Out of sheer curiosity we began to read the stuff during lunchtime. I can still recall the confused and empty feelings that filled my soul as we encountered question after question about selected doctrines and specific moments in the history of the Church. My senior companion was no different; he was as unsettled as I was. For weeks we did our work, but our hearts weren't in it. My mom and dad had a testimony, and I knew that they knew. That always seemed adequate. But now I was up against the wall of faith, and suddenly what they knew did not seem sufficient to settle my troubled heart. I prayed and pleaded for light and understanding. These vexations of the soul went on for about a month.

One day we came home for lunch, and my companion set about the task of heating the soup and preparing the peanut-butter sandwiches. I collapsed in a large chair in the living room, removed my shoes, and loosened my tie. As I began to reflect once more on my testimony problem, my heart ached. For some reason I reached to a nearby lamp table and picked up a copy of the pamphlet "Joseph Smith Tells His Own Story." As I began reading the opening lines, I was suddenly and without warning immersed in a comforting and soothing influence. It seemed at the time as if I were being wrapped in a large blanket as I began to be filled with the warmth of the Holy Spirit. I did not hear specific words, but the feelings within seemed to whisper, "Of course it's true. You know that now, and you've known it for a long time." Indeed, the feelings that swept over me were akin to what I had experienced some ten years earlier at the pulpit. In time, the answers to the hard questions did come. The Spirit touched my heart and told me things my mind did not yet understand, and I was then in a position to proceed confidently with my work until my head caught up with my heart.

I thank God for the formal education I have received, for the privilege it is (and I count it such) to have received university training and to have earned bachelor's, master's, and doctoral degrees. Education has expanded my mind and opened conversations and doors for me. It has taught me what books to read, how to research a topic, and how to make my case or present my point of view more effectively. But the more I learn, the more I value those simple but profound verities that soothe and settle human hearts. I appreciate knowing that the order of the cosmos points toward a Providential Hand; I am deeply grateful to know, by the power of the Spirit, that there is a God and that He is our Father in heaven. I appreciate knowing something about the social, political, and religious world into which Jesus of

Nazareth was born; I am deeply grateful for the witness of the Spirit that He is indeed God's Almighty Son.

I am a Latter-day Saint because I believe in the truth of the claims of Joseph Smith. I am a Latter-day Saint because I feel that The Church of Jesus Christ of Latter-day Saints provides answers to some of life's most vexing questions: Where did I come from? Why am I here? Where am I going after death? Those answers are as satisfying to my mind as they are soothing to my heart. To borrow the words of C. S. Lewis, I believe in these things "as I believe that the Sun has risen, not only because I see it, but because by it I see everything else."[1]

 Robert L. Millet is the Richard L. Evans Professor of Religious Understanding at Brigham Young University. He received his bachelor's and master's degrees from BYU in psychology and his Ph.D. from Florida State University in religious studies. Since joining the BYU faculty in 1983, Dr. Millet has served as chairman of the Department of Ancient Scripture, dean of religious education, and director of the Religious Studies Center. He is the author or editor of many books and numerous articles, dealing mostly with the doctrine and history of the Church. He and his wife, Shauna, are the parents of six children and reside in Orem, Utah.

1. *The Weight of Glory* (New York: Touchstone, 1996), p. 106.

ALEXANDER B. MORRISON

I was raised in western Canada, a son of Scots immigrants. Growing up on an isolated prairie farm, I had little formal exposure to religion, though I always believed in God. I knew nothing about "the Mormons," except for Zane Grey's lurid descriptions in his popular novel *Riders of the Purple Sage*. At age sixteen I went off to the University of Alberta, and my mind began to open up to the broader world of ideas and learning. Many of my fellow students were World War II veterans, disillusioned by their experiences. But I noted that one of my classmates, a man from southern Alberta, somehow seemed different. Where others were profane and rowdy, he was reserved and self-disciplined. Others were vocally cynical about sacred things, but he had a quiet faith. We became friends. I found he was a faithful member of The Church of Jesus Christ of Latter-day Saints, the first I'd ever met. My friend gave me two books about the Church and its doctrines to read. I devoured them avidly. Everything I read rang true to me. It seemed as though nothing I read was new. I realized that I was, in a sense, remembering truths I'd known subconsciously all along.

Two of the teachings of the Church particularly impressed me and resonated in my heart. The first, that "the glory of God is intelligence" (D&C 93:36), that the Latter-day Saints are to seek learning in all things "both in heaven and in the earth, at home and abroad" (see D&C 88:79), struck me with great force. My mind was beginning to grasp the wonders—the sheer beauty—of science and knowledge in general. The concept of a God who understood it all and wanted His children to do likewise thrilled and excited me. How wonderful it was to think that I could, and indeed *should*, spend the eternities learning and growing intellectually, seeking "out of the best books words of wisdom, learning both by study and by faith"! (See D&C 88:118.) That experience, I found, was intended to extend to *all* knowledge in *every* field imaginable. Indeed, Latter-day Saints are expected to embrace *all* truth without limitation and without concern as to its origin. "Truth is truth, where'er 'tis found / On Christian or on heathen ground."[1]

To go to school, in a sense, forever, seemed to me to be the noblest future to which anyone could aspire. That sublime truth has both inspired and sustained me for half a century.

Closely related to the concept of learning forever was the Latter-day Saint view that since truth is indivisible, there can be no conflict between valid expressions of it. I grew to understand, for example, that there is, in the end, no conflict between religion and science. I've learned to withhold judgment when the truths of science appear superficially, and from my limited knowledge, to conflict with those of religion. Someday, when I no longer "see through a glass, darkly," in St. Paul's felicitous phrase, I will understand that the truths of science and religion complement each other but are not in conflict. Truth, by its very nature, cannot be at war with itself. (See 1 Corinthians 13:12.)

The second great principle of "Mormonism" that attracted me mightily was the concept of eternal marriage, the idea that marriage is intended by God to be an eternal union between a man and a woman. Parents and children can be bound together in a union which neither death nor time can break. When I first heard that idea, I was courting, and deeply in love with, one who was to me the most beautiful and desirable of women. The thought that I could be with her and our hoped-for children forever—not just until death do us part—enraptured my soul. We've just celebrated our fiftieth wedding anniversary together, and I still feel the same way, both about my dear

1. See Conference Report, April 1926, p. 34.

wife and about the importance of eternal marriage. But I think I understand both better now than I did half a century ago!

Alexander B. Morrison was named a member of the First Quorum of the Seventy of The Church of Jesus Christ of Latter-day Saints on April 4, 1987, and became an emeritus member of that quorum in October 2000. At the time of his calling as a General Authority, he was a professor and chairman of the Food Science Department, University of Guelph, Ontario, Canada.

Elder Morrison is former assistant deputy minister of the Department of National Health and Welfare of the Government of Canada, Ottawa, Canada.

He was honored in 1984 as first recipient of the David M. Kennedy International Service Award from the Kennedy International Center at Brigham Young University, and he has received the Borden Award of the Nutrition Society of Canada and the Queen's Jubilee Award. He is a fellow of the Chemical Institute of Canada and of the Royal Society of Medicine. He earned his doctoral degree at Cornell University. Elder Morrison and his wife, the former Shirley E. Brooks, are the parents of eight children.

VIRGINIA H. PEARCE

꙰

My mother wears a simple, wide, gold band on her finger. She's eighty-nine years old, and she asked me last week if I knew the story about the gold band. "It's 18-karat gold, you know, more than one hundred years old, and I want to be sure you know its story."

"I do, Mother. But, let me repeat it to see if I have it right—the way Great-Grandma told it to you."

Martha Elizabeth Evans was seventeen years old when she first met George Paxman. He was new in town—lean, with a fine bone structure and deep-set blue eyes. She was a petite 5'2" young woman with smooth skin and an abundance of fine hair, unbelievably soft to the touch. They fell in love. Two years later, in the fall of 1885, after they made eternal promises to one another, he put the wide, gold band on the fourth finger of her left hand. She swooped her hair up onto her head, securing it with a few skillfully placed hairpins, in the fashion of a married woman. She would wear the ring on her finger and her hair pinned in soft feminine twists and curls for the rest of her life.

The hopeful young couple moved into a two-room adobe house with a dirt roof while George's carpenter skills played their part in building a majestic, white, limestone temple, towering on a hill above the little adobe village of Manti, Utah. The young husband worked eight hours a day and received scrip for a weekly $4.00 worth of goods in the local store and produce from the tithing office. But work on the temple was Martha and George's gift to God—a labor of faith and love.

On a June evening in 1887, a month before their first little girl turned one year old, George came home from working on the temple, where he had helped hang the large east doors. He was in terrible pain.

Alarmed, Martha loaded him into a wagon and made the strenuous trip through the mountains to a hospital, where he died three days later of a strangulated hernia. Eight months later Martha gave birth to a second little girl—my grandmother—whom she named Georgetta after her beloved George.

A twenty-two-year-old widow with two little girls, faith in God, and an 18-karat gold band on her finger, Martha faced the future.

But now, the story my mother wanted to be sure I knew: One day Martha was energetically engaged in her annual spring cleaning. Curtains, furniture, walls, bedding—all must be cleaned. Martha shook the mattresses out, replacing the old, matted straw with clean. Then, glancing at her left hand, she saw that her wedding ring was missing. Frantically she searched through the straw for the only item she had left to remind her of her young husband. She felt desperate at the loss and prayed. Then she looked down on the ground, and there was the ring.

Martha told and retold this story to her children and grandchildren. Her story convinced my mother that prayers are heard and that prayers are answered. Yes, the ring my mother wears is 18-karat gold. Yes, it is a loving link honoring marriage and family love. But most of all, it has become a family reminder about prayer.

I believe in prayer. I believe it is the way to open the conduit between God and me. For Martha that day, God granted her prayerful desire. But I believe that finding the ring was a miniature miracle when compared to the real message—that God was aware of her sadness and love for her long-gone sweetheart whom the ring represented. He was telling her that He knew and loved her. And stunningly, this reassurance of His presence and love is much greater than any event or situation.

In Martha's life, and surely in mine, God has not always granted those things that I have wanted—even asked for desperately. But He has frequently given me small but sure messages that He is there. And His presence—the indescribably settling quality of His great love—more than compensates for my tragedies and disappointments. And so the miracle of prayer doesn't reside in the ability to manipulate situations and events but in the miracle of a relationship with God.

My faith teaches me that every life will include suffering, pain, and loss. Unfair things will happen. We will be victims of the natural world, of political systems, of our fellow human beings, and even of our own weaknesses and selfish ways. But coached and nurtured by God, these difficulties, when placed at His feet, can be turned to our good. Even the great negatives of life can burnish us into a shining patina, not unlike that of my great-grandmother's ring. Through the lens of God's love, we can turn our backs on anger and bitterness and develop courage, compassion, and a host of other magnificent traits. I have seen it happen a thousand times. I have even felt those stirrings myself.

Happily for us, it is sometimes acceptable to God to give us the very blessing we desire. It seems to have been completely acceptable to give Martha her ring. Why doesn't He just do it, then, without requiring prayer? Why do we even bother to pray if it is already His will? I believe that a prayer becomes the simple, everyday work that we do which allows God to grant the blessings that He is already willing to grant but are conditional on our willingness to ask. I believe that He respects my will so profoundly that He wants me to exercise it whenever possible. No one requires me to pour out my soul; no one requires me to ask for certain blessings; no one insists that I kneel in reverence. So when I search my heart and willingly open it to Him, He rejoices and responds. And His gifts to me become even more wonderful.

Last week my sister's husband died suddenly and without warning. Searching the years and days just past, she is awestruck, recognizing specific skills and experiences put into her life by a loving Father, things that might have seemed circumstantial at the time but that have specifically prepared her to cope successfully with this heart-breaking loss. Rather than feeling abandoned and bitter, she feels cradled and cared for. Yesterday she said to me, "When I see how carefully Heavenly Father has prepared and planned for my present circumstance, how can I be frightened about my future? Surely He is putting into place today all that I will need to face the unknown times ahead."

Martha Elizabeth Paxman's picture hangs on the wall of our family room, her wedding band in plain view. Her picture is flanked on one side by pictures of her mother, her grandmother, and her great-grandmother. On the other side are pictures of her daughter Georgetta, then my mother, then one of me, then a group picture of my five daughters, and finally a picture of my granddaughters—eight generations of women. These women are linked by a genetic code, but even stronger is their link of faith. Each one believed that God lives and that He answers prayers. I believe that too, and when I want to feel more settled, more aware of God's love for me, and less fearful about the future, I look at Martha and say, "I know the story about your ring, Grandma, and I believe it, too!"

Virginia Hinckley Pearce was born in Denver, Colorado, and reared in Salt Lake City, Utah. She is married to James R. Pearce, a physician (internal medicine) in private practice. They are the parents of five married daughters and one son and the grandparents of fifteen.

She received a B.S. degree from the University of Utah, has taught classes in children's literature, and is a free-lance writer, having authored and co-authored several books, including a new children's book released in the spring of 2001. She recently edited a best-selling book about her mother called *Glimpses into the Life and Heart of Marjorie Pay Hinckley*.

Virginia received a master's degree in social work, also from the University of Utah, and has worked as a therapist in both public agencies and a private practice.

She has been a leader in The Church of Jesus Christ of Latter-day Saints, having served as first counselor in the General Young Women Presidency for five and a half years. She has also served on the Primary General Board. She is currently a stake Relief Society president.

She currently serves on a board for "The Brigham Young Academy" at This is The Place Heritage Park in Salt Lake City and on the Deseret Book Publishing Company Board of Directors.

DANIEL C. PETERSON

I first paid serious attention to the teachings of The Church of Jesus Christ of Latter-day Saints early in my high-school years because I found them attractive and intriguing. Very soon thereafter, I also began to suspect that they were true. I was impressed by a radical set of doctrines—radical in the best sense of the word, meaning deep down to the roots—that rested not upon inferences and speculation but upon credible witnesses. I continue to be exhilarated by the grandeur, vast scope, and cosmic sweep of "Mormonism," as well as by its dramatic history, and I have long been firmly convinced that it is all that it proclaims itself to be.

From the outset, my conviction that the startling claims of Joseph Smith and the church he founded are true has rested upon a mixture of intellectual analysis, empirical evidence, and what many would call flashes of intuition. (With my fellow Latter-day Saints, I would term these personal revelations.) In its most ordinary form, such intuition for me has resembled the *Sehnsucht* or sense of longing that C. S. Lewis describes in his autobiography, *Surprised by Joy*. Lewis recounts his quest for what he calls "pure northernness," for the immense, cold, clear, and fiercely beautiful world that he had glimpsed in various works of literature and—perhaps rather oddly to some—in the music of Richard Wagner.[1] I know exactly what he means. Experiences from youthful backpacking in the Sierra Nevadas of California, coupled with two years as a missionary in Germanic Switzerland, have made that very image a potent one for me, too. Like Lewis, I believe that

---

1. C. S. Lewis, *Surprised by Joy* (New York: Inspirational Press, 1994). The same theme also appears in his early work *The Pilgrim's Regress*.

such yearnings point validly to the possibility of their own fulfillment. If there were no actual object for such desires, we would not have them. Our hunger indicates the existence of food; our thirst demonstrates the existence of water.

Yet I am convinced, as Lewis was, that our spiritual yearnings will not and cannot be fully satisfied in this life, however desperately we may seek to quiet them with inadequate substitutes. Even the splendor of the Swiss Alps or the Canadian Rockies, even the exultation of Beethoven's *Emperor Concerto* or the majestic choruses of Puccini's *Turandot*, do not fully still the longing. But they do, I believe, hint at the existence of something that can. Augustine was right: Our hearts will continue restless until they rest in God.[2]

For, by contrast, the secular, naturalistic position seems to me a constricted, flat, and ultimately meaningless worldview that trivializes all of human life. I'm struck by Huston Smith's image, in a recent book, of a tunnel (which he uses to symbolize secularism) running beneath a gorgeous alpine meadow. (Again, coincidentally, there is the image of "northernness.") Travelers in the tunnel have literally no idea of the glory and vastness of the world through which or, rather, beneath which they are traveling.[3]

Not only is the cosmos that LDS theology discloses to me a rich one, but the doctrines are satisfyingly deep even when compared with other, more "major" religious traditions. The LDS faith is a profound way of looking at the world, seven days a week. It preserves all of the fundamental virtues of theism in general and of Christianity in particular, including the deity of Christ and His vital, saving role as Redeemer and Mediator. Indeed, buttressed by the testimonies of modern prophets and apostles, it provides solid backing for Christian

2. Augustine, *Confessions*, 1:1.
3. See Huston Smith, *Why Religion Matters: The Fate of the Human Spirit in an Age of Disbelief* (San Francisco: HarperSanFrancisco, 2001).

theism in a corrosively skeptical age. But it also bathes religious faith in a brilliant and exciting new light. (I cannot conceive of a more hopeful message.) And its claims withstand examination. I have attempted, and continue to attempt, to set out in writing some of the powerful empirical evidences, including marks of Semitic antiquity in the uniquely Latter-day Saint scriptural texts, that, to my mind, argue for the authenticity of Joseph Smith's prophetic calling and the inspiration of the movement he founded. I will have made only the merest beginning on that task when I finally turn my computer off.

At the same time, however, Latter-day Saint beliefs are remarkably open to the idea that God is at work in other communities beyond The Church of Jesus Christ of Latter-day Saints. While, as almost everyone who knows anything about us surely realizes, we are ardent missionaries, we do not condemn others to damnation. Although we declare, quite frankly, that the fullness of saving truth, religious ordinances, and priesthood authority has been entrusted to the Lord's restored Church, we also believe that truth and goodness are to be found elsewhere. God has inspired and does inspire others beyond the Latter-day Saint community, and most likely even unknown to us. In the course of my work editing and publishing classical texts of philosophy, theology, mysticism, and science from various Near Eastern languages, I'm frequently asked, "Why are the Mormons doing this?" I typically respond along the following lines: "You know us as an exclusivist group, dispatching tens of thousands of missionaries around the world, summoning others to accept God's modern revelation to living prophets and apostles. This is accurate. But it is incomplete. We are also, though the fact is far less well known, an inclusivist group, open to all truth and all people. Our own canonical scripture demands of us that we 'seek . . . out of the best books words of wisdom,' and our prophets have advised us to gather up truth wherever we can find it." (See D&C 88:118.)

Even more fundamentally, our view of missionary activity (extending beyond this life), and of vicarious service for those who have died without hearing our message, testifies to the impartial love of God for all of His children, no matter when or where they have lived. "Our Heavenly Father," the Prophet Joseph Smith taught, "is more liberal in His views, and boundless in His mercies and blessings, than we are ready to believe or receive."[4] And our expansive view of the eternal destiny of humankind means that, in the end, only those who defiantly and finally refuse God's love will be deprived of at least some level of salvation. This is, to me, an immensely comforting doctrine.

My experience with Latter-day Saint communities on five continents replicates, even in the very human problems that all of us experience (and cause), the life of the early Christian church that I see depicted in the biblical Acts of the Apostles and the letters of Paul. Latter-day Saint "wards" provide genuine community, a "haven in a heartless world," in which members of the Church live together in love and mutual caring. Lacking a professional clergy, each of us is responsible to lead and teach and serve. And the power of Latter-day Saint doctrines is especially evident at what might be called the great "nodal points" of human life, such as weddings, the birth of children, and death. Marriage and family are given not only social significance but also eternal weight, which powerfully sustains the vows that undergird them and charges even seemingly small daily acts with cosmic meaning. The Church's emphasis on the central concept of "covenant" seems to me especially relevant in our individualistic society. Additionally, we benefit from rituals of blessing on occasions of crisis and illness as well as at moments of new opportunity. And the gospel speaks with special eloquence at times of death, when, in the Latter-day Saint view, those who depart do so into a very real and

---

4. *History of the Church,* 5:134–36.

concrete world in which social ties and family relationships flourish even more richly than they do here, and where learning and growth continue into boundless eternity.

On a firmly practical level, the organization of the Church continues to astonish me with its brilliance and adaptability. Whether responding to catastrophes or sustaining individuals and families during rough times, it is remarkably effective. Specifically, in an era when female-headed households are on the rise in the United States and other Western nations, when the disappearance of fathers increasingly leads to what has been termed the "feminization of poverty," the Church, I think, does a strikingly good job at the difficult task of socializing males. From the very earliest stages of adolescence, priesthood callings (and especially missions) train them to serve, to grow up, to think of others rather than of themselves. And from their earliest days, they are taught that their most important role will not be as athletes or as CEOs but as husbands and fathers, and—notwithstanding the unfortunate connotations the word carries in some circles—as patriarchs, whose primary function is to serve and (literally) to bless their families. This seems to me clearly not a retrograde step but, in the climate of our time, a necessary and salutary one.

Are there dry periods? Yes. Of course. I believe that mortal life was designed to put us through such trials. And they're not always brief. During those times, though, I recall moments of piercing insight when, as Latter-day Saints sometimes say, the veil between this world and the next has seemed very thin. In my case, at least, these have often been connected with what we regard as the holiest places on earth, the temples built and dedicated by the Church. These sanctuaries are marked off as sacred and inviolate from the ordinary, compromising traffic of daily life and its mundane demands, and I have experienced them as beachheads of that other world in this one.

Do questions remain? Yes. But they intrigue and suggest; they do not paralyze. "For now," as the apostle Paul noted, "we see though a glass, darkly." We "know in part." But I have seen enough and understand enough to be assured that the day will come when we shall see "face to face." And "then shall I know even as also I am known." (1 Corinthians 13:12.) Until then, as the ancient American prophet Nephi said, although "I do not know the meaning of all things. . . . I know that [God] loveth his children." (1 Nephi 11:17.)

A famous and somewhat enigmatic fragment from the ancient Greek poet Archilochus says that "the fox knows many things, but the hedgehog knows one big thing."[5] It is my professional obligation, as a scholar, to know many things. (I wish I knew many more than I do.) But it has been the most fulfilling joy of my life to know one big and very important thing. The nineteenth-century zoologist Ernst Haeckel is reported to have said that if he could have just one question definitively answered, it would be, Is the universe friendly? My experience, my reason, and the teachings of modern prophets and apostles all concur in testifying that it is.

Daniel C. Peterson is a graduate of Brigham Young University in Greek and philosophy. His postgraduate studies include several years in Cairo and Jerusalem and a Ph.D. in Arabic and Persian from the College of Near Eastern languages and Cultures at UCLA.

Dr. Peterson teaches Asian and Near Eastern languages at BYU and serves as chairman of the board of trustees for the Foundation for Ancient Research and Mormon Studies (FARMS). He is also the director of FARMS' subsidiary CPART (Center for the Preservation of Ancient Religious Texts). He has published a number of books, including *Abraham Divided* and *Offenders for a Word*, and is the editor of the FARMS *Review of Books* and BYU's *Islamic Translation Series*.

---

5 . My translation. The Greek text is found in François Lasserre and André Bonnard, eds., *Archiloque: Fragments* (Paris: Société d'Edition Les Belles Lettres, 1958), p. 54.

ANNE OSBORN POELMAN

The warm summer nights in the small Midwestern town where I grew up invited stargazing. Many times I walked to the edge of town (never more than a few blocks in any direction) or down to the lake to sit and stare upwards, pondering the eternal questions people have asked for millennia. Why are we all here, and what is the purpose of our existence? Why am *I* here? Is there a God? And if there really is, will He answer the prayers of a curious child?

I pestered local ministers with my questions. The answers were indulgent smiles, a quizzical lift of an eyebrow, and heartfelt but unsatisfying generalities.

I had never been west of Kansas City, Missouri. When I left home to begin my freshman year at Stanford, it felt as though I were sailing off the end of the Known Universe, as on the old maps that showed the earth as flat with a mysterious void at the edge marked, "Here be dragons."

There weren't any dragons in California, of course. What I found was a deliciously inviting, dangerously exciting mix of intriguing ideas and inquiring minds. There were lots of questions, lots of ideas, endless late-night bull sessions in the dorm, and a gaggle of professors who seemed to feel it was their life's mission to shatter students' preconceived ideas and traditional beliefs. Challenged on all fronts, I soon realized I really didn't know what I believed. I tried out the campus chapel, which turned out to be a blend of High Church form and watered-down theology. When I visited a number of churches in the Palo Alto area, most seemed to function as hotbeds of social activism with little regard for religion itself.

Frustrated, and busy with my studies and more pressing concerns, I quit going to church. Sundays conveniently became free days.

I didn't think much about God, religion, or church until I started medical school. It wasn't the intricate wonders of the human body that awakened my dormant interest in religion. Not at all. It was the personal example of one of our best and most popular professors, a man whose interest in the students and their welfare was legendary.

He was a "Mormon."

A Mormon? An internationally renowned scholar? All I knew about the Mormons was the fleeting impression gleaned from a tourist stop in Salt Lake City and a quick (self-guided) tour of the famous Temple Square. A meeting was being held there in the old Assembly Hall, where a line of young people bore their "testimonies" one by one. I stood in the doorway and listened, fascinated at how so many— bound for all corners of the earth—could say with such certainty, "I *know* God lives; that Jesus Christ is His Son, our Savior and Redeemer; and that Joseph Smith [*Joseph Smith? Who's he?*] was a prophet."

Nothing came of my brief visit, but I never forgot the intensity and fervor with which those young people spoke. I wondered what could motivate them to interrupt their lives and their education to spend two years teaching strangers about religion.

I was too timid to ask our professor about his beliefs, but his kindness and concern for his students impressed me deeply. The summer after my second year of medical school, I took two weeks off to volunteer as a teacher at the Red Cross National Aquatics School in the Sierras. While I was there, I met another, much older man who had many of the same characteristics as our beloved professor. By chance I learned that he, too, was a Latter-day Saint.

Two people seemed beyond mere happenstance. Emboldened, I began asking him about his religious beliefs. Frankly, what he told me seemed a bit odd. I dismissed what he told me as fable. But what I couldn't explain away was the fact that whatever he, the professor, and those young people believed obviously made a big difference in their lives. That was the evidence. What I wanted to know was the *reason*.

When I returned to Stanford, I took a mental deep breath and visited a local Latter-day Saint congregation. The "service" (which was a Sunday School meeting) was a real eye-opener, unlike anything else I'd ever seen. The informality and warm, friendly chaos was stunning. So was the church itself. No cross, altar, or candles. No priest or minister in robes. Just a bunch of ordinary people doing quite extraordinary things. Regular people and a couple of kids giving talks. More kids passing Communion (the "sacrament").

Something profound was going on.

I felt touched and stirred in an unfamiliar way. In near panic, I got up and fled. As I rushed out of the church and into the parking lot, a voice inside my mind said as clearly as if it had been audible: "Anne, turn around and go back."

I did. And my life pivoted on that point, never to be the same again.

I took the missionary lessons, studied the gospel, and recognized what I'd been looking for all my life. It wasn't a sense of discovery as much as a feeling of recognition.

I'd come Home.

Thirty-plus years later, I'm still Home. While I use my mind and intellect daily in the care of patients with brain diseases, the things I know most surely come from the heart. Deep within my soul, I *know* that the gospel is true. Precisely how, I can't tell. But what I do know is that everything I've experienced in the intervening years since I became a member of The Church of Jesus Christ of Latter-day Saints has reinforced that deep conviction. It's real. It's right. And it makes all the difference in the world.

 Anne G. Osborn, M.D., is Distinguished Professor of Radiology at the University of Utah School of Medicine and Nycomed-Amersham Visiting Professor in Diagnostic Imaging at the Armed Forces Institute of Pathology in Washington, D.C. An internationally acclaimed teacher and lecturer, Dr. Osborn is one of the world's most prominent neuroradiologists and the author of the definitive reference books in her field.

Editor in chief of the *Yearbook of Diagnostic Radiology* and founding co-editor of the *International Journal of Neuroradiology*, Dr. Osborn has given more than 110 invited lectures all over the world, including China, Japan, Korea, Australia, India, South Africa, and Saudi Arabia. She has served as visiting professor at many of the world's premier medical institutions, including Harvard, Stanford, and Johns Hopkins Universities and the Karolinska Institute in Stockholm, Sweden.

Dr. Osborn has received numerous awards, including honorary membership in a number of international radiology professional societies, the Marie Curie Award from the American Association of Women in Radiology, the Gold Medal from the Chicago Radiological Society, the Rosenblatt Prize for Excellence from the University of Utah, and the Magna Cum Laude Scientific Exhibit Award from the Radiological Society of North America (RSNA). In November 2000 she was named the first-ever recipient of the RSNA's Outstanding Educator Award.

Dr. Osborn was the first woman elected president of the American Society of Neuroradiology, the largest subspecialty society in radiology. She has served as the first vice president of the Radiological Society of North America, currently chairs the committee that evaluates all the educational grant applications for the RSNA's Research and Education Foundation, and serves as historian/delegate-at-large for the World Federation of Neuroradiological Societies. She is married to Elder Ronald F. Poelman, emeritus member of the Quorum of the Seventy.

ART RASCON

I am reminded of one of my favorite Primary songs that my children used to sing in their church Primary class. The song is called "Follow the Prophet." Its beat and rhythm make it a favorite among Primary children, and its terrific lyrical chronology of Old Testament prophets makes it a wonderful song of learning.

There are eight verses in the song that briefly highlight the miracles and teachings of the prophets Adam, Noah, Abraham, Moses, Samuel, Jonah, and Daniel. As enjoyable and instructional as these verses are, it's the final verse that brings us to our current day and beautifully, or perhaps comically, reminds us of the condition of today's world:

> Now we have a world where people are confused.
> If you don't believe it, go and watch the news.
> We can get direction all along our way,
> If we heed the prophets—follow what they say.[1]

The song speaks a great truth. We live in a world where "people are confused," and if you don't believe it, "go and watch the news."

After working for nearly two decades as a reporter and covering global events for the national networks in dozens of countries, I believe I have come to know something of this world. Confusion, ignorance, speculation, and spiritual blindness are rampant. Pride, selfishness, greed, and a lust for power are driving forces of evil that send countries into war and deadly civil conflict. There is this great wave

---

1. *Children's Songbook* (Salt Lake City: The Church of Jesus Christ of Latter-day Saints, 1997), p. 111.

of filth—largely led by the media—that fills magazine racks, television screens, computer terminals, movie houses, and red-light districts, that drives individuals deep into sin, destroys families, and contributes to the overall degradation of society.

Why do I believe? Because I have witnessed the great contrast in those who have discovered the absolute truths about the Lord's restored teachings and those who have not. There is a certain happiness and peace that surrounds those who have placed their feet firmly in the true path toward God—despite their varied trials—and a degree of speculation that surrounds those who are confused about what truth really is.

I recall my travels with an international religious leader. Everywhere he went, he was met with many thousands of people yearning for truth. After one rather large open meeting, I spoke briefly with one of his most trusted and influential leaders, a kind, considerate man in his seventies.

"Sir, were you satisfied with the meeting?" I asked.

"Yes, indeed," he said. "There is a great need here of spiritual healing. Many of our members are leaving to join other denominations, and this deeply concerns us."

"What about the LDS Church?" I asked. "I understand that it's gaining members in extraordinary numbers."

"The Mormon Church has a powerful missionary force. They are good people. But we must return to the *truth* of Christ."

"Truth?" I questioned. "What is truth? Where does one find this truth?" He seemed surprised at the question.

"Truth," he said, "is what we feel, what we have in our hearts, and what we read in God's word. It is all that is around us."

"But is there not just one gospel truth?" I asked. "Is there not one sure way to find it?"

"No," he said, sounding confident. "What a person feels about the living word of Christ is *his* truth. Truth comes in many different forms. It is what one believes."

I thanked him for his time but felt sorry for this man from whom so many sought truth even though he himself didn't understand absolute truth or whence it comes. *Whatever happened to deep, thoughtful prayer as a way of finding truth?* I asked myself.

I have often learned great truth from those who might least be expected to have it. I can vividly recall my days in the refugee camps along the Kosovo-Macedonia border during the Kosovo War. Nearly a million Kosovar Albanians were brutally forced from their homeland—all with horrifying stories to tell. In the midst of this camp was a fifteen-year-old girl who was crying over her desperate circumstances. Her family had been forced from their home at gunpoint, many of her friends and relatives had been killed, and only part of her family was able to escape.

Her new home was a wretched refugee camp with a hundred thousand other Albanians. "This is where we sleep," she said, pointing to a plastic tent raised three feet off the ground by small twigs. It was nothing—yet it was the family's new home, and she was grateful for it. "We have nothing. We don't have any clothes, we have no food, we live in this awful place of sickness, and we are cold and hungry."

The condition of the family was pitiful. They looked sickly. I wanted to help but had nothing to give. A lump grew in my throat as I looked into the eager eyes of this lost and forgotten family. Then this young girl with knotted hair, ragged clothes, and a filthy appearance asked a sincere question: "May I give you a gift? It is customary that we give visitors a gift. I have nothing to give—but let me find something."

Give me a gift? I thought. I couldn't possibly accept anything. She insisted as she fell on her hands and knees and crawled about the dirt floor, rummaging under the plastic covering.

"I am sorry," she said. "I have nothing to offer except this small bottle of water." She handed it to me with the rest of her family motioning for me to accept it.

The lump in my throat grew larger, and I turned my head away to wipe a tear. *How was I to accept this bottle of water?* I thought. *I have so much, and they have nothing.* The water may have been the family's last possession.

"Please, take the bottle. It is our gift to you." She was genuine and sincere, and the look of compassion so touched me that I accepted the gift, fearing the family would be more crushed if I refused it.

"Thank you," I said, "and God bless you."

"No," she said, "God bless you. And God bless all the refugees."

I turned and walked away, clutching the bottle of water in my hand, and I wept. I had never before witnessed such selflessness, such love and charity. As in the story of the widow's mite, this girl and family had given more than I could ever give, because they gave everything they had. And then she wished God's blessings upon me. *Thank you.* I said to myself. *Thank you for teaching me the truth about love.*

Some time ago I was sent to a small town in rural northern Georgia that had been hit hard by a powerful tornado. As I walked down a small, dusty road, gazing in awe at the flattened trees and homes, downed power lines, and scattered debris, I noticed a home in the midst of the rubble that was still standing. I later learned the story behind the little house that would not fall.

Early that morning at 6:30, before the tornado hit, the father of the house had gathered his family, all members of the LDS faith, for morning prayer. He pleaded with the Lord for a blessing of protection upon his three children, his wife, and their home. After the prayer, when they had scarcely stood, they heard the thunderous noise of an approaching storm. They rushed to a corner, praying and huddling together for protection.

Within seconds, glass and debris were flying everywhere. They could hear the frightening sounds of the whirlwind and felt as if the world was crashing in around them. When the tornado finally passed, it was deathly quiet. As the family regrouped and glanced around at what had once been their neighborhood, tears came to their eyes as they realized how blessed they were. Their home, although extremely damaged, was the only one standing. Their neighborhood had nearly been destroyed, and sadly, five of their neighbors had been killed.

The anchor of support for this family was a deep faith in God and His restored gospel. They understood the plan of salvation and the purpose of life, and they had come to understand how overcoming adversity could bring forth the blessings of heaven. This family became the beacon that many in the community leaned on when the inevitable question surfaced: Why?

Allow me to contrast this story with a conversation I had with a woman later that day walking through the rubble of her home. She was holding tightly to a small doll and appeared teary-eyed and somewhat emotional. "Are you searching for something in particular?" I asked.

"Yes," she said tearfully, "just anything. Anything that looks like it's worth saving." She reached down and picked up a soggy stuffed animal with a pull-string and yanked it. The chime began to play "Twinkle, Twinkle, Little Star."

"Who does the toy belong to?" I asked, hoping she would not tell me of a child who was killed in the tornado.

"It's my four-year-old daughter's," she said. "She's at my parents' house right now. She got a few scrapes and bruises, but she's doing fine." I was relieved.

"Do you remember what happened?" I asked. "Could you tell me where you were when the storm hit?"

She began to get emotional. "I was in bed, and I heard something coming. I ran and grabbed my daughter and just hung on to her. The next thing I knew, I was over there." She pointed to a tree about seventy-five yards from where her mobile home had once stood. "I don't know how I survived," she said. "I just thank God I did."

"What do you attribute your survival to?" I asked, curious as to what she would say.

She paused and looked around at the splintered wreck of her home. "I guess faith in God," she said. "Faith in God helped me live." She continued but with a puzzled look on her face. "This type of experience makes you think about life. It makes you wonder what it's all for. It makes you think about death, and question whether there really is life after death." Her response made it clear that the tragedy had triggered a real introspection of her life. "I have so many questions now about everything," she said.

As I left this tearful woman, I couldn't help thinking of how the gospel could fill the great void in her life. She was divorced, a single mother, and she was hungry for answers to life's most pressing questions. As I thought of her and then considered the LDS family I had learned of earlier in the day, the contrast was clearly evident. One had a sure knowledge of where they came from, why they are here, and where they are going. The other was still searching.

I don't believe I have ever covered a story where I didn't believe the restored gospel would have helped those involved. As I learn more of the world, the Lord's promise echoes ever louder in my mind: "Ye shall know the truth, and the truth shall make you free" (John 8:32)— free from the shackles of sin and ignorance and filled with a knowledge of eternity.

The common thread in these shared experiences is simply this: By seeking guidance from above, and by following divinely restored gospel principles found in the LDS faith, we can be a happier people. I have witnessed too much to suggest otherwise.

Over the years I have interviewed literally thousands of people in a multitude of places, from the killing fields of Cambodia to the hate-filled streets of Haiti, from Central America to the Balkans, from the Middle East to nearly every state in the union. Some people have been rich and famous; others have been poor and desperate. I've met with raging dictators, proud elitists, humble immigrants, God-fearing souls, and the seemingly faithless wanderer.

As I look back on the many, many interviews, there is one that clearly stands out above the rest. It was an interview I had with a ninety-year-old, gray-haired man, who, despite his age, was, and still is, one of the most clear-minded, energetic, and passionate persons I've ever met. He was so loving and kind and yet so bold and absolute about his beliefs. There was no deception or speculation in this man as there is with most other people I interview. Everything he said spoke truth to me. Every gesture he made emphasized his points with star-tling conviction and clarity. The interview was with Gordon B. Hinckley, the president and prophet of the Lord's restored church.

How grateful I am that there is a prophet in these tumultuous days of uncertainty and skepticism. A knowledge and testimony of the Lord and His chosen prophet is the surest foundation one can have in the search for peace, happiness, and truth. There are so many good, God-fearing people in this world, but sadly there are also too many others who are bent on rage, selfishness, and brutal control. If we are to live in a world where there is true love of God rather than love of evil, we must come to a realization that the God of heaven has a mouthpiece who is charged with exemplifying and teaching truth. By doing so we will find greater peace in our hearts and greater truth in our souls of how the Lord would have us live.

Each story I encounter teaches me something about life, death, people, places, things—and about how a person can better prepare for what lies ahead: Eternity.

As a Latter-day Saint, I believe that the underlying gospel principle that brings us closer to God and His restored truths is faith. Oh, how much brighter, more compassionate, and more peaceful the world would be if there was greater faith in God and His wonderful truths! Faith that we are His children and that He loves us. Faith in His Son, Jesus Christ, and in His glorious resurrection. Faith that God's church exists today, with Jesus Christ as its cornerstone. And faith in modern-day revelation and a living prophet. It is this faith that has driven me to learn the truth, accept it, and live by it. This is why I believe.

Art Rascon is an Emmy-winning journalist who has reported on everything from political infighting to civil wars. His reporting has taken him to nearly every state in the United States and to more than fifty other countries throughout the world. He has been nominated for fourteen Emmy awards, winning four, and has also received more than two dozen other local and national awards. The national *Hispanic Business Magazine* named Rascon as one of the hundred most influential Hispanics in America. Rascon was born in El Paso, Texas, and reared in Denver, Colorado. He graduated from Brigham Young University with a degree in communications-journalism and studied humanities and European politics in Madrid, Spain. He also authored the book *On Assignment—The Stories behind the Stories*. He and his wife, Patti, have seven children, including a young man they have taken in from Kosovo. Rascon currently serves as a bishop in Houston, Texas, while working at the ABC-owned station KTRK-TV.

ANDY REID

As head football coach of the National Football League Philadelphia Eagles, I am very proud of the players, the coaches, and all who work in this fine organization. However, the thing I am most proud to be associated with is my membership in The Church of Jesus Christ of Latter-day Saints.

I was raised in Los Angeles, California, where I grew up just under the bright lights of Dodger Stadium. My youthful energies were directed into sports. My eyes, however, were exposed to many city distractions. I saw friends destroyed by drugs and alcohol, some potentially great athletes among the victims. I kept my goal to play professional football close to my heart and realized that drugs and alcohol were not the way to go if my dreams were to come true.

Colleges and universities noticed my abilities to play football. I took my five allotted recruiting trips. The one university that was different from the others and best suited me was Brigham Young University. BYU is nestled nicely into the Rocky Mountains along the Wasatch Front in Provo, Utah, about an hour south of Salt Lake City. BYU was just what the doctor ordered for a college athlete who was looking to separate himself from those big-city distractions. Here was a school with an honor code that all students were required to follow, yet it had a dominating, tough football team. The students were asked to stay morally clean and abstain from taking drugs or drinking alcoholic beverages. There is more to it, but this was the part I liked the best. In other words, keep your body as a fined-tuned machine that could, with hard training, become the best athletically possible.

My life gained substance at BYU. My junior year I met my future and present wife, Tammy Ann Reid. This 5'3" ball of energy helped reinforce the many spiritual lessons I had been taught about the LDS faith. Her true love and dedication to her Heavenly Father never wavered as she dated me, a nonmember football player. You could only respect her focused approach toward the Church.

After a school year of dating, I returned home to L.A. for the summer. I proceeded to take the missionary discussions, far from Tammy, who was at home in Arizona, but close to my family and friends. If I was going to truly convert my heart and soul to The Church of Jesus Christ of Latter-day Saints, I had to do it among my roots. The two missionaries were special. Elder Wiemer was the perfect missionary to teach me the discussions about the Church. He had played high-school football in the L.A. city league at the same time I had and was a star quarterback of his team. His family had moved to Texas during his senior year, and he was called back to the City of Angels to serve his mission. We hit it off right away. I truly believe Heavenly Father had a plan for me, and Elder Wiemer was again playing the quarterback position to that plan.

At the end of the summer of 1980, I called Tammy and told her I was ready to be baptized. I asked her if her father, Big Jim, would do the honor. My only regret in having Big Jim baptize me was that Elder Wiemer and Elder Muir could not be in Arizona to help with the baptism. They had spent many hours praying *with* and I'm sure *for* me, and many hours teaching me the gospel principles that I would need to be spiritually rich in my earth life and my post-earth life. Well, Big Jim and I climbed down into the baptismal font, both of us 6'4" and 260-plus pounds, and the water quickly jumped over the protective glass and into the first row of seats. The spirit I felt in that small church in Glendale, Arizona, was overwhelming.

I was very excited to be a new member of The Church of Jesus Christ of Latter-day Saints in the summer of 1980, and I can say twenty-one years later that I'm still as excited as ever. My life had direction; there was a plan. I knew exactly what I needed to do to return to my Heavenly Father at the end of my earth life.

Many trials and tribulations have occurred in my life since 1980. Tammy and I have said many prayers and have had many prayers answered. We have been blessed with a beautiful family, three boys and two girls. Through hard work and the Lord's helping hand, we are able to teach our children the gospel and how to live the gospel in their day-to-day lives.

We are blessed to live in Philadelphia, which is not only one of the oldest and largest cities in America but also has several diverse cultures. We are able to see Heavenly Father's work daily as the Church continues to grow in the area. The members of the Church are great examples to those they come in contact with.

We have also been blessed with my job. Philadelphia is passionate about its professional sports teams. It truly is a privilege to be the head coach of the National Football League Philadelphia Eagles. We spent much time on our knees in prayer before accepting this job. We knew we could only do the job with Heavenly Father's strong, supporting hand to guide us.

Philadelphia fans are known around the league for being brutal to visiting teams, and sometimes they are even brutal to their own team if they are not playing well. My first year in Philadelphia was the 1999 season, and we did not win many games. We actually started the season with four losses. I was not a popular person in the City of Brotherly Love. I had come to Philadelphia with a plan that I thought could help change the worst team in the NFL into a respectable one. I knew it wouldn't be an overnight process, and I also knew that I would have to stick to my guns during the tough times. I was very glad I could fall back on the great example of strong people in the scriptures and Church history for support. I was able to stay strong during this time and prayed that better days were ahead.

The 2000 season was a reward for all my players and coaches who believed we were going to be okay if we worked hard. We all did just that and ended the year 11–5 and headed for the playoffs. We ended up losing in the second round of the playoffs to the New York Giants. We had taken our 5–11, 1999 record and reversed it in one year. Heavenly Father's supporting hand and teachings were a big part of my plan. My faith in a higher purpose and plan and a reason for living lives of integrity make all the difference. What seemed so mystical to those who watched the plan unfold was so ordinary to what we learn in church daily. This is how we live—with direction, with a purpose, and with a final goal of returning to our Heavenly Father.

Andy Reid, head coach for the Philadelphia Eagles, attended Brigham Young University, where he earned a bachelor's degree in physical education and a master's degree in professional leadership in physical education and athletics.

Reid has coached at San Francisco State, Northern Arizona, Texas-El Paso, and Missouri, and he came to the Eagles after spending the previous seven seasons as an assistant coach with the Green Bay Packers. After a 5–11 mark in his first season, he led the Eagles to the greatest turnaround in franchise history, finishing second in the NFC East at 11–5 and earning a trip to the NFC Divisional Playoffs. For his efforts, he was named the NFL's Coach of the Year by the Maxwell Football Club, *Sporting News*, and *Football Digest*.

He and his wife, Tammy, are the parents of five children.

HARRY REID

For me, the title of this book would better be *Why I'm Glad I Believed.*

I was born and raised in Searchlight, Nevada, a mining town of about two hundred people. Mining was not the main industry in Searchlight when I grew up; the number-one business was prostitution. At one time in my youth there were thirteen separate bordellos in town.

I went to a two-room school, and most of the time one teacher taught all eight grades.

I thought we had one of the best homes in Searchlight. But on reflection, I realize that it had no hot water, only an outside toilet, and was heated by a wood stove.

During all the time I spent in Searchlight there was never a church or, as I remember, even a church service. So when I went away to high school in Henderson, some forty-five miles away, it was a real adjustment. I hitchhiked or obtained rides in other ways to and from Basic High School. I would stay with people during the week and go home on weekends.

My first boarding site in Henderson was with my father's brother, Uncle Joe. His wife was Aunt Rae, who many in the family thought was a little strange because she was a Latter-day Saint.

Aunt Rae was very good to me. She was strict but fair. One thing she suggested was my going to something called seminary. A boy named Ron was nice to me and said he also went to seminary. I thought it unusual to go to class before school started, but because of Ron and Aunt Rae I agreed to try this thing called seminary.

The seminary instructor was named Marlan Walker. He was also a high-school Spanish teacher and, as I learned later, an LDS bishop. To say he was a good teacher is a gross understatement. He was mesmerizing. For the first time in my life, I heard the message of Jesus Christ.

In my high-school years, I took two years of Spanish from Marlan Walker as did my wife-to-be, Landra Gould. Marlan went out of his way to be kind to everyone, especially to me and my Jewish girlfriend, Landra. He set an example in kindness that was impressive.

I obtained an athletic scholarship to attend the College of Southern Utah, where I lived in a dormitory with two of my Nevada friends. It was a room for four, so we were assigned a roommate named Larry Adams, who was a Korean War veteran and a returned missionary. He always acted as a returned missionary should.

Because Landra's parents did not want her to marry a non-Jew, we decided, following my sophomore year in college, to elope. Our former Spanish teacher, still a bishop, heard of our secret marriage plans and said he would save us the twenty-five dollars for a justice of the peace and would himself marry us, in his LDS chapel, no less.

After he married us, we two nineteen-year-olds went to Utah State University to complete our education. My brilliant wife sacrificed her remaining college to work so I could become a lawyer.

Landra rose before dawn each day to take a bus to Thiokol Chemical Company about fifty miles distant, where she worked to pay for my college education. The bus driver, Mr. McPherson, was a stake missionary. Because of his teaching and his patience, we were baptized into The Church of Jesus Christ of Latter-day Saints.

After more than forty years, Landra and I believe our joining the Church to be among the best decisions we ever made. We accepted the Church and a new life because of the power of example. Many contributed to the change, from Aunt Rae to Marlan Walker, from Larry Adams to the stake missionaries. They were effective because they lived their lives as shining representatives, even models, of the life of Jesus.

Our blessings are many. We have five children and soon will have twelve grandchildren. All five of our children have attended BYU, and all have been married in the temple. Each child has been a positive example for us.

After these many years I believe that the Church has been a steady, positive blueprint for my life. Without the direction of the Church, I would have been without a compass.

So you see, I am glad I believed.

 United States senator Harry Reid (D-NV) was born in the small mining town of Searchlight, Nevada, on December 2, 1939. He graduated from Utah State University in 1961 and earned a law degree from George Washington University. His law-school years acquainted Harry Reid with Capitol Hill, where he worked nights as a police officer to pay for school.

Harry Reid married Landra Gould, his high-school girlfriend, in 1959. The Reid family eventually grew to include five children and will soon include twelve grandchildren. Senator Reid was first elected to the House of Representatives in 1982. In 1986 he was elected to the United States Senate, where he currently serves as the assistant Democratic leader.

MITT AND ANN ROMNEY

In Detroit, the Hudson's Thanksgiving Day Parade was a very big deal, with bands, floats, horses, and, most important to a young boy, new cars. The turkey dinner and the traditional Lion's game on TV were big, but the parade was bigger.

My first memory of the parade was when I was four. Even when we moved some twenty miles into the suburbs when I was six, we'd journey back into the city on Thanksgiving morning to see the parade.

Among the boys at school, bragging rights attached to how good a view you had at the parade. I didn't talk much about that myself. The Romney family's parade perch was almost an entire city block away, midway up an apartment building where you could only see the parade cross the side street. We'd take turns poking our head out the window, craning our heads to the left to take in as much of the parade as we could.

Our station was the apartment of Pearl Peterson, an eighty-year-old widow with white hair, a maroon dress, and a large lace collar. It was hard for me to understand why, with so much sidewalk available next to the parade route, our family regularly chose such a disadvantaged site. I remember complaining a bit and being told by my mom that we went to Pearl Peterson's apartment because it brought happiness to her Thanksgiving Day.

After the morning parade shared from her window, Pearl would join us at home for turkey dinner. As I grew older, I noted that there was far more joy in her face as we crowded into her small home than when we gathered at our large and abundant table. Mom talked to or saw Pearl almost every week, but besides at church, Thanksgiving was the only day I really saw her. And yet, as I remember the brightness in her face, the steaming hot chocolate, and the crowding together at her open window, I remember the feelings of love for her that grew in my heart. While the view was obstructed, my heart was opened.

Our annual visits to the home of Pearl Peterson are my first memories of service outside my family. Of course, no one ever called it service. It felt like love.

I've sometimes wondered whether my parents took me along to teach me an important lesson. I don't think so. They were merely doing what they enjoyed doing, and as I did it with them, I began to enjoy doing it too. Sharing or giving of yourself in behalf of another person may begin as service, but it quickly becomes love and produces a fountain of good feelings even inside the heart of a little boy.

During my growing-up years, I was pulled along by my parents as they shared their love for others by serving them. And I grew to know and savor the feelings of joy it brought to my heart.

THE CHURCH AND SERVICE

As much as anything in our religion, we are thankful for the opportunities our faith provides to serve and therefore love other people. Of course, no religion could credibly make a case that its adherents give the most service or express the most love. One need only think of Gandhi, Bishop Tutu, Mother Teresa, Albert Schweitzer, or Madame Curie to recognize that great icons of service come from many backgrounds of faith. In fact, many who have studied the world's religions have noted the remarkable similarity of teachings relating to service of others and what has come to be known in Christianity as the Golden Rule.

To members of our faith, it is no surprise that faiths that predate the mortal life of Jesus Christ contain so many of His teachings. We believe that Adam was taught the plain and simple truths of what we now call the gospel, including the fundamental principles of love and service. While generations of flood and Babel and darkness intervened, the basic message of eternal truths was preserved by good and righteous men and women of our planet's many lands. Lao-tzu, a Chinese philosopher predating Confucius, provides the first recorded expression of what would become the Golden Rule: "The good I meet with goodness; the bad I also meet with goodness."[1]

In our view, what is remarkable about The Church of Jesus Christ of Latter-day Saints as it relates to the love and service of others is certainly not that it is the first, or only, or most devoted in loving and serving others, but the extent to which it provides to us and to its members opportunities and motivation to so love and serve. We are deeply thankful to our faith that it has led us to experience so many forms of love and service of others and has therefore opened to us such rich feelings. And as we survey the large and growing membership of our faith, we are struck by the enormous breadth of service and caring from so many people. Thousands, even millions, are making an effort to include in their lives the fruits of Christian love. The breadth and scale of their millions of unpublicized good deeds with no thought of personal gain or desire for acclaim is possibly unique in all of Christianity.

The roots of the Latter-day Saints' service to others begin with the teachings of Christ and His past and present disciples. The words of the Master establish the foundation: "Thou shalt love the Lord thy God with all thy heart, and with all thy soul, and with all thy mind. This is the first and great commandment. And the second is like unto it, Thou shalt love thy neighbour as thyself." (Matthew 22:37–39.) The connection, the unity of these two commands was then powerfully taught by the Lord in His description to His disciples of who

---

1. Thomas Cottam Romney, *World Religions in the Light of Mormonism* (Independence, Mo., Press of Zion's Printing and Publishing Co., 1946), p. 379.

would inherit the kingdom of the Father: "I was an hungred, and ye gave me meat: I was thirsty, and ye gave me drink: I was a stranger, and ye took me in: naked, and ye clothed me: I was sick, and ye visited me: I was in prison, and ye came unto me. Then shall the righteous answer him, saying, Lord, when saw we thee an hungred, and fed thee? or thirsty, and gave thee drink? When saw we thee a stranger, and took thee in? or naked, and clothed thee? Or when saw we thee sick, or in prison, or came unto thee? And the King shall answer and say unto them, Verily I say unto you, Inasmuch as ye have done it unto one of the least of these my brethren, ye have done it unto me." (Matthew 25:35–40.) By caring for and serving the children of the Father, we are serving and loving God Himself. And so, serving and loving God and our neighbor become one.

The Master's teachings leave no doubt about the preeminent place He holds for those who served. In the parable of the Good Samaritan, He noted that the supposedly holy man passed by the man in need, presumably in his preoccupation with caring for the affairs of the church. More lofty and more righteous was the occupation of the Good Samaritan for the needs of his fellowman.

The principles of service and care for the needy were also taught by the prophets who preceded Jesus and who looked forward to His coming. Through Moses, the Lord commanded the Israelites not to harvest the corners of their fields: "Thou shalt leave them for the poor and stranger." (Leviticus 19:10.) Similarly, some 125 years before Christ, a prophetic king in the new world who likewise looked forward to the coming of Christ taught His people, "When ye are in the service of your fellow beings ye are only in the service of your God." (Mosiah 2:17.)

Of course, there can be no more compelling teaching regarding the divine admonition to care for and serve one another than that expressed in the life of the Savior Himself. His miracles healed and comforted and blessed the lives of His brothers and sisters, all children of the same Father in heaven. And in the end, He laid down His life for all the sons and daughters of God. "Greater love hath no man than this, that a man lay down his life for his friends." (John 15:13.)

The Apostle Paul preached the Master's principles in what has become a familiar couplet: "And now abideth faith, hope, charity, these three; but the greatest of these is charity." (1 Corinthians 13:13.) A Latter-day Saint's perspective on charity is far more expansive than the familiar admonition to care for the poor. Writing some four hundred years after the death of Christ, Moroni, a Book of Mormon prophet, explained that "charity is the pure love of Christ, and it endureth forever." (Moroni 7:47.) Fundamentally, then, serving others is an expression of our love of Christ and His love for us. Again, the commandments to love God and to love our neighbor become as one.

PROVIDING OPPORTUNITIES TO SERVE

To a member of our faith, these and other admonitions to love and serve our fellowmen have become very familiar. The words of the Master and His disciples as recorded in the Bible are repeated for Latter-day Saints again in His words recorded in the Book of Mormon. As we both grew up in Michigan and attended a school that was affiliated with the Episcopal faith, we know that teachings of love and service are certainly not unique to the Latter-day Saint faith. More than teachings about service, however, what we value most highly is that our church has led us to taste the fruits of service in so many aspects of our lives. Whether between husband and wife, among family, as part of community life, in caring for the poor, in our careers, or in our worship itself, each area of life is imbued with opportunities for love and service, and in each our church has helped us to see more clearly the opportunities to serve.

LOVE AT HOME

We fell in love when we were young, very young. We both dated a number of other people and felt the thrills of romance and discovery when we went out with new people. But when we began dating each other, the interest and the feelings we felt for one another never seemed to go away. In the days we spent together, and through the expression of literally thousands of letters (Mitt's attendance at far-off Stanford University and then his two-and-a-half-year mission to France meant that letters would become the staple of our communication), our minds were opened to one another in a way that transformed us. Genuinely, fundamentally, we cared for the other more than we cared for ourselves. Perhaps that was the test of true love, that the other's happiness dwarfed our concerns about ourselves. Our church taught us that the feelings and relationship we shared were not a mortal convenience. Rather, our marriage was the precursor of an eternal companionship that would last beyond the grave and into the eternities.

The division of work and responsibility in a marriage is largely based upon cultural roots. Nevertheless, we each genuinely enjoy doing things for and serving one another. I (Mitt) get a kick out of picking up Ann's clothes on the floor next to her bed on the rare occasion when she leaves them there, exhausted and anxious to get to sleep. I (Ann) enjoy making Mitt's favorite dinner of meat loaf and mashed potatoes. In small ways, and in very large ways, we serve each other. And somehow as we do so, the feelings of love we have for one another only seem to grow stronger. Two years ago, it was apparent that something was very wrong with how Ann's body was working. Doctors diagnosed her problem as multiple sclerosis. As we cried together, holding each other, in the doctor's office, we acknowledged that any problem would be okay as long as we could be together and not be separated by death. Regardless of our circumstances, we can each serve one another to the extent of our ability. And the joy that flows from serving one you love continues uninterrupted.

Bringing children into the world is in and of itself an act of service. For me (Ann), the decision to have a child would mean a distended body and passage into the valley of the shadow of death. Even more, it initiated a career of intense service to a child. The modern-day leaders of our church have plainly taught us that success at home exceeds any other kind of success. In other words, assuming that our financial circumstances were sufficient, one of us would remain home to raise a child. There was simply nothing more important than leading a child back to its heavenly home. The scriptural instructions to parents about their children are clear: "Ye will teach them to walk in the ways of truth and soberness; ye will teach them to love one another, and to serve one another." (Mosiah 4:15.)

I had not planned to choose motherhood as a career. The all-girl's high school I had attended set high academic expectations: like my friends, I assumed I would use what I had learned to pursue a professional career. When Mitt and I moved to Boston, the rising voice of feminism and concerns about population growth meant that some people would resent my choice to have a family. Not having grown up in the LDS faith, I hadn't given much thought to becoming a mother. When our tiny son was placed in our arms, however, I took on the work of the ages. The responsibility for my child's physical, mental, and social development became mine and Mitt's. There is so much routine in motherhood—you feed, you wash, you clean, and then you do it again and again. But between the routines were defining moments when I taught and molded and built character. There were unpredictable moments when my son's mind and heart were open to me. It is then when the most important work of our society is carried out. While there are many women who have achieved and deserve respect for their contribution, for me there could be no more fulfilling and exhilarating career.

Our church did not leave us without guidance to achieve the success in the home it directed us to seek. We were encouraged to set apart every Monday night for family home evening, an experience of games, teaching, and family-only time that served a myriad of purposes. Family prayers were to begin each day. Through the Church, our children would enjoy Sunday classes beginning at three years old. Then, during their teenage years, they would add weekday and weekend activities as well as five-day-a-week, early-morning religious instruction before school.

Because Mitt and I had five sons in eleven years, I knew it would be some time before I would join my friends in the workplace. As it turned out, my diagnosis of MS has limited my work to church and charitable endeavors. I am so glad I chose to first become a mother.

When I consider the joy my sons have brought me, when I experience their strength of character and devotion to God, I silently weep with gratitude. I am so thankful for scriptures and prophets and a church that encouraged my choice of having children and devoting myself to teaching and caring for them.

Just as my last sons were getting ready to leave the nest, my parents came to Boston for their annual checkups. Despite the absence of any symptoms, both learned that they were afflicted with cancer. In the almost two years that followed, I learned how difficult and exhausting can be the care of a deteriorating and dying parent. Again, the emotional fruits of caring for one's family were more abundant and sweet than I could ever have imagined.

One of the living apostles of Jesus Christ has noted, "No service in the church or in the community transcends that given in the home."[2] We will be forever grateful for the counsel we received from our faith and from our parents that led us to choose having five sons and focusing our energies first and foremost upon them and upon each other. I now fully understand Mitt's dad's answer to a question we posed to him together. We asked, "What has brought you the greatest satisfaction in your life?" George Romney had been a three-term governor of Michigan, a presidential candidate, a member of the president's cabinet, and a highly successful mega-corporation CEO. His answer encompassed none of those: "My life's greatest achievement and satisfaction has come as my sweetheart and I have raised our four children."

TURNING OUR HEARTS TO THE FAMILY BEFORE US

The biblical prophet Malachi quoted Moses and the Lord as prophesying that the hearts of the children would turn to their fathers. (See Malachi 4:6.) We believe this refers not only to our parents here in mortality but also to the fathers and mothers and ancestors who preceded us. In addition to our church's admonition to identify our ancestors and learn about their lives, it also provides an opportunity for us to serve them.

In our temples, members of our faith can serve as proxies in performing ordinances such as baptism and marriage for our ancestors. This explains something of the feeling members of our faith have for the more than 100 temples that dot the globe. They remind us of the solemn vows we ourselves have made, and they fill our hearts with the feelings that come from serving others. President Gordon B. Hinckley, the living leader of our Church today, remarked that "in temple work is found the very essence of selfless service. . . . This blessing of the

---

2. Boyd K. Packer, in *Ensign*, November 1997, p. 6.

spirit becomes literally a medicine to cure many of the ailments of our lives."[3]

NEIGHBORS IN THE COMMUNITY

Spencer W. Kimball, a previous president of our church, expressed a sentiment I (Mitt) heard repeatedly at the Romney dinner table: "We urge Latter-day Saints everywhere to become actively engaged in worthy causes to improve our communities, to make them more wholesome places in which to live and raise a family."[4] The sense of obligation is so strong that observers of our faith frequently comment on how often Latter-day Saints serve in PTAs, Scouts, youth coaching, and local government. My dad went the whole nine yards, having served as head of a Detroit Schools advisory board, governor, and U.S. cabinet member. There was no question in the minds of those who knew him about the source of his motivation. It was not ego; he was a man without guile. It was out of an irrepressible sense of duty to serve.

More frequent than opportunities to serve in civic positions are those that arise from every day living. My (Ann's) brother Jim learned that a sixteen-year-old girl in his neighborhood was about to lose her fight with cystic fibrosis. Doctors suggested a radical new surgery— removing her lungs and replacing them with lobes from the lungs of two living donors. Jim was one of the two volunteers whose tissue type sufficiently matched the young girl's. Giving her a lobe of his lung shortened his breath but lengthened the greatness of his soul.

One of the men in our ward (we Latter-day Saints call a congregation a ward) learned on TV of a devastating tornado in Oklahoma City. He surmised that the Red Cross would take several days to accumulate the necessary supplies and transport them to the homeless.

---

3. *Ensign*, August 1982, p. 3.
4. *Ensign*, June 1976, p. 85.

Being moved to do something himself, he drove his old Ford van to a local bakery owned by a friend. Together they loaded it with as much bread as it could carry. The friend suggested that he call a local radio station and ask them to invite others who felt as he did to join him in downtown Salt Lake City with vehicles or items that would be needed by the tornado victims. Before the morning was over, 320,000 pounds of emergency essentials had been brought to the appointed parking lot. Seven semi-truck trailers followed Tom on his drive to Oklahoma. The tears of joy Tom and his fellow Samaritans shed with the victims in Oklahoma evidenced a depth of emotion that will never be forgotten.

NEIGHBORS TO THE POOR AND AFFLICTED

Our church helps even the most financially humble of its members to be able to help the truly poor. Once a month, members of the Church are asked to fast for twenty-four hours. The savings from the expense of the meals not eaten are then donated to a fund for the poor. Further, farms and distribution centers for clothing and food are maintained by local congregations of our church to provide the basic necessities to those in need.

As a boy in my early teens, I journeyed to a Church-owned farm in upper Michigan to care for the crops that would be provided to those in need. As a teenager I probably spent too much time horsing around for me to truly feel the spirit of giving to others. My personal empathy for the plight of poverty came overwhelmingly five or six years later. I had been asked by my bishop and called by the president of the Church to serve a mission in France. One day my companion missionary and I went from door to door in a massive low-income apartment complex. Our hope was to find someone who might have interest in learning more about our faith. But at one door, a very old and emaciated man stood before us. Behind him was an empty and freezing cold apartment. The pain in his face and the poverty of his circumstances took my breath from me. As I stood there speechless, he yelled at us to leave him alone, and he slammed the door. I left the building and returned to my apartment to gather some money I might take back to him. But upon returning to the complex, I was unable to find again the man's door. I knocked upon several but received no response.

As I rode home, still moved by the disparate circumstances of my life and his, I told myself that I would never again pass a hungry person, a person in need whose hand was outstretched to me. I do not know what I would do if I visited a place such as India where mobs of people would overwhelm someone handing out money. But I don't visit India; I visit cities in America. And that commitment, so many years ago, has been a blessing to my life.

NEIGHBORS IN THE WORLD

When we watch those TV ads of impoverished children from around the world, we are overwhelmed with sorrow and with a sense of helplessness. How can what we give possibly make any difference in the face of world affliction?

Some years ago we came to reason that while we might be unable to make a difference to the poor of the world, we could make a difference to the poor and afflicted whom we encountered. The Samaritan had cared for the man he met on the way he was traveling.

We have found throughout our life that God places people on our way that He expects us to succor. One Christmas Eve, we received a call from a distraught mother who lived in a different state than ours. We didn't know her or her family. She explained that her daughter and grandchildren were living in an apartment near the ocean in Boston. They were without funds and without heating oil to keep them warm. As we listened, we felt that this was someone who may have been placed in our way for a purpose. Our young sons loaded logs from the garage into our car and took them to that unheated apartment. Remarkably, the apartment had a workable fireplace, which we were quickly able to light. The next day we returned with other necessities that we noticed had been missing. It was a Christmas we will not soon forget.

Some members of our faith are moved to look well beyond the way placed before them. A friend from our home in Belmont, Massachusetts, helped lead a convoy of trucks delivering medical supplies to Bosnia and pioneered a medical safari to Africa, where she used her nursing skills to care for the sick. Our congregation in Belmont provides the funds for an orphanage and for a leper colony, the Belmont Mercy Home, in Madras, India. Children in that faraway land bless the lives of the many people in Belmont who can afford to clothe and feed them.

SERVING IN THE CHURCH

Of course, the Church itself can receive the service of its members. Quoting Emerson, President Gordon B. Hinckley noted that "every great institution is but the lengthened shadow of a great person."[5] To a great extent, all Christian churches are the shadow of the Master. In The Church of Jesus Christ of Latter-day Saints, Christ's frequent admonitions to serve one another, to strengthen the fellow Saints, or members of His church, are given ample exercise. By virtue of the fact that all the administrators and teachers and counselors and musicians and so forth in a congregation are drawn from the lay membership itself, each member receives an assignment to serve others in the Church.

One of the most important assignments each man and woman receives is to visit the home of other members to teach, inquire

---

5. *Ensign*, August 1982, p. 3.

whether there is some service that is needed, and offer friendship. Each month, a man and a young companion visit several families in their congregation that have been assigned to them. These assignments may last over many years. When they do, deep friendships develop. Likewise, the women in our congregation visit other women once each quarter in their homes. These one-on-one talks among women can be a source of strength and comfort and counsel.

Of course, much of the service in the Church is unrelated to assignments and callings. When we lived in Cambridge, Massachusetts, two elderly women were living examples of the Master's parable of the widow's mite. Alberta Baker and Helen Rhodes were themselves widows, probably in their eighties, and living alone in their apartments. Our plan to build a new chapel generated an occasional bake sale and encouraged those in a position to do so to make building contributions. Helen took in sewing so that she would have money above her modest retirement funds to give to the new chapel. Alberta collected scraps of wool from old dresses and suits which she tore in strips and knotted into a rag rug that could be sold at auction to provide building funds. "This poor widow hath cast more in, than all they which have cast into the treasury." (Mark 12:43.)

THOSE MISSIONARIES

There are probably few places in the world where people have not encountered two young men or two young women with their dark suits and plastic name tags. Being a missionary was far from the self-concept of each of our five sons. They grew up in an affluent household, and by age nineteen, the time when young men are typically called to serve as missionaries, their lives were centered on themselves: education, clothes, music, and girls.

Each was asked by our church to serve a mission for two years. They would live in very humble circumstances, eat only two meals a day to save money, and walk or ride a bike in sun, rain, or cold. And most difficult of all, they would be treated worse than a door-to-door salesman: knocking on doors, disturbing people's peace at home, they would repeatedly and deservedly be told to go away—sometimes forcefully.

Incredibly, each of our sons has said that his mission was the most formative period of his life. It was a time to learn something about humility. Our sons beseeched God, in behalf of others, and learned that He was always there. They worked harder than they had ever worked before. And they tasted the sweet fruits of service at a time when their lives could have otherwise been directed toward solely selfish pursuits. At that critical juncture in time, when young people may turn entirely inward, the Church asked them to serve their fellowman. As Robert Frost said in a similar context, "And that has made all the difference."[6]

SHAPING THE SOUL

Understanding our Father in Heaven's purposes may well be beyond human capacity. Even so, reason suggests that eternal purposes are linked to the two great commandments, loving God and loving our neighbor, that Jesus taught.

What first comes to us is the fact that in many instances we, God's children, act as His hands on the earth. While scriptures and experience witness His direct intervention, they also report of the many times when His will is fulfilled by His children's actions. A man was inspired by the Holy Ghost to welcome and care for Saul of Tarsus following his remarkable vision on the road to Damascus. So too, every Good Samaritan fulfills God's will. How great would be the alleviation

---

6. In "The Road Not Taken," *The Poetry of Robert Frost*, edited by Edward Connery Lathem (New York: Holt, Rinehart and Winston, 1969), p. 105.

of hunger and suffering if God's children all sought to care for the poor and afflicted of the world. As President Thomas S. Monson has said, "The Lord knows each of us. Do you think for a moment that He who notes the sparrow's fall would not be mindful of our needs and our service?"[7]

There may also be eternal purpose through the effect that service has on those who provide it. The Lord taught, "Whosoever shall seek to save his life shall lose it; and whosoever shall lose his life shall preserve it." (Luke 17:33.) Simply put, "He who lives only unto himself withers and dies while he who forgets himself in the service of others grows and blossoms in this life and in eternity."[8] If our life's purpose is to become more like Christ, there are many qualities we must develop to achieve such a transformation. "Perhaps the most essential godlike quality is that of compassion and love—compassion shown forth in service to others, unselfishness, that ultimate expression of concern for others we call love. Wherever our Father's children magnify their opportunities for loving service, they are learning to become more like Him."[9]

And finally, there is at least one more purpose that may stand behind our Father's command to love and serve Him by loving and serving His children. That purpose is to bring to us, who are given the chance to serve, greater happiness and fulfillment in our own lives. Paradoxically, it seems that those who abandon selfishness, taking no thought for themselves, and devote themselves to service of others are richly rewarded. Each act in our life where we have given to another has brought a richness of emotion we had never imagined. The profound nature of our marriage, the bonds we share with our sons and

---

7. Ensign, November 1989, p. 45.
8. Gordon B. Hinckley, in Ensign, August 1982, p. 3.
9. Spencer W. Kimball, in New Era, March 1981, p. 49.

their wives and children, our relationships with our parents, our friendships, and even our connection with Deity are all profoundly affected by the opportunities and motivation our faith has provided for service.

Ann Romney, mother of five and grandmother of four, is co-chairman of the Faith in Action Committee of Boston's United Way. She serves on the boards of Families First, Best Friends, and the Massachusetts General Hospital Women's Cancer Advisory Board.

Mitt Romney is the president and CEO of the Salt Lake Organizing Committee of the Olympic Winter Games of 2002, a position he has held since February 1999. Formerly, he was CEO of Bain Capital, a private investment holding company with $13 billion of capital under management. He was also CEO of Bain & Company, Inc., a leading international management consulting firm with 2,500 employees worldwide. In 1994 he was the Republican nominee for Massachusetts for the United States Senate.

GORDON H. SMITH

In 1842 the Prophet Joseph Smith published thirteen statements of belief, known today as the Articles of Faith. I learned them all by heart in my youth. Each article begins with the declaration "We believe," except the eleventh. It reads, "We claim the privilege of worshiping Almighty God according to the dictates of our own conscience, and allow all men the same privilege, let them worship how, where, or what they may."

Not until I grew older did I fully appreciate the significance of the eleventh article. Its "claim" was actually a cry for tolerance and understanding by a persecuted and peculiar people. Explicit also in the claim is the offer to tolerate and respect the beliefs of others.

Central to my service in the United States Senate is a commitment to tolerance. While I have lived most of my life in places where Latter-day Saints are a minority, I have never known the persecutions that caused my pioneer forebears to flee the United States for the hardships of the American frontier. Yet I have felt the sting of discrimination for my faith. My reaction to physical and psychological persecution has been to understand the eleventh article in personal terms and to practice tolerance toward others, asking only the same in return.

I believe in the American tradition of separating church and state. Our Constitution fosters tolerance by guaranteeing freedom of worship while guarding against the establishment of a state orthodoxy. I am not a Latter-day Saint senator; I am Oregon's senator. Yet I am free to believe and live as a Latter-day Saint. It is an important distinction if I am to represent all believers and nonbelievers alike. I do not check my values at the door of the Senate, nor do I pursue a sectarian agenda.

So if the reader can remember that I recognize and respect the first human right of conscience, the right of others to believe and disbelieve in religious traditions different from my own, just as fervently as I believe, then I will tell you why I believe in the message of The Church of Jesus Christ of Latter-day Saints.

For as long as I can remember, I have had a confirming sense that God lives, that Jesus Christ is His Son and my Savior, and that the Church was established to help me find my way home to my Father in Heaven. I suspect that I was given a spiritual gift of faith. (See 1 Corinthians 12:9.) But that gift has been nourished throughout my life by experiences with reason and revelation. Let me explain.

I like to be happy. I love the promise of America's founding Declaration to "life, liberty, and the pursuit of happiness." Being obedient to the teachings of Jesus Christ and His Church helps immeasurably in my pursuit of happiness.

I have found that happiness is the natural consequence of having and pursuing noble purposes. The Lord's Church teaches that we are God's children and that He has placed us here on earth as part of His eternal plan. Our purpose is to experience life by receiving our physical bodies and by making choices between good and evil, right and wrong. How we spend our time on earth affects the happiness we enjoy in mortality and eternity.

I believe that the commandments of God are not given as restrictions but as warnings and guides to keep us safe and help us grow, so that we may know happiness more abundantly. For example, we are taught that our bodies are sacred. By obeying the laws of health, I enjoy more energy and enthusiasm for every stage of my life. By avoiding addictive substances, I am able to control my mind and body, and I am better able to resist sickness and disease.

By living the laws of chastity—abstinence before marriage and fidelity thereafter—I experience all the fulfillment of family life. My twenty-five years of marriage to Sharon Lankford Smith is founded upon trust and love. My children Brittany Anne, Garrett Lee, and Morgan Spencer are able to look to me for consistency and security. To hold these children as infants, to help with lessons, to cheer them on, and to wipe away their tears is to feel something of divinity and to understand why God loves us as well. Reason tells me that most of the lasting happiness I will know in this life will come from my family relationships, from making commitments and keeping covenants.

Each of the Lord's commandments also teaches and refines me. I find that by paying tithes and offerings to the Lord's church, I am blessed in personal and powerful ways.

With each offering I am reminded that God is the source of all my blessings and that I have a duty to help the poor and build His church. But more, obedience to this commandment helps me to keep in better balance the spiritual and the material, to discern better the difference between wants and needs, and to be more prudent in financial matters.

In addition, serving in Church responsibilities helps me to serve others and to realize that my problems become smaller when I help others in carrying theirs. Whether teaching a class, administering the sacrament, or presiding over a priesthood quorum, the act of serving and enjoying the attending power of the Lord's Spirit is an endless source of happiness.

Deductive reasoning from life's experiences teaches me that obedience to God's commandments brings forth blessings and happiness. But I realize that many fine faiths teach true principles, so why The Church of Jesus Christ of Latter-day Saints? In a word, revelation.

The bridge between reason and revelation is not easily explained to everyone's satisfaction. Indeed, the Apostle Paul warned the Saints of his day that spiritual things would seem as foolishness to some. To me, however, spiritual things are as real as tangible things. Though this is not easy to explain, let me try. Revelation is a feeling like a fire burning in your heart; it is clear communication to your mind, pure knowledge, and new information, and it is peace to your soul that passes understanding and removes doubt.

Such confirming experiences can come at odd times and places, but usually to those who earnestly seek to know the truth and who are not disqualified from feeling revelation by serious transgressions. Prayer is an essential ingredient and, for me, the holy scriptures are often the catalyst. I love to read, and I have read many books in my life. From them I have drawn education, entertainment, even enlightenment. But no books affect me in the transcendent and transforming ways as do the Bible, the Book of Mormon, the Doctrine and Covenants, and the Pearl of Great Price. I first realized this at the age of eight.

On the Sunday following my baptism into the Church, the children's Primary organization presented me with my own personalized copy of the Book of Mormon.

That night I could not sleep, so I turned on my night-light and opened my book at the beginning. I began to read: "I, Nephi, having been born of goodly parents, therefore I was taught . . ." (1 Nephi 1:1.)

As though it were yesterday, I still remember my reaction. I put down the book because I could no longer read the words. My eyes filled with tears, my spine tingled, my heart burned, and I knew with perfect clarity that the Book of Mormon was true, that it was a gift of God, and that like Nephi, I had been taught by goodly parents.

Many years later I found myself serving as a nineteen-year-old missionary for the Church in faraway New Zealand. When Christmastime approached, and I was thousands of miles removed from family festivities, for the first time in my life, I was overcome by a sense of loneliness and homesickness. On the morning of December 25, 1971, I felt forgotten and disconsolate. I turned to the Christmas story as recorded by Luke. I began to read: "For unto you is born this day in the city of David a Saviour, which is Christ the Lord . . ." (Luke 2:11.)

I had read these words before, but never before had I been so powerfully impressed by their truth and majesty. In an instant I felt transformed. My homesickness was banished by gratitude; depression was replaced by joy indescribable. I knew again that Jesus Christ was my Savior, that He lives, and that I was His servant, privileged to be in a land so beautiful. I felt His presence. I was filled with peace and with feelings of goodwill toward all. It was an unforgettable revelation to me that I cannot doubt or deny.

Many years later, in a poignant circumstance, another scripture revealed to me the miracle of forgiveness and the reality of the atonement of Christ. I was serving as a bishop in the Church with responsibility for the welfare of some 600 souls.

A fine woman asked to see me. She told me that, in spite of my high opinion of her, many years earlier she had committed a grievous sin. From that moment on, over a period of many years, she had lived a life of faithfulness and rectitude. But she had always felt too restrained by fear of societal consequences and church discipline to ever confess her transgression to a church authority. Now, however, she wanted to lay down her terrible burden, no matter the consequence. Her heart was broken, and her spirit contrite; she yearned for forgiveness and was prepared for any Church sanction.

I was saddened that she had carried her burden alone so long. My heart was breaking for her when there came into my mind a passage from the Doctrine and Covenants. I read it to her: "Behold, he who has repented of his sins, the same is forgiven, and I, the Lord, remember them no more. By this ye may know if a man repenteth of his sins—behold, he will confess them and forsake them." (D&C 58:42–43.)

I was impressed to tell her on behalf of the Church that the matter was closed, her repentance was complete, and the Lord would remember it no more—and neither should she. She left my office a new person. She had been reborn, and I had been party to something miraculous. I better understood what had been accomplished by Jesus in the Garden of Gethsemane and on Calvary's cross—the atonement of Christ.

For these reasons and revelations and many, many more, I believe in the truth of The Church of Jesus Christ of Latter-day Saints. It was restored by God through the Prophet Joseph Smith. Its proof is found in prayer, in the words of prophets, and in obedience to true principles. For me it has been part and parcel of my pursuit of happiness. It may be for you as well.

Born on May 25, 1952, in Pendleton, Oregon, Gordon Harold Smith graduated from Brigham Young University in 1976 and earned a law degree from Southwestern University in 1979. After working as an attorney in private practice, Smith assumed management of his family's frozen vegetable processing company, a position he held until his election to the U.S. Senate.

Smith entered politics in 1992 when he was elected to the Oregon Senate. His colleagues recognized his leadership abilities by electing him minority leader and then president of the state Senate during his first term in office. Senator Smith and his wife, Sharon, have three children. They maintain homes in Pendleton, Oregon, and Bethesda, Maryland.

CATHERINE M. STOKES

When I was only three or four years old, I listened to my two older brothers question whether there was a God and then conclude that if there was a God, "He don't know nothin' 'bout us." This conclusion was unaffected by television, movies, or books depicting lives of plenty beyond the stark poverty and social and racial status of the descendants of slaves in rural Mississippi in the 1940s. Regardless of such discussions, we went to church—religiously. There was nothing else to do other than work at our chores in the field or at home. Our people were strong in faith, especially my grandmother's generation, always telling us, "The Lord will provide."

And He did provide. He provided me with a deep and enduring faith. At what point did I believe? I don't recall. Sometimes I think I always did, even during the questioning of young adulthood, because I always prayed, as far back as I can remember, and music has always spoken to me spiritually. Did I come to this earth with an undeniable belief mechanism in place? I think so, but it did not truly flourish until, after various levels of participation in many religious traditions, I came home—spiritually, religiously, practically—to The Church of Jesus Christ of Latter-day Saints.

This is why I believe.

When I joined the Church, most of my friends and acquaintances thought I had taken leave of my senses. Some early comments were, "I thought you were smart until you joined the Mormon Church." "Are you the only black member they have?" "If you're going to give that much money to a church, why would you give it to a white church?"

Are there diverse opinions about race among members of the

Church? Of course there are, and they run the spectrum. At the same time, there is a no more welcoming, loving, helping place. You have to come and see for yourself.

This is why I believe.

Recently, on what has become an annual visit to see friends in Mesa, Arizona, I accepted an invitation from the mother of one of the missionaries in my area to visit Thatcher, Arizona. When I learned that it would require a three-hour drive, one way, I expressed my reluctance to trouble anyone to that extent. Fortunately, the missionary's sister was living in Mesa and wanted to go to Thatcher anyway. It was an eventful trip. Our drive began in the rain. Next, as we went through the Superior Mountains, snow began to fall in earnest. The next thing we knew, the car had stopped and wouldn't go into gear. Fortunately, we were less than an hour from Thatcher. The young lady's father came to get us. As I met the father, mother, and both sets of the young missionary's grandparents, I extended my hand, and in return it was not just received warmly, but in addition I was gently enfolded in a welcoming embrace. Were there any other Blacks in Thatcher? I doubt it. My world of urban, inner-city Chicago and Thatcher, Arizona, could not have been farther apart. But, there we were, in the words of Paul, "being knit together in love." (Colossians 2:2.) The two younger children hugged me recklessly throughout the visit as if the hugs were transferable to their big brother. My hostess had even tied a quilt for me to take home as a memento of the trip. And then a loaf of bread was given with a generous bag of the local pecans—shelled, no less. Our day ended with good-bye hugs all around. I hope they will come to my town. The commonality of membership in the Church brings an instant rapport and is a true expression of Christian love.

This is why I believe.

Through my faith, I have come to know the sweetness of forgiving and letting go of old hurt. When I would visit my relatives in Mississippi as a young girl, I was puzzled about why we had to step off the sidewalk when a white person approached from the opposite direction. At that time, I had no issue of injustice or outrage; I just did not understand why we did that. My relatives quickly told us to go back to Chicago and not bring me back because I would get us all lynched. As I got older, this memory provoked anger and outrage, and I walked with a hostile determination not to step aside or off the sidewalk for whites. Fortunately, in Chicago, I could do that and live. A few years ago while visiting my daughter in Wichita, Kansas, I was taking an early-morning walk to enjoy the sunrise. Having become a faithful walker, I had learned something about walkers and runners. Walkers are generally friendly and accommodating. They speak, and they smile. Runners are generally singularly focused on the run. Most do not speak or smile or acknowledge on-comers in any way. On this particular morning, the narrow sidewalk appeared to be all mine until a young white woman came into view, running straight toward me. To my astonishment, *I stepped off the sidewalk.* As she ran past, I returned her smile and nod. I marveled at how easily and gently the old hurt was released. This young woman had no idea how big a step I had taken. Sweet tears of thankfulness came as joy filled my soul. Forgiveness is central to the teachings of the Church.

This is why I believe.

Too often we hold on to the hurt, and in holding on we not only allow the hurt to continue but we also reinforce it. Oh, that forgiving would flow for all of our hurts. I am convinced that our survival of slavery and all that followed has been because we have been forgiving. This appears to be changing. It's painful for me to know of some of our young college students shunning those who choose not to segregate themselves. Similarly, it is beyond my capacity to understand why some criticize white people who adopt black children. Would they rather that these children languish in institutions or inadequate foster care? I remember a time I was visiting friends in Pleasant Grove, Utah. When we attended church, I observed a white woman with two black tots who were obviously not her birth children but *were* obviously her children. I am so grateful for her, and I thank our Father in Heaven for her. Throughout our time in this country, Black women have cared for everybody's children with unfeigned love. Why would this privilege be denied to white women or to any woman?

Several of my white LDS friends who have adopted black children have asked that I help them, especially on matters cultural. So I am an "adopted" aunt and grandmother for them. I hasten to add that I also have white and black nieces, nephews, and grandchildren who don't think I'm adopted. One of these blond, blue-eyed ones asked his mother why I was not in her childhood family pictures. His mother asked why he thought I should be in the pictures. His response: "Isn't she your sister?" "Being knit together in love" is real in my life and in my church.

This is why I believe.

About ten years ago, a young, white member of my local congregation said to me, "We need to do something about these kids in the summer." "These kids" were children beset by the ills of urban, inner-city life. His statement marked the beginning of the Inner City Youth Charitable Foundation, which provides full-time camp experiences for boys and a day camp for girls from our congregations in the Chicago area. Subsequently Ricks College, in Rexburg, Idaho (now BYU—Idaho), joined in this effort by providing counselors. These young college-student counselors have an experience in urban America that changes their lives through the extending of their understanding. These activities are funded by the generosity of donors solicited by present and former board members. In the Church we not only believe but practice that "inasmuch as ye have done it unto one of the least of these my brethren, ye have done it unto me." (Matthew 25:40.)

This is why I believe.

Brigham Young (the second president of the Church) said that if your religion can't help you in this life, it won't save you in the next. My religion helps me in my life. It is a twenty-four-hour, seven-days-a-week religion that supports me in my goal to serve my God.

This is why I believe.

Today, at age sixty-four, my appreciation for time and my time left on this earth is especially intense. That God is and that He loves us, for me, is best expressed in the words of the Apostle Paul in Romans 8:38–39: "I am persuaded, that neither death, nor life, nor angels, nor principalities, nor powers, nor things present, nor things to come, nor height, nor depth, nor any other creature, shall be able to separate us from the love of God, which is in Christ Jesus our Lord." And again in the words of the Apostle Paul in Philippians 4:13: "I can do all things through Christ which strengtheneth me."

I want to make the most of my remaining time in ways that matter, particularly in healing the wounds—the ruptures—the breach in race relations in this land. I love the words of a familiar gospel song: "Give me a pure heart that I may serve Thee, Lord, fix my heart so that I may be used by Thee . . ." This is my desire. I counsel with the Lord to know His will for me for the time left. I pray that this will include being among those described in Isaiah 58:12: "They that shall be of thee shall build the old waste places: thou shalt raise up the foundations of many generations; and thou shalt be called, The repairer of the breach, The restorer of paths to dwell in."

That we might wax stronger and stronger in humility and firmer and firmer in faith, yielding our hearts in God's service to repair the breach, is my prayer.

This, I believe.

Catherine M. Stokes describes her life as a delightful but incredible journey. She is a registered professional nurse who has held a diversity of positions in health care, from bedside nursing, office nursing, teaching, and public health to her current position as an assistant deputy director in the Office of Health Care Regulation of the Illinois Department of Public Health.

Mrs. Stokes lives in Chicago, and she loves to cook, travel, facilitate group singing, and read Anne Perry mystery novels. She and her former husband have one daughter, Ardelia, who lives and works in Wichita, Kansas.

HEIDI S. SWINTON

⤳

I was twenty-seven and pregnant with twins. They were due April 10; spring was a nice time of year to have babies. Like many expectant mothers, I worried that my baby—in this case, babies—would have the right number of fingers and toes. I wondered what physical features would dominate. Would they be smart? I never imagined that one of my babies would die.

Christian Horne Swinton was born February 10, 1976, at 2:08 in the afternoon. He died at 10:07 the next morning. I was in one hospital; he was in another. Four days later my husband, Jeffrey, and I buried him, our oldest child, while his twin brother, Cameron, fought for his life on a respirator in the newborn intensive care unit blocks away.

Identical twins, they were born two months early before the development of sophisticated fetal monitors, ultrasound, and drugs to accelerate lung development. Immediately following the delivery, doctors stabilized the two boys and then, with hopes of saving their lives, whisked them away to another specialized hospital. They couldn't breathe and were blue from lack of oxygen; each weighed just three pounds and was about the size of my hand. I held Christian only once. By then, he had been dead an hour.

Not wanting Christian to be alone, we decided to have him buried with my grandmother, who had borne three sets of twins of her own. I can still picture the scene at the cemetery: the grief on the faces of our families and friends who were circled around us; the miniature blue-velvet casket suspended over the grave; the hearse just off to the side, seeming so big for such a small cargo; and the flowers adding some pink, yellow, and red to the lifeless winter landscape. I can still hear the wind whipping the branches of the birch tree just a few yards from where we were standing. It was cold.

My belief in Jesus Christ, in His gospel, and in His church is rooted in what I learned that day as a young mother watching my dreams slip away. I learned that Jesus Christ is with us, and that His presence is our salvation. The prophet Isaiah said it so well: "When thou passest through the waters, I will be with thee; and through the rivers, they shall not overflow thee: when thou walkest through the fire, thou shalt not be burned; neither shall the flame kindle upon thee. For I am the Lord thy God, the Holy One of Israel, thy Saviour." (Isaiah 43:2–3.)

I am not sure I fully grasped the power of "the Lord thy God . . . thy Savior" before those dramatic first days and weeks of being a parent. Before the twins were born, I understood the plight of Hannah, who "had no children." (1 Samuel 1:2.) I had lost five children in miscarriages, and I imagined that these two were going to make things right. The Lord was giving us a bonus. So how could I accept such disappointment and death in that light? How could I believe in a God that would let this happen? What had I done to deserve this? I am one who loves "happy endings," and this experience did not appear to have one. Or did it?

My religious background prompted me in those desperate days to turn to the Lord for help, and His intervention was immediate. The circumstances didn't change, but my resolve and capacity to cope did. I know I was never without the love of God. Clearly, I felt His presence and His power in the cemetery at Christian's grave. I felt His Spirit with me in the hospital day after day as I sat beside Cameron's isolette, unable to hold him, watching him be fed through a tube, and hoping, praying, that he wouldn't die as well. Since then, Christ has done for us what He promised: "I will go before thee, and make the crooked places straight." (Isaiah 45:2.)

To this day I recoil when a doctor calls me on the phone. My thoughts flash back to the call from the neonatologist on duty in the intensive care unit as he described Christian's brain hemorrhage and the desperate condition of Cameron's heart and lungs. I remember my obstetrician coming into my hospital room and pulling a chair up to the bed. Taking my hand, he said, "There will be a time when your son here is a teenager, and you will look back, gratefully, knowing you have one all the way home."

I was raised a member of The Church of Jesus Christ of Latter-day Saints. But it was the impact of losing one son and nearly losing another that shaped my whole-souled belief in Jesus Christ and His power. That wintry afternoon I began to understand how the Lord touches and teaches each of us: "Peace I leave with you, my peace I give unto you: not as the world giveth, give I unto you. Let not your heart be troubled, neither let it be afraid." (John 14:27.)

Jesus Christ spoke those words to His disciples at the end of His mission. They are imprinted on my soul as if He had spoken them to me. I felt peace in the cemetery. I felt peace in the hospital. I have felt that peace many times since when I have faced other perilous experiences. Sometimes, I feel peace of mind or peace in my heart. There are days when that peace reminds me that "all is well,"[1] even though nothing seems right or fair. This singular spiritual peace comes from believing that Jesus Christ lives, that He is the Savior, and that His mission is to connect us inseparably to heaven.

I know now what I didn't know then: "Family relationships are perpetuated beyond the grave."[2] At our service for our son, my brother-in-law spoke of a teaching revealed through Joseph Smith, the first prophet of the LDS Church: "The Lord takes many away even in

1. The well-known refrain from "Come, Come, Ye Saints," in *Hymns* (Salt Lake City: The Church of Jesus Christ of Latter-day Saints, 1985), no. 30.
2. "The Family: A Proclamation to the World," September 23, 1995, in *Ensign,* November 1995, p. 102.

infancy that they may escape the envy of man, and the sorrows and evils of this present world; they were too pure, too lovely, to live on earth; therefore if rightly considered instead of mourning we have reason to rejoice as they are delivered from evil, and we shall soon have them again."[3]

With that understanding of the eternal family as a footing, I have raised our four boys to look forward, to count on Christ and His promise that we will all be united with Christian when we live again with our Father in Heaven. I have always pointed them to the Lord for that strength and direction. I have shared with them my belief that Jesus Christ lives and that He is my Savior—and theirs.

More than a decade ago, I prepared a compilation of the testimonies of Jesus Christ given by the all the presidents of the LDS Church. As I researched and read their words, I was moved by the majesty of their personal witness and the simplicity of the descriptions of their belief. I was impressed that my testimony of Jesus Christ had come in a way similar to theirs. Joseph F. Smith, who served as president of the Church in the early years of the twentieth century and who had lost a handful of his own children in their early years, expressed so succinctly the essence of belief: "I have received the witness of the Spirit in my own heart . . . that I know that my Redeemer lives." Rather than fanfare, it was the heartfelt witness of the Spirit that had spoken to him and affirmed the reality of God.

Such peace and affirmation of truth comes as a quiet, sacred communion amid the press of life, much like what Elijah experienced on the mount: "The Lord passed by, and a great and strong wind rent the mountains, and brake in pieces the rocks before the Lord; but the Lord was not in the wind: and after the wind an earthquake; but the Lord

3. *Times and Seasons* 3 (15 April 1842):751–53.

was not in the earthquake: and after the earthquake a fire; but the Lord was not in the fire: and after the fire a still small voice." (1 Kings 19:11–12.)

Earthquakes may shake mountains, though sometimes we are the only ones that feel the ground moving. I, too, have stood on a windy mount and heard the still, small voice. That voice of peace speaks softly: "Be still, and know that I am God." (Psalm 46:10.)

Heidi S. Swinton is an award-winning author and screenwriter of *American Prophet: The Story of Joseph Smith*. She also wrote the award-winning PBS documentary *Trail of Hope: The Story of the Mormon Trail* and is currently writing the documentary and companion book *Sacred Stone: Temple on the Mississippi* to be aired on PBS in 2002.

Heidi serves as a member of a writing committee for The Church of Jesus Christ of Latter-day Saints, as vice chair of This is The Place Heritage Park, and as a member of the Advisory Board of BYU-TV and the BYU Women's Conference Committee. She graduated from the University of Utah and attended Northwestern's Graduate School of Journalism.

She and her husband, Jeffrey, have five sons.

DIETER F. UCHTDORF

It was in post-World-War-II East Germany where I first learned about The Church of Jesus Christ of Latter-day Saints. My mother and her four children, I being the youngest at age four, fled Czechoslovakia in the winter of 1944, before the arrival of the Russian front, finding support and relief with my grandmother in the German kingdom of Saxony. My father served at the western front, and my oldest brother, fifteen years old, was drafted into the military service during these chaotic final months of World War II. My brother became a prisoner of war for a short period of time; however, both returned safely in the summer of 1945.

In the aftermath of this horrible war, my grandmother was left a widow and was searching for answers to the eternal questions: "Can there be a God?" "Who am I?" "What is the purpose of life?" "What happens after death?"

Through a wonderful lady by the name of Ewig (translates to *Eternal*), my family was introduced to The Church of Jesus Christ of Latter-day Saints, and answers to those pivotal questions followed: "Yes, there is a God, and He loves us. Jesus, our Savior, is the Christ."

I played in bombed-out houses as a child and grew up with the ever-present consequence of a lost war, but the gospel, even in those early childhood years, brought hope and peace into our lives. The teachings of the Bible helped our family in the challenging times: "For God hath not given us the spirit of fear; but of power, and of love, and of a sound mind. Be not thou therefore ashamed of the testimony of our Lord." (2 Timothy 1:7–8.)

Later, in my professional life, as I traveled around the world as an airline captain in a Boeing 747, and as an executive of a major

European airline, I visited numerous countries and met many wonderful people. Often they asked how I became a member of the Church. Some of my peers frequently suggested that I must have learned about it during my professional stay in the United States.

It gave me pleasure to explain that this is a universal faith, an international church, with values and beliefs that are true and right and helpful, irrespective of culture, nationality, political system, tradition, language, economic environment, or education. Reflecting on my life, I give full credit to the teachings and the programs of the Church for what has happened to me. It has helped me raise my sights out of the destruction and rubble of the war. It also has the timely answers to overcome today's evils of pornography, abortion, drugs, permissiveness, and corruption. It brings us closer to God and the commandments He has given us. It helps us to be true to our virtues and values and will strengthen our faith and give us hope even in serious times of challenges.

UNIVERSALITY

Our church is a great teacher and builder of values. It lifts, sustains, and strengthens people. It makes life more complete, rich, and happy as we move through this vale of tears. It is a great reservoir of eternal truth, building faith in things that are eternal. It is here to help us come to a solid, certain conviction concerning the place of each of us in the plan of the Almighty. We are children of God, with a divine inheritance and an eternal destiny.

The history of this church reflects an impressive ability to adapt and succeed in different cultures and under difficult circumstances. The doctrinal principles remain constant in every culture and give answers to important questions of human relationships and our existence.

At times I've been asked, "Why did the restoration and establishment of the Church take place in America and not in other more civilized parts of the world? Why in America?"

Our church is different from many others, in that we believe that the church that Jesus established in New Testament times eventually disappeared from the earth, primarily because of persecution of the Christians and the death of the apostles. Essentially, it fell into apostasy. Thus, the authority of the priesthood, part of the gospel of Christ, and sacred ordinances and covenants were lost. We believe that the original church of Christ was restored again and organized in 1830 through authority given by heavenly messengers to a young man named Joseph Smith in upstate New York. He had asked God for direction about which church to attend, and he received visions, heavenly tutoring, and a charge to reorganize the original church as it had been organized during Christ's time on earth.

The great confidence with which Americans often announce their country to be choice above all other lands is sometimes irritating to citizens of the rest of the world. However, in regard to the forthcoming of the new religion, the Constitution of this land and the Bill of Rights provided ideal circumstances for true freedom of religion, speech, press, and assembly. The restoration would not have been possible in Europe or on any other continent. The tradition of intertwining political authority and church, in some countries still a recognizable influence in our day, would have prohibited such a bold development. Democracy; freedom of religion, speech, press, and assembly; and separation of church and state were prerequisite for reestablishing the religion.

Europe had its time in preparing for the restoration of the original Church of Jesus Christ in important previous centuries, especially with Gutenberg's invention of the printing press in the mid-1400s and Columbus's voyage to the Americas in 1492. These activities helped set the stage for another great spiritual movement, the Protestant Reformation. Wycliffe, Hus, Luther, Zwingli, Calvin, Knox, and others prepared the way for the Pilgrims before they fled to America in search of further religious liberty, which finally led to the restoration of the gospel of Jesus Christ.

POWERFUL EUROPEAN INFUSION

In the early days after the Restoration, Europe again played an important role in establishing the worldwide Church of Jesus Christ. An infusion of new, dedicated members was needed for the crucial periods that lay ahead, especially for the pioneering exodus to the West. From 1847 to 1869, more than 32,000 British and Irish converts to the Church left their homelands for a new life in pioneer America.

The novelist Charles Dickens made some interesting remarks about these Latter-day Saint emigrants against whom, as he stated, he had a negative predisposition. He had seen them on the ship *Amazon* before it set sail in 1863: "What would a stranger suppose these emigrants to be? . . . I should have said they were in their degree, the pick and flower of England."[1]

He stated this despite the fact that in the early years, most European converts came from the middle and especially the working classes. The Church lifted them up and helped them prepare for a better life, with an educational and spiritual vision. Attempts to interest dignitaries of various countries, the traditional nobility, the moneyed aristocracy, and the powerful secular intelligentsia fell on deaf ears and sometimes even led to the missionary's banishment.

The European converts, in certain ways, saved the early Church in its struggles with persecution and apostasy. They turned out to be exceptionally good pioneers. They brought with them a solid religious conviction and faith, an unusually strong work ethic, a usable and practical quality of artisanship, and a desire to blend into the new society and religion.

---

1. In *The Uncommercial Traveler*, in the chapter "Bound for the Great Salt Lake."

By 1880, out of a total Utah population of 144,000, 43,000 (about 30 percent) were foreign-born. If children born in America to foreign-born members were included in the figure, it would exceed 60 percent. But emigration and anti-Mormon pressures and persecution took its toll on the membership in Great Britain. In 1892, Church membership on the British Isles declined to 2,600 and rose very slowly to only about 6,000 through 1950.

Scandinavia was typical for the challenges the Church and its members faced in more progressive parts of Europe. Constitutions and laws guaranteed, as early as 1845, religious freedom and freedom of speech and press. But local courts ruled that Latter-day Saints could not enjoy protection because they were not considered Christians. Missionaries were arrested and fined for preaching, baptizing, or administering the sacrament. Unable to pay, they had to go to jail, where they studied the scriptures, sang hymns, and taught the gospel to the jailers, who were often sympathetic and provided them with the best cells. From 1850 to 1950, more than 27,000 members emigrated from Scandinavia.

In spite of mob disturbance and occasional brief imprisonment of the missionaries in Scandinavia, the Church grew. The persecution, hopelessness, poverty, and starvation of the nineteenth century motivated people to seek a better life with their fellow Church members by joining the gathering headed to the promised land in Utah.

Despite constant persecution, there were also conversions in Germany. One exceptional convert, Karl G. Maeser, came from Saxony. In 1855 Maeser, a schoolteacher, found an anti-Mormon tract that aroused his curiosity. Maeser's persistent requests led to the visit of two missionaries in his hometown. Foreign missionaries were outlawed in Saxony. The meetings had to be in secret. Under cover of darkness, Karl G. Maeser and some of his friends and family were baptized. Conditions were so prohibitive, however, that they all decided to emigrate in 1857.

In 1876 Brigham Young appointed Maeser as the principal of the forerunner of BYU, the Church-owned university, which has more than 27,000 students today. Heber J. Grant, the seventh president of the Church, stated, "If nothing more had been or ever would be accomplished in Germany than the conversion of Dr. Karl G. Maeser, the Church would have been well paid for all the efforts and means expended in that land."

PROGRESS IN A CHANGING WORLD

After World War I and with the downfall of the former oppressive government, the Church's future looked promising in Europe, especially in Germany. During the 1920s the strongest congregations outside the United States were established in Germany. Thousands immigrated to America and contributed great spiritual and temporal strength to the Church in Utah. The members who stayed in Germany formed exceptional congregations. At no time previously had the Church outside America had such stability and success.

With the growing influence and power of the German National Socialist Party (Nazi), times became difficult. Gestapo agents spied on the Church's members and church services. Hymns could not be sung that mentioned "Israel" or "Zion." In 1939 all missionaries had to leave the country, and Church members suffered immensely. Heinrich Worbs from Hamburg was arrested by the Gestapo and died six months after his release, having endured numerous tortures. Another member, Helmuth Hübner, a gifted student, concluded that he and his teenage friends must oppose the Nazi regime. He took notes of the BBC broadcasts, typed handbills on the typewriter he used as a Church clerk, and duplicated them on the Church's mimeograph machine. In 1942 the Gestapo arrested him and his friends, Karl-Heinz and Rudi, as they had learned about their connection with the Church. They were tried before the feared Blood Tribunal in Berlin and convicted of conspiracy to commit high treason. Helmuth was sentenced to death, and his friends to hard labor in a prison camp. Shortly before he was beheaded by guillotine at the Berlin prison Plötzensee in October 1942, Helmuth wrote to loved ones, "I am very thankful to my Heavenly Father that this agonizing life is coming to an end. My Father in Heaven knows that I have done nothing wrong. . . . I know that God lives and He will be the judge. Until our happy reunion in that better world."

Countless stories of faith and endurance could be told of members who suffered in all parts of Europe. Bombing raids destroyed their meetinghouses, so they held services in their homes, aiding and encouraging one another as best as they could.

After the war, Ezra Taft Benson, one of the Church's twelve apostles, arrived in a devastated Europe in 1946 to evaluate how Europe could best be helped through the welfare and humanitarian efforts of the Church. He stated at that time, "The wreckage to lovely government buildings, universities, monuments, museums, parks, and business block cannot possibly be understood unless seen. . . . My heart is heavy as I reflect on these awful, never to be forgotten, scenes. Truly, war is hell in all its fury."[2]

Comparing the members of the Church to other Germans who were still in deep depression, Ezra Taft Benson noted, "Our [members], on the other hand are full of hope, courage, and faith, and everywhere they look cheerfully forward with expressions of deepest faith. . . . It was one of the greatest demonstrations that we have ever seen on the real fruits of the gospel in the life of men and women."[3]

2. Ezra Taft Benson, *A Labor of Love: The 1946 European Mission of Ezra Taft Benson* [Salt Lake City: Deseret Book Co., 1989], p. 60.
3. Ibid., p. 65.

After World War II as Europe was starving, quick and generous help was provided though the Church in clothing and food. I still remember the sweet taste of wheat and peaches and the touch of soft clothes that were given to us in Zwickau, East Germany. One hundred and thirty-three boxcars of food, medicine, and clothing were shipped to the cold and starving people in Europe. This desperately needed aid saved lives, rescued the dispirited, and brought new hope for the future. It helped us to regain physical strength, but even more, it gave us hope for the future.

In November of 1947, ten large trucks with seventy-five tons of potatoes left Holland for Germany. The war was still in everybody's memory. Germany had occupied the Netherlands, but the conflict was over, and the Dutch members couldn't help but have compassion and so sent potatoes that they had grown for their own people to German members who were in even greater need.

HOPE AND HELP VERSUS POLITICS AND PERSECUTION

The massive devastations of World War II naturally hindered missionary work in Europe after the war. England took the lead in member growth and Church strength. Leaders observed, "Never has there been so much favorable sentiment toward the Church and such opportunities to interest people in our message!" In 1947 Church population worldwide had reached one million members. But in all of Europe, the membership had declined from its previous twentieth-century peak in 1939 to less than 29,000 in 1950 because of war casualties and postwar immigration to the United States.

Faithful living, according to the principles of the gospel and the courage of the members, brought fruit in the late 1970s and early 1980s. For the first time in history, a temple was approved behind the Iron Curtain, and it was finished in 1985. Ninety thousand visitors toured the new edifice before it was dedicated. What a miracle it was to have such a Christian, sacred sanctuary built in a declared atheistic country.

Prominent political leaders of communist Germany gave an insight into why these miracles were possible: "We have observed you and your people for twenty years. We know you are what you profess to be: honest men and women." The faith and devotion of the members in that nation had not gone unnoticed by God. The long period of preparation had passed, and the future of the Church in Eastern Europe unfolded.

Official recognition of the Church was also reached step by step in all of the western countries of Europe. However, the people of Europe stopped short of completely embracing this "American sect," as many still see the Church. Rapid changes in society, earning a living, acquiring possessions, and leisure activities take precedence over any interest in religion. Religious devotion is still dominated by tradition.

Thus, for members to join the Church requires courage, faith, and a strong belief in the truth of the new religion. Children and youth are often the only members of the Church in their school. These challenges are often considered blessings because they lead to a more cognizant living and exploration of the faith.

Standing up for something builds character and gives moral strength to individuals of any age. The renewing enthusiasm connected with the growth of the Church at this crucial time brought a stability and solidarity into the congregations of Europe.

THE WIND BENEATH MY WINGS

Coming back to the question of why I, a European, became a Latter-day Saint makes me think again of comments I heard from friends, colleagues, and peers. Some said, "Well, you became a Latter-day Saint as a six-year-old child when the rest of your family joined the Church, and you grew up in your religion; it gave you a safe harbor and a solid spiritual foundation—it is a family tradition for you."

Others said, "You could have been attracted by the many

character-building activities offered by your church for the young people." These include the Primary, a faith-promoting and fun organization for children up to age twelve, and the Young Women and Young Men organizations, which help youngsters between twelve and eighteen to develop their talents in multiple fields, including sports, arts, social competence, and leadership skills, with a clear focus on intellectual as well as spiritual values.

Still others said, "During your idealistic adolescent years, you recognized that this church has the best record per capita in serving the less fortunate through humanitarian and welfare efforts in all the world." Indeed, the humanitarian efforts of the Church are far-reaching in impact and scope. To name just a few, these have included aid to many thousands of people after earthquakes in China and Japan, a cyclone and flooding in Bangladesh, a volcanic eruption in the Philippines, drought in Africa, conflicts in Bosnia and Croatia, a crop failure in North Korea, and problems in Rwanda, Mozambique, and Zimbabwe.

Others speculated, "Perhaps the challenging but spiritually rewarding commitments expected of members in a church with no paid clergy made sense to you." Members are expected to teach, to organize, and to take responsibility in this great organization, all this without temporal reward. Living the law of the tithe, fasting once a month, giving generously to the needy—these similarities between the biblical church and the restored church are impressive.

Other possible reasons mentioned by my associates and friends for joining the Church have included the following:

• No premarital sex, fidelity in marriage, a health code with no alcohol, drugs, tobacco, coffee, or tea—all extraordinary expectations and values with great potential to refine and enhance one's life.

• The clarity, logic, and common sense shown in the organization of the Church and its teachings.

• The immense efforts of the Church to encourage self-reliance and promote education. The Church is providing a ladder by which people can climb out of impoverishment, gain self-respect, earn respect in society, and be empowered to make contributions of significance to the nation of which they are a part.

Yes, these are all valid and compelling reasons for me to be a member of The Church of Jesus Christ of Latter-day Saints. But there is more to it, much more. In my profession as an airline captain, I had to know, trust, and apply many procedures, technical details, and parts pertaining to the aircraft I flew. This knowledge was imperative for a successful and safe flight crossing the oceans and continents. But the most important part, as I used to call it, was the "wind beneath my wings." Without it, there was no life, no climb, no flight into the wild blue yonder or to faraway, beautiful destinations.

Similar to this supporting wind, and absolutely basic to my religion and my membership in this church, is my firm conviction of the divinity of the Lord Jesus Christ and His place in the eternal plan of God, our Eternal Father. Jesus Christ is the key figure in our faith. We are Christians. Jesus Christ is the resurrected, living Son of God, our Eternal Father. He is the source of the good news of the gospel. He is the author of our salvation. He taught us the way, the truth, and the life through which we may go on to immortality and eternal life. He gave Himself as a sacrifice for the sins of all mankind. His redeeming love is bringing the transcendent, messianic message of hope to all the world. He has reestablished His church. Jesus Christ is its living head, giving us hope that through the grace of God, we may once again return to our Heavenly Father with this wonderful promise and blessing that families can be forever, even beyond this earthly existence.

On the way home to our Heavenly Father, we are entitled to be taught, directed, and uplifted, not only by the written word of God as found in the holy scriptures but also by living prophets as in times of old. What a privilege and blessing to have living prophets of God among us today!

Joseph Smith was called to restore the Church of Jesus Christ in 1830, and Gordon B. Hinckley guides us today. The prophets can have a positive influence on the present course of our civilization, if we will only listen. They give us a divine and eternal perspective to solve personal, national, and international problems by following their inspired counsel and living an honest and moral life. They testify of the reality of God the Father; His living Son, Jesus Christ, our Redeemer; and of the Holy Ghost.

These are some of my firm, core beliefs and convictions that really are the "wind beneath my wings." It is a universal, divine wind, transcending continents, cultures, traditions, and political and economic circumstances. This church and its teachings are here to bless individuals, families, and people. It has done this in the past and will continue to do so in the future.

Dieter F. Uchtdorf was born in 1940 in Ostrava, Czechoslovakia. He grew up in East and West Germany and saw firsthand the effects of World War II and its political consequences. A professional pilot for thirty-six years, he finished his career as a B-747 captain and was senior vice-president of flight operations and chief pilot of Lufthansa German Airlines. He has served as a General Authority since 1994. He and his wife, Harriet Reich Uchtdorf, have two children and four grandchildren.

PETER VIDMAR

I don't lay claim to fame of any significance. Certainly there are better-known and more accomplished contributors to this book. But I did have my fifteen minutes of fame many years ago at the 1984 Olympics in Los Angeles. Standing on the victory stand with my teammates as we received the men's Olympic Team Gymnastics gold medal, I was overwhelmed with tremendous feelings of gratitude. I was grateful for the many people who played such an important part in my development as an athlete. My teammates and I lived a dream together as we shared those many hours in the gym. My mother was a devoted chauffeur for many years, driving me back and forth to the gym and sacrificing much of her free time for my training. (What a thrill it was for her when I got my driver's license!) Although my father has lived his adult life as a polio victim, with a leg that serves only to support his weight, he has never complained about what other people would call a disability. His example taught me to never complain in the gym, to willingly submit to the demands my coach placed on me. My coach saw something in me that led to his devoting twelve selfless years of his life helping me to reach my dream. I cannot repay him for all he has done for me. My wife, a former UCLA gymnast, was with me throughout the entire year leading up to the games. Her emotional support helped me deal with the pressures of Olympic competition. I am indebted to all of these people and others too numerous to mention. But most important, I was grateful to my Father in Heaven for blessing me with all that led to that moment on the victory stand.

I was born and raised in The Church of Jesus Christ of Latter-day Saints. Some of my ancestors were pioneers who crossed the plains to flee religious persecution, enduring great hardships for their faith. My grandfather John Vidmar was an orphan, often homeless, who as a child was taken in by a family who were members of the Church of Jesus Christ. Their kindness led to his own inquiry and then baptism into the Church. He married a pioneer daughter, and their descendants have been active members of the Church.

The youngest of six children, I grew up in Los Angeles, and although I trained seriously in gymnastics, I lived a fairly normal life. I attended high school, I surfed many mornings at local beaches, I attended Church youth activities, and I went out with my friends. But I never experimented with drugs or alcohol. As an athlete I valued my health, but more important, my faith taught me to avoid all of those things. Once, when I was competing in a very prestigious event in Europe, I won the vault event. As I stood on the victory podium, I received a gold medal, flowers, and gifts. I was thrilled. Before walking off the podium, I noticed another individual coming forward with a silver cup, and I thought, "Another gift? I'll take it!" But as the presenter moved closer with this cup, I noticed that it was full of wine. Turning to a German friend and competitor, who was standing on the third-place stand, I asked what it was for, and he explained that tradition called for the champion to drink out of the cup and to pass it to the next athlete. I told him, "Well, I don't drink." He responded, "Then just take a sip and hand it to the next person." Then I explained, "No, it's against my religion, and I can't even take a sip." My friend proceeded to explain to the officials in their language that I wouldn't drink it, but they insisted I take the cup. So I took the cup and held it high in the air for the crowd to see. And then, without taking a sip, I handed it down to the next person, amid the laughter of the crowd. Although it was an awkward moment, it was easy to turn down the wine because I was taught years before that it was something to avoid.

Aside from lessons taught in the home and the example set by my parents, I attended early-morning seminary classes before high school. The lessons I learned about Jesus Christ, the life He lived, the service He rendered, and the sacrifice He made had a tremendous impact on me. I wanted to have the peace that came from trying to live a Christlike life. I have participated in community service projects, volunteered to feed the homeless, and help in Church canneries. I studied the Bible and the Book of Mormon, I prayed, and I gained a personal testimony that what I was learning and trying to do was based on true principles and could make a difference in my life and in the lives of others.

In many areas my belief has given me strength to live what I was taught. Many readers may be familiar with the Academy-Award–winning movie *Chariots of Fire*. Much of this film is based on a true story of Great Britain's Eric Liddle, who chose not to run the 100 meters because it was held on Sunday. He instead ran the 400 meters and won the gold medal. To me, it's a lesson about keeping one's principles regardless of what the rest of the world thinks. I had my own little *Chariots of Fire* experience with my coach, one of the finest persons I know.

My coach started me in the sport at age eleven, and for twelve years I trained under him. Although he won't admit it, he made tremendous personal sacrifices for me. Today, we have enjoyed almost thirty years of friendship. When I was thirteen years old, my coach asked me to train on Sundays. His intentions were only good. He saw potential in me and wanted to take me as far as I could go, which meant training as much as possible. I was thrilled to be under his tutelage. I was in love with gymnastics and dreamed daily of going to the Olympics. But I told him no. For me, Sunday was the Sabbath, and I didn't engage in recreational activities or sports on Sunday. I needed to keep this day holy. I did a poor job of explaining this to him, and he was very disappointed. He was not of my faith and didn't appreciate

that I would refuse this extra training time. He always gave 100 percent to his athletes and wanted that same devotion in return. He asked
me to leave. I was devastated. But deep in my heart I knew I needed
to keep this commandment. After a few weeks my coach met with me
and my parents. If there is one thing my coach understands, it is commitment. To this day I have never met a more devoted coach in any
sport. When he realized how committed I was to this principle, he
probably thought he could channel that discipline to gymnastics. He
allowed me to return, and I trained so hard Monday through Saturday
that I truly earned my day of rest on Sundays!

Why at the age of thirteen would I take a stand like that?
Certainly my parents raised me to live this way, but I didn't consult
with them on the issue. They were willing to let me choose for myself.
Indeed, I think the key to my coach's accepting me back to the gym
was the fact that it was *my* decision to not train on Sundays, not my
parents' decision, and maybe my coach was impressed with that.

I felt at peace then, and I feel at peace now, when I do my very
best to live the principles that were taught by Jesus Christ. As a member of The Church of Jesus Christ of Latter-day Saints, I have been
taught from my youth to live a certain way that seems outdated to
many people. But I don't feel hemmed in or burdened by rules. I feel
free.

As a parent, I enjoy seeing my children grow when they understand a principle that was taught by the Savior and then put it into
action. I have a lot to learn and much more to do, but I have found
great peace in my life as a member of the Church of Jesus Christ.

Over the front door of our home we had painted the saying *Return
with Honor*. It is a reminder to every member of our family to return
home from school, work, or travels with the same values, character,
and integrity we learn in the home.

In 1984 Peter Vidmar captained the U.S. Men's Gymnastics Team to its first-ever Olympic gold medal. He also captured the gold in the pommel horse, scoring a perfect 10, and he became the first American to take a medal (silver) in the individual all-around men's competition. His winning performances averaged 9.89, making him the highest-scoring U.S. male gymnast in Olympic history.

In addition to his Olympic success, he has numerous NCAA and international titles, an economics degree from UCLA, and experience as a television announcer for CBS. He also serves on the Executive Committee of USA Gymnastics and the Governor's Council on Physical Fitness and Sports for the State of California.

Peter now lives in California with his wife, Donna, and their five children. He translates his skills as a leader and motivator into inspirational presentations for Fortune 500 companies looking to benefit from his gold-medal performances.

MARK H. WILLES

∽

"Ye shall know the truth, and the truth shall make you free." (John 8:32.)

Good journalists are preoccupied with seeking the truth. At Times Mirror we had hundreds of reporters and editors working hard to uncover, report on, and make sense of what was really going on in the world around us. Since I was new to the newspaper business, I spent a lot of time talking with them about how they practiced their craft. I quickly came to deeply admire their relentless search for truth.

As we did surveys to find out what our readers wanted to see more of in our papers, we found a growing desire for greater coverage of religion. Being a religious person myself, I was heartened by these findings. But then I began to wonder if even good journalists could really cover religion in an effective and appropriate way.

Consequently, I found myself pondering a question: How would a good journalist verify the story of the birth of the Savior? After all, His birth, life, death, and resurrection are central to Christian religions around the world. If true, these events are the most important things ever to take place in the history of mankind. How, therefore, would a first-class journalist find out the truth about these remarkable occurrences?

As I thought about this, I turned to the account of the Savior's birth contained in Matthew:

"Now when Jesus was born in Bethlehem of Judaea in the days of Herod the king, behold, there came wise men from the east to Jerusalem, saying, Where is he that is born King of the Jews? for we have seen his star in the east, and are come to worship him." (Matthew 2:1–2.)

Then, being sent by King Herod to Bethlehem to search for Him, they again saw the star, whereupon "they rejoiced with exceeding great joy. And when they were come into the house, they saw the young child with Mary his mother, and fell down, and worshipped him." (Matthew 2:10–11.)

A good journalist would have some serious problems with these verses in the Bible. For example, Matthew's age and circumstances do not seem to indicate that he was actually there at Jerusalem and Bethlehem when the wise men came. Therefore, he did not personally witness what he was reporting on. By using "unnamed sources" as the basis for his account, Matthew was committing a real journalistic no-no.

But what if we could solve this problem by uncovering manuscripts containing the writings of the best journalists alive at the time of the birth of Jesus? What might we find? What would these reporters have done when they heard stories of stars and wise men?

World-class reporters would have immediately tracked down the wise men and interviewed them. They might have asked, "Where and when did you first see the star? How did you know it was a special star signaling the birth of the Savior?"

The wise men most likely would have told the reporters that the star was a bright, new star—that it was the star written about by the prophets. Therefore, they knew by a burning feeling within them when they saw it that it was *the* star heralding the birth of the Christ Child. It was this burning feeling that testified of Jesus and caused them, like the disciples on the road to Emmaus, to rejoice. (See Luke 24:32.)

These reporters might have been touched by the story of the three wise men. Or they might have been skeptical. In either event, in order to get confirmation or add balance to their accounts, they would quickly seek out others and interview them. They would undoubtedly find many who had been so preoccupied with their daily affairs that they had not even looked up to see the star. After all, with family, business, and other pressures weighing so heavily upon them, how could they find time to gaze at the stars?

These reporters might find others who had in fact seen the star. Upon probing, the reporters might learn that some had dismissed the appearance of the star because they were not aware of the prophecies about it and therefore simply thought it was a curiosity. A few others might indicate that they were aware of the prophecies but quickly dismissed them. After all, miracles like that could not possibly happen in their time.

The reporters might find others who saw the star, knew the prophecies, and even felt the same burning confirmation in their hearts that it was His star. But they had not followed it to see the Savior because the timing wasn't right. They had important things to do. Perhaps they would go later, at a more convenient time.

Finally, the reporters would seek out star experts. These experts would likely give a learned explanation as to why there indeed had been a new star but that it most likely had nothing to do with anything important here on earth.

The reporters would take all of these interviews and with the help of trained editors prepare long, "balanced" articles giving all of the different points of view about the star. They might conclude that the wise men had witnessed the most momentous thing ever to happen in the history of the world to that point. Or they might conclude that since so many others did not see the star or doubted the claims of the wise men that it was a special star, perhaps the wise men were either duped or were simply seeking publicity. Most likely, the reporters would not really have concluded anything. They would have reported all points of view and left it up to readers to decide whether or not there was really anything special about the star and the experiences of the wise men.

If reporters would have difficulty verifying the story of the wise men, how would they ever deal with the unique nature of the conception of the Savior or the fact that some shepherds saw angels? And what could they possibly make of the fact that wise men, shepherds, and others kept talking about a "burning in their hearts" that helped them "know" the truth of what they had seen and heard?

As I thought about all of this, I realized that while good journalists can report on and write about the *practice* of religion, they cannot effectively deal with the *essence* of religion. They can report that some profess to have faith, but they can't report on or explain the power of faith. They can report on the fact that some people pray, but they can't explain how prayer connects people to God. They can report on people's adherence or lack thereof to God's laws, but they can't effectively deal with the reality of the Lawgiver. Of course, the practice of religion, which has to do with actions and observances, is important to be sure. But the essence of religion is what we feel and know in our hearts. It has to do with things unseen. It is, after all, spiritual, and therefore deeply personal. And it is the essence of religion that prompts and brings meaning to the things we do in the name of religion.

Consequently, journalists, who have the responsibility to write the truth, cannot effectively deal with what many of us believe are the most important truths of all. Perhaps that is one reason why the Lord has said, "My thoughts are not your thoughts, neither are your ways my ways. . . . For as the heavens are higher than the earth, so are my ways higher than your ways, and my thoughts than your thoughts." (Isaiah 55:8–9.)

So why do I believe? It has nothing to do with interviews or opinions. I am grateful that others believe, but their belief provides comfort, not a burning conviction. Some do not believe. I respect their views, but their disbelief does not provide refutation.

I believe that Christ was born in Bethlehem because I have asked, in prayer, and received a *burning* in my heart that told me it was so.

I know that the Christ Child is the God of this world and that He loves each of us and all of us. I know because I have read His words and a *burning* in my heart has told me they are true.

I know that He is the Prince of Peace because I have bowed before Him and felt His love and the deep feelings of peace that only He can give.

Likewise, I believe that Joseph Smith was a prophet because miracles happen in modern as well as ancient times. As I have studied his teachings and his testimony of the Savior, I have felt a *burning* in my heart that told me they were true.

Finally, I believe that every president of The Church of Jesus Christ of Latter-day Saints, up to and including President Gordon B. Hinckley, have been and are living prophets of God. I have asked, on bended knee, and received a *burning* confirmation of their divine calls.

I am grateful for outstanding journalists who help us better understand the world in which we live. I am also profoundly grateful that it is possible, through study, prayer, and faith, to understand the truth of things that transcend this world and at the same time give deeper meaning and purpose to the time we spend here.

I believe in Christ because He lives. I love Him, honor Him, and worship Him.

Mark H. Willes retired as chairman, president, and chief executive officer of Times Mirror in April 2000.

He joined Times Mirror as CEO in June 1995. In addition, he served as publisher of the *Los Angeles Times* from October 1997 to June 1999. Prior to joining Times Mirror, he was vice chairman of General Mills, Inc., Minneapolis, Minnesota. A fifteen-year veteran of the company, he served as president and chief operating officer from 1985 to

1992, when he was named vice chairman. Mr. Willes previously served with the Federal Reserve System. He was president of the Federal Reserve Bank of Minneapolis from 1977 to 1980 and first vice president of the Federal Reserve Bank of Philadelphia from 1971 to 1977. He began his career as an assistant professor of finance at the Wharton School, University of Pennsylvania, from 1967 to 1969.

Born on July 16, 1941, and raised in Salt Lake City, Utah, Mr. Willes received his A.B. degree from Columbia College, New York City, and his Ph.D. from the Columbia Graduate School of Business.

Mark Willes is married and the father of five grown children. He is presently serving as president of the Hawaii Honolulu Mission for The Church of Jesus Christ of Latter-day Saints.

STEVE YOUNG

In the game of American football there are huge men who are paid to hit the quarterback. Many times when I had only a few seconds, I would drop back to pass the ball, and these huge men would make it impossible for me to see any of my receivers. This forced me to run with the ball or desperately throw it away.

After each game the whole team watched the wide-angle replay that is filmed from the top of the stadium. This provided the coaches and players an "eagle-eye view" of all the action on the field. This permitted us to see every player and learn where mistakes were made or to reinforce good decisions. I always hated watching these films; inevitably there were so many things that I would have done differently had I been able to see the action. In fact, it is very frustrating for a quarterback to hear the fans yell from the stands, "How could you miss that one? It was as obvious as the nose on your face." My answer was always the same: "If I could have seen him, I would have thrown him the ball."

The more troubling criticism came from the coaches. They knew how hard it was to see the whole field. The fact that I couldn't see around the big guys didn't seem to matter. In fact, one coach pulled me aside and said some very profound words: "You'd better find a way to see better or you'll never make a great player."

I came to realize that seeing is not believing, but believing is needed to start seeing. In other words I needed to start throwing the ball where I believed Jerry Rice (one of the game's great receivers) was, even when I couldn't actually see him. At first it was nearly impossible—in fact, frightening—to throw the ball when I wasn't sure, but I knew I had to get this right or my job could be in jeopardy. The great news was that the mere act of throwing, even when I wasn't sure, led me to develop a deeper sense of the playing field. Over time, I got so good at throwing to the spot that I believed was right, that my faith in this process was soon proven by our success.

As I look back, it was this one skill that made the greatest impact on my career. Developing the faith that my senses were right on the field became a metaphor for me. First believing, then having the faith to throw the ball, I came to realize I had been doing this spiritually my whole life. You see, I was born in Greenwich, Connecticut. I had a house, a mother, a father, three brothers, one sister, and a dog. I went to a local elementary school, middle school, and high school. I had a paper route and ate at McDonald's. I played Little League ball and rode my bicycle for hundreds of miles. I was in Boy Scouts, and I went to church every Sunday of my life. I had the greatest friends, and we would throw the ball for hours and hours; only the dark of night sent us home to make excuses for being late and to eat a hot dinner. I was a typical American boy—or so I thought. Then one day I looked around and saw that not everyone was going home to a family, a hot dinner, and a dog. And so I began to wonder why there were so many differences. Some of the differences were obvious and didn't matter much: my friends' homes were different, and my friends worshipped differently, but we were still much the same. We cared about each other and shared our pocket treasures, fixed each others' bikes, and caught the same school bus. But my world broadened, and riding into the big city I became acutely aware that not everyone had a home, not everyone had a mom and dad, and not everyone had a hot dinner. Some differences mattered a lot! So I began to question, I began to wonder, and at times I began to challenge.

Every night I said my prayers. They were pretty routine, using the same words: gratitude, help us to win our next ball game, bless Mom and Dad, and help me not to be afraid. Being afraid was my secret, mine and my Heavenly Father's. It seemed that any new change was hard for me, much harder than for my friends. I hated being left at kindergarten,

I dreaded Scout camp, and the first day of school each year was absolute pain. And so I not only prayed by my bed each night, but I also prayed when I got off the school bus, and when I was packing my sleeping bag, and when I went to visit my cousins. I worried about each ball game, fearing I wouldn't be good enough. So my prayers became my private anchor and my strength, and more times than I can remember a peace came over me as I embarked upon life's "growing up" and "growing out" experiences. This peace I can never deny; this peace was real. I felt it when I was very young, and I knew that somehow my Heavenly Father, my God, heard my prayers and in some miraculous way heard everyone's prayers. How simple was my faith! Even when life became very complex, how powerful was this conduit to a real and accessible power. I remember reading about George Washington in school; he was my hero, and I studied more than just what our school offered. I was impressed by this account and a quotation from his own journal:

> George Washington gratefully credited God with preserving the American army through the trials of the devastating winter. Deep thanks, he wrote, are "due to the great Author of all the care and good that have been extended in relieving us in difficulties and distress." Washington had pled repeatedly with that "great Author," seeking relief for his suffering men. Those prayers at Valley Forge have almost been given the status of legend. Yet, the General really did pray during that dark winter. According to the record, two eyewitnesses (General Henry Knox and the man with whom Washington was quartered at Valley Forge, Isaac Potts) tell of the General retiring to a quiet grove where he could be alone to seek the help of God. But this man of great faith was not motivated to pray at Valley Forge simply because of the horrors of that winter. Washington prayed at Valley Forge in large part because it was his habit to pray. Quoting his

grandson, George Washington Parke Custis, "Throughout the war, as it was understood in his military family, he gave a part of every day to private prayer and devotion."[1]

He prayed from the time of his youth and he continued that practice throughout his life. His prayers then were but one strand in a lifetime of devotion.[2]

I remembered thinking that I knew how he felt, this powerful man of destiny. He, too, prayed to the same God in heaven; he, too, was afraid; he, too, needed something beyond his own strength; he, too, sought the source, "the great Author," for courage and peace. From that point on, I searched for others who humbly recognized the hand of a Supreme Being in the existence of nations and peoples, but also and even more humbling were the accounts of the hand of a loving Father concerned for the needs of every living individual, with each soul considered by Him as His own child. I knew it to be true; I had felt it, and I could say it with conviction. However, just as I believed with all my young faith, I still had so many questions. My belief in God answered many questions, and my belief in God created many questions. One of my first was, "Why?"—why so many inequities, why so much disaster, why am I here on this earth at this time, and what can I do to make a difference? I sought these answers, and the answers continuously confirm why I believe.

History repeatedly records human existence and the evolution of religion—how similar in countless ways and how different in others! Most doctrines seem to have originated from the same source and over

1. George Washington Parke Custis, *Recollections and Private Memoirs of Washington* (New York: Derby & Jackson, 1860), p. 493.
2. Jay A. Parry, Andrew M. Allison, and W. Cleon Skousen, *The Real George Washington* (Salt Lake City: National Center for Constitutional Studies, 1991), pp. 273–74.

time were distorted, adapted, and changed, yet continually people searched for the inner longing of a caring supreme entity in which to focus their faith. Only the wealthy and prosperous cultures seemed to take all power to themselves as sophistication no longer needed direction, except for their own. The study of human nature seems to reflect the cycles of humility and pride and repeats itself time after time. Granted, many have never felt the need for or had exposure to organized religion, yet something internal recognizes the need for goodness, values, and charity. I know there is an intrinsic worth to every living being, and virtually every living thing testifies of a loving God, familiar and exact. Of course, there have always been those who have seen hypocrisy among a few and so have discarded the whole. They fix their faith on science, abstractions, or prominence. I was impressed when Spencer W. Kimball, educator and spiritual leader, clearly explained:

> Expertise in one field does not automatically create expertise in another field. Expertise in religion comes from personal righteousness and from revelation. Man cannot discover God or his ways by mere mental processes. One must be governed by the law which controls the realm into which he is delving. Why, oh why do people think they can fathom the most complex spiritual depths without the experimental and laboratory work accompanied by compliance with the laws that govern it. Absurd it is, but you will frequently find popular personalities who seem never to have lived a single law of God, discoursing in interviews on religion. And yet the financier, the politician, the college professor or the owner of a gambling club thinks because he has risen above his fellowmen in some field, he knows everything in every field. One cannot know God nor understand his works or plans unless he follows the laws which

govern. The spiritual realm which is just as absolute as is the physical cannot be understood by the physical. You do not learn to make electric generators in a seminary neither do you learn certain truths about spiritual things in a physics laboratory. You must go to the spiritual laboratory, use the facilities available there and comply with the governing rules. . . . It matters little whether one is a plumber, a banker, or a farmer, or a college professor [or a football player] for these occupations are secondary, but it is most important what one knows and believes concerning God and his past and his future and what he does about it.[3]

In order for people to act upon their beliefs, they must have personal freedom—agency, the right to discover for oneself one's origin and life's purposes and to recognize theory or fact by deduction partly, by personal revelation completely! As the nations of the world seek and sacrifice for democracy, the opportunity to choose their course is their purpose, but their right to find God and know who they worship is their divine gift.

And so I say, to all who are interested in why I believe, that my throwing a football for the 49ers professional football team does not make me an authority on any other subject than throwing a football. But if my experience, my going into a "spiritual laboratory" and seeking, pleading, studying, and repenting can bring you one step closer to the true and living God, let me tell you that I do believe. I believe because I practiced my faith first without knowing and then felt the answers in my heart. Over time this faith produced conviction that I know more than anything else in my life, seen or unseen. I have felt God, I savor His written word, I love and listen to His ordained prophets, and He speaks

---

3. BYU address, September 6, 1977.

to my heart. I have tested His words, and they bear good fruit both immediately and proven by time. I believe I understood and made certain choices before this life on this earth and that what I do now for my fellowman matters in the hereafter. All you have to do is start "throwing the ball without seeing," and that faith will develop until you know that our Father in Heaven and His son Jesus Christ live and are our hope individually and the hope for the whole world.

 A professional athlete for fifteen years, Steve Young is best known as former quarterback for the San Francisco 49ers. His achievements include recognition as the highest-rated quarterback in NFL history, Super Bowl XXIX Most Valuable Player (MVP), the NFL's MVP in 1992 and 1994, and seven consecutive pro-bowl appearances. Off the football field, Young uses his visibility to raise awareness and funding for children's charities. He is founder and chair of the Forever Young Foundation (FYF) and is the broadcast host for the Children's Miracle Network's annual telecast. A charismatic, inspiring speaker, Young is also author of the children's book *Forever Young*. He and his wife, Barbara, are the parents of one son.

Appendix A: Glossary

Area Authority Seventy. Policies of the Church's First Presidency and Quorum of the Twelve are implemented mainly through other senior leaders known as Seventies. Many of the Seventies reside in different nations around the world, overseeing the growth and development of the Church. These leaders are known as Area Authority Seventies.

Bishop. A Church leader who presides over a local congregation and with whom rank-and-file members most frequently interact.

Book of Mormon. The Book of Mormon is a testament of Jesus Christ, along with the testaments recorded in the Bible. It contains religious writings of civilizations in ancient America between about 2200 B.C. and A.D. 421, including an account of the ministry of Jesus Christ on the American continent after His resurrection. The Book of Mormon was published in 1830 after being translated by Joseph Smith from an ancient record kept on plates of gold.

Brigham Young. Born June 1, 1801, at Whitingham, Vermont, Brigham Young joined The Church of Jesus Christ of Latter-day Saints in 1832. As the senior member of the Twelve Apostles, he succeeded Joseph Smith as leader of the Church. In February 1846 he led the Latter-day Saints across the frozen Mississippi River into unsettled Iowa territory and established a settlement called Winter Quarters, near modern-day Omaha, Nebraska. Pursuing Joseph Smith's vision, Brigham Young prepared his people—perhaps 17,000 of them by that time—for a historic trek across the wilderness to the Rocky Mountains, 1,300 miles to the west. The first pioneer company left Winter Quarters early the next spring and arrived in the valley of the Great Salt Lake on July 24, 1847.

Brigham Young directed the colonization of hundreds of communities in western America and served as president of the Church until his death on August 29, 1877.

Calling. An inspired request from a Church leader to a member to serve in an office or position in the Church. Callings may include administrative, teaching, and service opportunities and are a way for members to share their talents, gain new skills, and serve the Lord.

Conference Report. Published proceedings of the semiannual general conference of the Church, consisting mainly of addresses delivered by General Authorities and General Officers of the Church in the way of counsel, instruction, and revelation to members of the Church.

Doctrine and Covenants. A compilation of revelations given to and declarations made by various presidents of the Church. Part of the Church's standard works (canonized scripture), it is often referred to as the D&C.

Endowment. A course of instruction, ordinances, and covenants, with a bestowal of spiritual power, given in temples of The Church of Jesus Christ of Latter-day Saints. James E. Talmage, a member of the Quorum of the Twelve, explained, "The temple endowment . . . comprises instruction relating to the significance and sequence of past dispensations, and the importance of the present as the greatest and grandest era in human history. . . .

"The ordinances of the endowment embody certain obligations on the part of the individual, such as covenant and promise to observe the law of strict virtue and chastity, to be charitable, benevolent, tolerant and pure; to devote both talent and material means to the spread of truth and the uplifting of the race; to maintain devotion to the cause of truth; and to seek in every way to contribute to the great preparation that the earth may be made ready to receive her King,— the Lord Jesus Christ." (The House of the Lord [Salt Lake City: Deseret Book Co., 1968], 84.)

Family History Research. Genealogical and historical research to identify one's ancestors, primarily for the purpose of performing vicarious ordinances (such as baptism) for them in Latter-day Saint temples. The Church maintains the world's largest family history library, which is open to the public. The Church also provides electronic records for family history research over the Internet and in Latter-day Saint meetinghouses throughout the world.

First Presidency. The Church of Jesus Christ of Latter-day Saints is headed by the president of the Church and two counselors, together known as the First Presidency. The First Presidency and Twelve Apostles are prophets, receiving divine revelation to guide the Church. Together the Council of the First Presidency and the Twelve Apostles comprise the principal policy-making and administrative body of the Church.

First Quorum of the Seventy. One of the presiding councils of the Church, along with the First Presidency and Quorum of the Twelve.

General Authority. A member of one of the presiding councils of the Church, including the First Presidency, the Quorum of the Twelve, and the Quorums of Seventy.

Gold Plates. The ancient record, kept on plates of gold, from which Joseph Smith translated the Book of Mormon.

Joseph Smith. Joseph Smith was born December 23, 1805, in Sharon, Vermont, and later moved with his family to Palmyra, New York, where in 1820 a religious revival was taking place. Confused by the conflicting claims of the various faiths, Joseph went to the Bible for guidance and read James 1:5, which instructs those who lack wisdom to "ask of God."

Following this counsel, he prayed for guidance in a wooded grove near the family farm. In the most dramatic revelation since biblical times, God the Father and his Son, Jesus Christ, appeared to the boy and commanded him to join none of the existing churches but to continue as he was until directed further. That direction came in 1823, when Joseph Smith was visited by an angel named Moroni, a resurrected inhabitant of ancient America, who told him of the existence of the gold plates from which the Book of Mormon was later translated.

After a series of revelations and dramatic visitations to Joseph Smith and others, The Church of Jesus Christ of Latter-day Saints was organized on April 6, 1830, in Fayette, New York.

Joseph Smith died at the hands of a mob on June 27, 1844, at Carthage, Illinois.

Law of chastity. The Lord's commandment to shun sexual immorality, including adultery and fornication.

Mission president. An elder of the Church called by the First Presidency to serve, with his wife, as president of a geographical mission area. The period of service is usually three years. Typically, the president is a high priest with extensive prior service in the Church. His wife is likewise experienced in Church leadership and teaching. Under supervision from Church headquarters, he establishes mission rules, study patterns, goals, and discipline. His assignment requires constant travel to zone conferences every six to eight weeks. The president and his wife have direct contact with the missionaries by phone, mail, and personal visits. They continually foster programs of goodwill, service, and understanding. (See *Encyclopedia of Mormonism*, edited by Daniel H. Ludlow [New York: Macmillan, 1992], 914–15.)

Mutual. The weekday activity meeting attended by young men and women of the Church. In the Church's early days, its youth organizations were known as "mutual improvement associations."

Pearl of Great Price. A short collection of inspired translations and other documents from the Prophet Joseph Smith, including his history and the Church's Articles of Faith. It is part of the Church's standard works (canonized scripture).

Presiding Bishopric. The Presiding Bishopric consists of the presiding bishop and his two counselors. Serving under the First Presidency, they are responsible for many of the Church's temporal affairs, including involvement in receiving, distributing, and accounting for tithes, offerings, and contributions; administering programs to help the poor and needy; designing, constructing, and maintaining places of worship; and auditing and transferring membership records. The Presiding Bishopric also presides over the Aaronic Priesthood. (See *Encyclopedia of Mormonism*, edited by Daniel H. Ludlow [New York: Macmillan, 1992], 1,128.)

Priesthood. The priesthood is the authority to act in God's name. It includes two divisions, the Aaronic Priesthood and the Melchizedek Priesthood. Those ordained to the priesthood "must be called of God, by prophecy, and by the laying on of hands by those who are in authority, to preach the Gospel and administer in the ordinances thereof." (Articles of Faith 1:5.) Young men twelve to eighteen years of age, and older men who are new converts, are ordained to offices in the Aaronic Priesthood, "which holds the keys [governing or delegating authority] of the ministering of angels, and of the gospel of repentance, and of baptism by immersion for the remission of sins." (D&C 13.) The Aaronic Priesthood is preparatory to receiving the greater authority and blessings of the Melchizedek Priesthood.

"The Melchizedek Priesthood holds the right of presidency, and has power and authority over all the offices in the church in all ages of the world, to administer in spiritual things" (D&C 107:8), including the bestowal of the gift of the Holy Ghost.

Those holding the Melchizedek Priesthood are also ordained to an office within the priesthood, usually that of elder. They may later be ordained to the office of high priest or patriarch as their Church callings require. Those called as General Authorities for the whole Church are ordained seventies or apostles. (See *Encyclopedia of*

Mormonism, edited by Daniel H. Ludlow [New York: Macmillan, 1992], 882–83.)

Priesthood quorum. Any duly organized group of priesthood holders, including (on the general level) the First Presidency, the Quorum of the Twelve, and the Quorums of Seventy, and (on the local level) quorums of high priests, elders, priests, teachers, and deacons.

Primary. The Church's organization for children, which helps parents teach the principles of the gospel to their children ages 3 through 11. The children meet weekly to receive religious instruction and enjoy social interaction. Children 18 months to 3 years may attend the Primary nursery on Sundays.

Promptings of the Spirit. Personal guidance from the Holy Ghost, to which Church members are entitled if they live faithfully.

Regional representative. A priesthood leader who presides over a certain geographical area as a representative of the Quorum of the Twelve Apostles. This position has been superseded by that of area authority seventy.

Relief Society. The Church's organization for women, it is one of the oldest and largest women's organizations in the world. It was established in 1842 to help the poor, the sick, and others in need of compassionate service. During its weekly meetings, the organization provides instruction on a variety of topics, including theology, home and family education, compassionate service, social relations, and home management. The Relief Society also administers a literacy program in several countries.

Sacrament. The Lord's Supper, known in some churches as the Eucharist or Communion. Among Latter-day Saints, the sacrament consists of bread and water as emblems of the Lord's body and blood. (See Matthew 26:26–28.) They do not believe in the doctrine of transubstantiation. By partaking of the sacrament, Latter-day Saints renew their baptismal covenants, promising to take upon themselves the name of the Savior, to always remember Him, and to keep His commandments. (See D&C 20:75–79.)

Stake/District. A stake is a local Church unit comprising several wards and presided over by a stake president and his counselors. In developing areas where stakes and wards are not yet organized, small Church branches (local congregations) are organized into districts.

Sunday School. An organization for members of the Church 12 years of age and older that provides religious teaching for the different age-groups.

Testimony. A spiritual assurance of the reality and goodness of God, of the mission of Jesus Christ, and of the divine calling of latter-day prophets. The core of LDS religious experience, it goes beyond assent, conviction, or belief. It is a personal confirmation from the Holy Ghost and is interrelated with faith in God as demonstrated by dedication and discipleship. (See *Encyclopedia of Mormonism*, edited by Daniel H. Ludlow [New York: Macmillan, 1992], 1,470.)

Testimony meeting. A monthly meeting in which Latter-day Saints express their testimonies of the gospel as they are individually inspired to do so. This is known as "bearing testimony."

Tithes and offerings. The voluntary payment of one-tenth of one's income to the Church constitutes a tithe. Latter-day Saints also pay other offerings, including the fast offering, in which they fast for two meals each month and contribute the cost of those meals to the care of the poor.

Urim and Thummim. An instrument provided by the Lord to enable Joseph Smith to translate the Book of Mormon from the gold plates. He described the instrument as "two stones in silver bows—and these stones, fastened to a breastplate, constituted what is called the Urim and Thummim." (Joseph Smith—History 1:35.) The Bible gives no explicit description of this revelatory instrument, which was used anciently by the high priest of Israel, but notes that it was placed in a breastplate over the heart. (See Exodus 28:30; Leviticus 8:8.) Urim and Thummim is the transliteration of two Hebrew words meaning, respectively, "light(s)" and "wholeness(es)" or "perfection(s)."

Ward/Branch. A ward is a local congregation of Latter-day Saints, presided over by a bishop. In developing areas where wards are not yet organized, members attend small Church branches, which are usually part of a Church district.

Work for the dead. Temple ordinances (such as baptism) performed vicariously for family members who are no longer living.

Young Men. The young men's organization of the Church, which provides spiritual training, social and cultural activities, and, in some nations, Scouting. Young men ages 12 through 17 meet in classes on Sundays for religious study and several times during the month for social, cultural, and recreational activities.

Young Women. The young women's organization of the Church, which provides spiritual training and social and cultural activities. Young women ages 12 through 17 meet in classes on Sundays for religious study and several times during the month for social, cultural, and recreational activities.

Appendix B: Foundational Documents

The Articles of Faith of The Church of Jesus Christ of Latter-Day Saints

1. We believe in God, the Eternal Father, and in His Son, Jesus Christ, and in the Holy Ghost.

2. We believe that men will be punished for their own sins, and not for Adam's transgression.

3. We believe that through the Atonement of Christ, all mankind may be saved, by obedience to the laws and ordinances of the Gospel.

4. We believe that the first principles and ordinances of the Gospel are: first, Faith in the Lord Jesus Christ; second, Repentance; third, Baptism by immersion for the remission of sins; fourth, Laying on of hands for the gift of the Holy Ghost.

5. We believe that a man must be called of God, by prophecy, and by the laying on of hands by those who are in authority, to preach the Gospel and administer in the ordinances thereof.

6. We believe in the same organization that existed in the Primitive Church, namely, apostles, prophets, pastors, teachers, evangelists, and so forth.

7. We believe in the gift of tongues, prophecy, revelation, visions, healing, interpretation of tongues, and so forth.

8. We believe the Bible to be the word of God as far as it is translated correctly; we also believe the Book of Mormon to be the word of God.

9. We believe all that God has revealed, all that He does now

reveal, and we believe that He will yet reveal many great and important things pertaining to the Kingdom of God.

10. We believe in the literal gathering of Israel and in the restoration of the Ten Tribes; that Zion (the New Jerusalem) will be built upon the American continent; that Christ will reign personally upon the earth; and, that the earth will be renewed and receive its paradisiacal glory.

11. We claim the privilege of worshiping Almighty God according to the dictates of our own conscience, and allow all men the same privilege, let them worship how, where, or what they may.

12. We believe in being subject to kings, presidents, rulers, and magistrates, in obeying, honoring, and sustaining the law.

13. We believe in being honest, true, chaste, benevolent, virtuous, and in doing good to all men; indeed, we may say that we follow the admonition of Paul—We believe all things, we hope all things, we have endured many things, and hope to be able to endure all things. If there is anything virtuous, lovely, or of good report or praiseworthy, we seek after these things.

JOSEPH SMITH.

THE LIVING CHRIST:
THE TESTIMONY OF THE APOSTLES

As we commemorate the birth of Jesus Christ two millennia ago, we offer our testimony of the reality of His matchless life and the infinite virtue of His great atoning sacrifice. None other has had so profound an influence upon all who have lived and will yet live upon the earth.

He was the Great Jehovah of the Old Testament, the Messiah of the New. Under the direction of His Father, He was the creator of the earth. "All things were made by him; and without him was not any thing made that was made" (John 1:3). Though sinless, He was baptized to fulfill all righteousness. He "went about doing good" (Acts 10:38), yet was despised for it. His gospel was a message of peace and goodwill. He entreated all to follow His example. He walked the roads of Palestine, healing the sick, causing the blind to see, and raising the dead. He taught the truths of eternity, the reality of our premortal existence, the purpose of our life on earth, and the potential for the sons and daughters of God in the life to come.

He instituted the sacrament as a reminder of His great atoning sacrifice. He was arrested and condemned on spurious charges, convicted to satisfy a mob, and sentenced to die on Calvary's cross. He gave His life to atone for the sins of all mankind. His was a great vicarious gift in behalf of all who would ever live upon the earth.

We solemnly testify that His life, which is central to all human history, neither began in Bethlehem nor concluded on Calvary. He was the Firstborn of the Father, the Only Begotten Son in the flesh, the Redeemer of the world.

He rose from the grave to "become the firstfruits of them that slept" (1 Corinthians 15:20). As Risen Lord, He visited among those He had loved in life. He also ministered among His "other sheep" (John 10:16) in ancient America. In the modern world, He and His

Father appeared to the boy Joseph Smith, ushering in the long-promised "dispensation of the fulness of times" (Ephesians 1:10).

Of the Living Christ, the Prophet Joseph wrote: "His eyes were as a flame of fire; the hair of his head was white like the pure snow; his countenance shone above the brightness of the sun; and his voice was as the sound of the rushing of great waters, even the voice of Jehovah, saying:

"I am the first and the last; I am he who liveth, I am he who was slain; I am your advocate with the Father" (D&C 110:3–4).

Of Him the Prophet also declared: "And now, after the many testimonies which have been given of him, this is the testimony, last of all, which we give of him: That he lives!

"For we saw him, even on the right hand of God; and we heard the voice bearing record that he is the Only Begotten of the Father—

"That by him, and through him, and of him, the worlds are and were created, and the inhabitants thereof are begotten sons and daughters unto God" (D&C 76:22–24).

We declare in words of solemnity that His priesthood and His Church have been restored upon the earth—"built upon the foundation of . . . apostles and prophets, Jesus Christ himself being the chief corner stone" (Ephesians 2:20).

We testify that He will someday return to earth. "And the glory of the Lord shall be revealed, and all flesh shall see it together" (Isaiah 40:5). He will rule as King of Kings and reign as Lord of Lords, and every knee shall bend and every tongue shall speak in worship before Him. Each of us will stand to be judged of Him according to our works and the desires of our hearts.

We bear testimony, as His duly ordained Apostles—that Jesus is the Living Christ, the immortal Son of God. He is the great King Immanuel, who stands today on the right hand of His Father. He is the light, the life, and the hope of the world. His way is the path that leads to happiness in this life and eternal life in the world to come. God be thanked for the matchless gift of His divine Son.

THE FAMILY: A PROCLAMATION TO THE WORLD
THE FIRST PRESIDENCY AND COUNCIL OF THE TWELVE APOSTLES
OF THE CHURCH OF JESUS CHRIST OF LATTER-DAY SAINTS

We, the First Presidency and the Council of the Twelve Apostles of The Church of Jesus Christ of Latter-day Saints, solemnly proclaim that marriage between a man and a woman is ordained of God and that the family is central to the Creator's plan for the eternal destiny of His children.

All human beings—male and female—are created in the image of God. Each is a beloved spirit son or daughter of heavenly parents, and, as such, each has a divine nature and destiny. Gender is an essential characteristic of individual premortal, mortal, and eternal identity and purpose.

In the premortal realm, spirit sons and daughters knew and worshiped God as their Eternal Father and accepted His plan by which His children could obtain a physical body and gain earthly experience to progress toward perfection and ultimately realize his or her divine destiny as an heir of eternal life. The divine plan of happiness enables family relationships to be perpetuated beyond the grave. Sacred ordinances and covenants available in holy temples make it possible for individuals to return to the presence of God and for families to be united eternally.

The first commandment that God gave to Adam and Eve pertained to their potential for parenthood as husband and wife. We declare that God's commandment for His children to multiply and replenish the earth remains in force. We further declare that God has commanded that the sacred powers of procreation are to be employed only between man and woman, lawfully wedded as husband and wife.

We declare the means by which mortal life is created to be divinely appointed. We affirm the sanctity of life and of its importance in God's eternal plan.

Husband and wife have a solemn responsibility to love and care for each other and for their children. "Children are an heritage of the Lord" (Psalms 127:3). Parents have a sacred duty to rear their children in love and righteousness, to provide for their physical and spiritual needs, to teach them to love and serve one another, to observe the commandments of God and to be law-abiding citizens wherever they live. Husbands and wives—mothers and fathers—will be held accountable before God for the discharge of these obligations.

The family is ordained of God. Marriage between man and woman is essential to His eternal plan. Children are entitled to birth within the bonds of matrimony, and to be reared by a father and a mother who honor marital vows with complete fidelity. Happiness in family life is most likely to be achieved when founded upon the teachings of the Lord Jesus Christ. Successful marriages and families are established and maintained on principles of faith, prayer, repentance, forgiveness, respect, love, compassion, work, and wholesome recreational activities. By divine design, fathers are to preside over their families in love and righteousness and are responsible to provide the necessities of life and protection for their families. Mothers are primarily responsible for the nurture of their children. In these sacred responsibilities, fathers and mothers are obligated to help one another as equal partners. Disability, death, or other circumstances may necessitate individual adaptation. Extended families should lend support when needed.

We warn that individuals who violate covenants of chastity, who abuse spouse or offspring, or who fail to fulfill family responsibilities will one day stand accountable before God. Further, we warn that the disintegration of the family will bring upon individuals, communities, and nations the calamities foretold by ancient and modern prophets.

We call upon responsible citizens and officers of government everywhere to promote those measures designed to maintain and strengthen the family as the fundamental unit of society.

THE RELIEF SOCIETY DECLARATION

We are beloved spirit daughters of God, and our lives have meaning, purpose, and direction. As a worldwide sisterhood, we are united in our devotion to Jesus Christ, our Savior and Exemplar. We are women of faith, virtue, vision, and charity who:

Increase our testimonies of Jesus Christ through prayer and scripture study.

Seek spiritual strength by following the promptings of the Holy Ghost.

Dedicate ourselves to strengthening marriages, families, and homes.

Find nobility in motherhood and joy in womanhood.

Delight in service and good works.

Love life and learning.

Stand for truth and righteousness.

Sustain the priesthood as the authority of God on earth.

Rejoice in the blessings of the temple, understand our divine destiny, and strive for exaltation.

Young Women Theme

We are daughters of our Heavenly Father who loves us, and we love him. We will "stand as witnesses of God at all times and in all things, and in all places" (Mosiah 18:9) as we strive to live the Young Women values, which are: faith, divine nature, individual worth, knowledge, choice and accountability, good works, and integrity.

We believe as we come to accept and act upon these values, we will be prepared to strengthen home and family, make and keep sacred covenants, receive the ordinances of the temple, and enjoy the blessings of exaltation.

PHOTO CREDITS

Danny Ainge: NBA Properties, Inc.

Nolan D. Archibald: The Black & Decker Corporation

Thurl Bailey: Skip Schmiett

Clayton Christensen: Brooks Kraft

Kim B. Clark: Brooks Kraft

Jane Clayson: Tony Esparza

Paul Alan Cox: Susan Middleton & David Liittschwager

Richard Paul Evans: Kent Miles

Gladys Knight: Many Roads Records

Kieth Merrill: Andrew DeLory

Alexander B. Morrison: The Church of Jesus Christ of Latter-day Saints

Virginia H. Pearce: The Church of Jesus Christ of Latter-day Saints

Andy Reid: Ed Mahan

Dieter F. Uchtdorf: The Church of Jesus Christ of Latter-day Saints

Mark H. Willes: Lee Salem Photography, Inc.

Michael K. Young: Bob Narod

Steve Young: Dave Bush Photographers

Other photo credits were not available. All photos are under copyright and may not be used without permission.